THE RELUCTANT MERCENARY

THE RELUCTANT MERCENARY

The Recollections of a British ex-Army Helicopter Pilot in the anti-terrorist War in Sri Lanka

Tim Smith

The Book Guild Ltd
Sussex, England

First published in Great Britain in 2002 by
The Book Guild Ltd
25 High Street
Lewes, East Sussex
BN7 2LU

Typesetting in Times by
Acorn Bookwork, Salisbury, Wiltshire

Printed in Great Britain by
Bookcraft (Bath) Ltd, Avon

A catalogue record for this book is available from
The British Library.

ISBN 1 85776 514 1

Contents

Introduction

There have been many books written by Americans about the American debacle in Vietnam. One could be forgiven for thinking that they have some sort of monopoly on debacles, heroism and muscular Christianity, or of being emotionally and psychologically screwed up by personal involvement in acts of inhumanity, death, destruction and violence committed during a time of conflict.

Inevitably the British followed their lead in glorifying the Falklands cock-up and then that mincing, political television show in the Gulf. All of it under the protective, authoritarian shield of being 'in the right'; doing it for Queen and Country, the Battalion, the Regiment et al.

There has, however, been other even tackier wars that our government has indirectly supported. Sub-contracted out, so to speak. The 'soldiers' involved weren't recognised militarily or politically. Indeed, our Government's representatives denied their very existence. Without leadership, loyalty, support, or a flag to face they were, nonetheless, a shadowy final extension of political power. All without that protective shield about them.

Unrecognised by their country, their government, their company, and even the people they 'worked' for, they were also involved in acts of violence, death and destruction. The fact that they haven't spoken about it has a lot to do with our latest social disease, the Television War; a sickness that embraced the Falklands, the Gulf War, Bosnia etc. All wonderfully televised buckets of crap that were captured on film by a news-hungry media and beamed into homes around the world by satellite link. (No wonder that the books written about them have followed the same televised 'through the bushes' heroic vein.) How could our shadow soldiers possibly keep up with such muscular-Christian, khaki-clad heroes?

On the other hand, it is not easy to recognise a member of Britain's Shadow Army. They don't wear a uniform. They don't appear on television. The only place you'll find anything written about them will be in *Newsweek* or a quarter column in the Foreign

News section of *The Times*, a speculative article in *The Soldier of Fortune*, maybe. Unrecognised, denied, rejected by all and sundry, they are not easy to find, are generally a bit flaky and probably reticent about their involvement in things that were 'just a little untidy.'

So, having discovered one, how do you find out what went on? How do you get him to speak to you about it?

Try asking him at some unguarded moment in the privacy of his own home, or in the impersonal security of a crowded pub. In all likelihood the reaction you get will be somewhat different to that which you expected. If you are quick you may see the shield drop into place or brief looks of shock or apprehension come across his face. You may be told to piss off, but then that's his option, for they are all different.

You haven't asked me to tell you 'all about it', but somebody should, just for the record. At the end you might, just might, understand how our shadow soldiers (quite ordinary men) are sent out in hope to fight in wars you've never even heard about. And return home with a gutful of frustration, fear, anger, despair and an overwhelming sense of sadness at Man's inhumanity to his fellow man.

In telling this story now I tell it once; hopefully, only once, and thereafter I'll be left in peace.

The author

1

A Hole in the Roof

In early January of 1990 I spent the evening in the Golden Bridge Chinese Restaurant, down near the docks in Grimsby. It was a family affair to celebrate my son's 18th birthday. The evening went well. I was happy to sit back, fat, dumb and happy, and enjoy the happy chatter of the younger members of the group as they set about their meal.

Towards the end of the evening, as dessert was being served, a small internecine war broke out as to who had sovereignty over the banana fritters. Adopting a unilateral stance of political noninvolvement, the opportunity was taken to have a look about the place. Brightly lit though it was around our table, the remainder of the restaurant was blanketed in shadows.

On the wall opposite me was a painting of a native-built wooden fishing boat, a junk maybe, drawn up on a palm-fringed beach. Behind it was a small fisherman's shack built of atap leaves.

Suddenly it was June, 1986. Trying hard to stifle a small gasp of surprise, I struggled hopelessly to cover the looks of bewilderment and shock that I knew were crowding over my face.

Sitting across the table from me, my wife Eileen sensed, somehow, that something was wrong. Looking up from her plate, she turned and followed my gaze to the picture on the wall. Immediately she knew what was going on inside my head.

Filled with the solid thump of rotor blades and the hacking rattle of machine guns, my mind was running a savage mental replay. A native-built wooden fast-boat lay at the waters' edge, burning yellow and red amid a pall of black smoke. A body hung over the side, caught by one leg.

A young man, clad only in a dhoti and a flapping shirt, was running for cover towards the beached fishing boat.

Unwillingly, incessantly, the machine guns rattled on inside my head. Sand leapt in fountains around his feet and legs. He stumbled but staggered on as the bullets struck him. His shattered body was thrown in a convulsing heap behind the boat.

The hacking rattle of machine guns continued to fill my mind.

Great splinters of wood flew from the sides of the boat. 'Gunners, cease firing,' screamed a voice, 'for God's sake stop. Leave his mother something fit to bury.'

The helicopter rolled away to the right and thundered off to the west, leaving the beach quiet again except for the crackle of burning wood at the water's edge.

Similar flashbacks still occur, and with such monotonous regularity that I can now, after several years of practice, outwardly pass off such occasions with some aplomb. First, let me go way back; tell you really who I am, what it's all about.

Born and brought up to a large extent in rural Wiltshire, I found some difficulty in adjusting to inner-city life when my family moved to Bristol. As soon as I was old enough I escaped from those back streets and the Old Man's belt.

At the age of 15 I buggered off out of it and joined the Army. Do you know, even then the old bastard made sure I signed on for the 3rd Royal Tank Regiment? Having boxed and cycled and ran like a deer for two years, I finished with the Boy's Service and Passed Off, with a leg in plaster, into Man's Service.

For several years I scrabbled about on the lower rungs of the promotion ladder. At the age of 24, having achieved the grand heights of Lance Corporal, I decided it was time to do something better with my life. Actually I got involved in yet another fight. Sometimes I think that more time was spent fighting out of the ring than in it.

Just before Christmas of 1966, I got myself caught up in an attempt to repair a rift between a couple of friends of mine. Calling at the Married Quarters of one of them, I tried to patch up their disagreement. Actually, if he didn't come clean, I was gonna punch his lights out.

Paddy's wife answered the door. She flew at me without warning, teeth bared and talons extended. There was a great danger of getting my eyes scratched out by an enraged female. Simply reacting to years of boxing training, I applied two cracking left jabs and a right hook to the situation. She hit the floor like a sack of spuds. Utterly disgusted with the reception that I'd received on such a vital mission of Christmas Goodwill, I legged it before she came round.

Several days later, on First Parade, the Squadron Sergeant Major invited me to 'Get my arse down to the Regimental Guardroom and present myself to the Provost Sergeant, immediately'. Go to Jail, do not pass Go, do not collect £200. In the Monopoly Game of Life, I had landed on the wrong bloody square again.

Fortunately the Provost Sergeant was also the Regimental Boxing Team's Manager-cum-Trainer and, although extremely impressed with the speed and accuracy of my punches, he was more than somewhat pissed off with my choice of target. He asked me dead straight, as the Boxing Team Manager, what had gone on and why. I was honest with him. He then told me equally straight as the Provost Sergeant that I was deeply in the shit, but that he would do what he could to lessen the depth.

It's a shitty fact of Army life, isn't it, that the Army will teach you to fight like the devil and then when you do, they punish you for it. It's called discipline.

(Take note that something similar, but in a strangely different order, would make life a bitch later on in this tale of woe.)

At my subsequent appearance before the Commanding Officer two days later he interceded on my behalf, and I was really quite fortunate to lose my imminent promotion to Corporal and get myself posted to Recce Squadron as a Land-Rover driver for my sins.

It was there that I became involved for the first time with helicopters. In no time at all I was put into the left-hand seat of a Skeeter to operate the radios and read the maps for the pilots. After several months of watching and learning I eventually decided that if a drunken Tank Regiment Staff Sergeant could manage to fly one without crashing, then so could I.

They even got round to promoting me.

Chatting about it to a pal over a beer one evening (he was a clerk in Regimental Headquarters) revealed the fact that the necessary rank and the education qualifications needed to apply for the Army Pilots Course were already in my sticky little fist. Without any further buggering about, I applied for the course.

It was not without some difficulty that I was eventually accepted. Apart from the fact that it took me nearly 18 months to pass the medical, the CO didn't think that I was Sergeants' Mess material;

Corporal RTR

maybe he was right. It took me nearly two years to convince him otherwise.

Eventually I got my wish, and at the age of 26 passed the course and took up my first posting as a Sergeant Pilot with my parent Tank Regiment. Having struggled like hell to get away from the tanks there I was, after three bloody years, back at square one.

Finally I managed to get a transfer into the Army Air Corps. At last I'd managed to escape from the Tank Regiment. Being accepted into the Permanent Cadre meant that I would carry on flying wherever they chose to send me, the Far East, West Germany and, of course, the inevitable tours in Northern Ireland.

With no great effort I managed to make my way up the ranks to Warrant Officer II and QHI (Qualified Helicopter Instructor). At the tender age of 40, with a lot of life still left in the old dog, I wasn't discouraged from taking my pension and legging it into civvy street.

After 22 years in the Army I had amassed a grand total of two ex-

Same job, less pay

wives, half a house, half a car, and half a golden handshake. Bloody marvellous!

However, stuffed in my trouser pocket was an Air Transport Licence for Helicopters and my Flying Instructors Rating.

As a civilian it took me only two years to do it all over again. Two disastrous love affairs, and I was another £5000 down. To cap it all my 13-year-old son had returned home to me some time before, leaving his mother in Germany; home to Dad, seeking the security that he felt his father could provide.

Sheeit, but it really was time to settle down. However, my job as a Flying Instructor was in the balance. The company that I was working for was currently teaching a group of Iraqi Officer Cadets how to fly helicopters. The end of the contract was coming up. The Boss and his short-sighted bean counter decided that he had made his money and was about to close the flying school. It was a great shame really, for they were the finest bunch of flying instructors that I have ever come across.

Fortunately for me, there was the chance of another job, still locally, as Chief Helicopter Pilot with an embryonic charter company. Clutching at straws, I took the job, yet another pay cut, and worked like hell to make the job go.

Smaller job less pay

Unfortunately, the more work that I put in the less time there was to chase up new business.

The boss' wife spent endless hours in the office on 'telephone duty,' knitting; it was like waiting for the guillotine to fall. What was badly needed was a lot more security at work and at home.

A smaller, more affordable, house was found with yet another wife. I was a sucker for punishment. If you can't provide security, I had thought, then go out and buy it.

Life, they say, is a bucket of shit, but it's the only one you've got. Just to bring mine to the point of overflowing, my latest ex-wife-to-be informed me, a couple of days before the wedding, that she was pregnant.

Right then and there I should have buggered off out of it. But, quite frankly, I had run out of any sort of enthusiasm or good ideas for the future. It was a case of just stoically plodding on.

One evening, after several months of remarried life, I was sat watching the television. A log fire burned cheerfully in the grate (it was cheaper than coal). With a can of beer in my hand I was as complacent as buggery. I sat there just listening to the rain on the windows.

The sound of gently running water seemed to seep into my mind. Vaguely curious, I took a stroll into the hallway to find where it was coming from. Following the dripping sound, I went upstairs. It seemed to be coming from under the roof. Grabbing some stepladders and a torch, I took a brief look into the roof space. A few minutes later, when I came back down, the future had been settled.

There was a small hole in the roof; a couple of broken slates where the rain came in. It had trickled down the wall and through the ceiling onto the banister rail. From there it ran down into the hallway in a tiny rivulet, where it formed a particularly nasty little puddle under the mat before running out under the door and into the street.

That was on Saturday night. On Monday afternoon the roofing contractor's surveyor emerged from the roof space and casually informed me that '£3000 would cover the job just nicely.' Three bloody thou! I was bloody skint. I couldn't afford three quid. The house was all that I had and the Building Society owned most of that.

Complete and utter bloody despair set in. Very naturally I was hoping, no, I was bloody well praying, that some easy way out of this mess would jump out of the woodwork; and when it did, I went straight for it.

When the telephone rang a couple of days later, I was just about ready for anything.

'Smudger, my old lad, it's Greg here, I'm calling from Sri Lanka. How are you, are you still working for Doug?' It sounded like he had his head in a dustbin.

'Greg, I'm fine, we're all fine. How are you, what the hell are you doing in Sri Lanka?'

'I'm working with the Sri Lankan Air Force, instructing. How do you fancy a nice easy tax free job teaching Officer Cadets to fly Jet Rangers for the Sri Lankan Air Force?'

'Easy,' I thought, 'where the hell is Sri Lanka?'

'Tell me more,' I said, as I mentally packed my suitcase with instruction manuals, insect repellent, Diocalm and anti-malaria tablets.

I hadn't seen or spoken to Greg for ages, not since the SFT Flying School had packed up. Greg had been one of the instructors at the school, in fact he had been one of the instructors when the company first started up, one of the 'original four', and had finished up as Chief Instructor on the Jet Ranger Section. We went back a few years.

Greg explained very briefly that he had got the job from a box-numbered advert in *Flight* magazine, and had been out there several months already.

'Let's hear it for box-numbered adverts.' I muttered to myself. By all accounts he was having a ball. He was teaching Basic Helicopter Flying on Jet Rangers in the cool of the early morning and the late afternoon, with a midday siesta in between. Evenings were pleasantly passed on the veranda of the bungalow where he lived in the camp, or in the best hotels in Colombo and Negombo, eating mediocre steaks and drinking VSOA, Very Special Old Arak. The Sri Lankan Air Force badly needed more instructors.

'Yes, yes of course, count me in old buddy' I said excitedly, almost dribbling in anticipation of the old team getting back together, not to mention getting the hole in the roof fixed. Grabbing a pencil, I scribbled furiously as he passed me a handful of names and some phone numbers to call.

'Who's it with?' I asked eventually.

'KMS,' he replied, 'they're a bit like AirTran, doing jobs for the Government.'

'Yeh, um, OK. What's KMS stand for?' I asked, hoping perhaps to look the company up in the Helicopter World Business Directory.

'Uuh, Keenie Meenie Services, I think it's Maori, or something like that, for little, they're all ex-squaddies. It's an offshore-based company with offices in London,' he went on, his words echoing down the satellite link.

It was all a bit vague and seemed almost too good to be true. At that stage of the game I wouldn't have given a toss if they were green-skinned, double-headed, baby-eating monsters, provided the pay was half-decent.

Ricocheting off a piece of metal in space, Greg's other-world voice assured me that the rates of pay were very good and that life was about to take a turn for the better. I believed him. Oh boy, but I really *wanted* to believe him.

The following day I made a few phone calls to London.

After some fairly terse and guarded conversations I eventually persuaded them that I actually was an old friend of Greg's and was finally invited down for an interview, and lunch, at their offices in the West End.

Quite who 'they' really were I still wasn't sure. Actually, I didn't give a toss. A Flying Instructor's post in South East Asia on North

Abingdon Road

Sea rates of pay wasn't to be sneezed at. You couldn't possibly catch a cold doing that, now could you?

A week or so later I managed to arrange some time off from work and took the Night Sleeper from Carlisle to London. Still being totally skint, I took the tube across town to save money and sought out the company's office in Abingdon Road, Kensington. I walked past it twice before I eventually found it.

Discreetly set back off the main road and up a set of dirty concrete steps, the bare and anonymous door opened only after a brief and furtive conversation with an electronic gadget on the wall. (Note: the steps are clean these days and a new door graces the front of a late-Victorian brown brick building.)

I felt utterly bloody stupid standing there, apparently talking to a scruffy heap of bricks and concrete. Normally I don't talk to scruffs.

A very well-endowed secretary with a charming smile met me on the stairs and escorted me to an upstairs waiting room that was thankfully more welcoming than the uninviting door downstairs had led me to expect.

Anonymous Door

The interview that followed was more like an interrogation. Nevertheless, I considered it to have gone off quite well. On the other hand I was a complete novice when it came to such things.

Dave Prichard, or was it Richards, I didn't find that out either, and Mike were as charming and efficient a pair of suits as you would ever care to meet. They were obviously the products of Sandhurst and some Guards Regiment or other, and, in all probability, the SAS to boot.

I wasn't sure which one was which and never would find out. They were like a pair of eggs, a Tweedledum and Tweedledee

They fired all manner of questions at me, probing into my

military background and my more recent civilian life. The fact that I had, until quite recently, been quite happily teaching Iraqi military students to fly Jet Rangers and Gazelles with some success seemed to go a long way with them.

Throughout it all I tried to make some sense out of Greg's hurried briefing on the phone but was given little chance to ask any pertinent questions. I thought it better to wait until after lunch to find out more about my prospective employers.

Some upside-down letterhead reading would do for a start.

Lunch was taken at a 'very select club' that seemed to be peopled by a variety of City and Military types, all very much Officers and Gentlemen. A large proportion of the clientele sported blazers with Regimental badges. There was also a good scattering of broken noses and cauliflower ears. They were a healthy looking bunch, to say the least. The badge that went with them was generally the Parachute Regiment. This, I thought with a barely suppressed giggle, must be the stiff upper lip of the Old Boy Network.

Dave and Mike, excusing themselves for a couple of minutes, eased off and chatted to some more grey suits on the far side of the room.

Left to my own devices, I had a look around me. A set of tweeds was heading straight towards me, a face that was vaguely familiar from my Army Air Corps days.

After a few moments of thought it came to me, a Welsh Guards chappie that had flown an Auster at weekends for fun. Aye, that was him, Captain Collins, Tommy Collins. He'd had a bad do with a Scout helicopter in Northern Ireland.

'Sergeant Major, how are you? How nice to see you again. What are you doing in Town?' he asked.

Why do 'they' insist on maintaining a military rank structure, even when you're a civvy? I suppose it's meant to keep us of the lower orders in our place.

'Hullo Sir, it's good to see you again,' I replied, shaking his hand. 'I'm here on an interview for a job.' I gave myself a swift mental kick in the arse for almost tugging my forelock. How come it's so hard to break the old rank structure mould?

'Flying still?' he enquired, politely curious.

He had always had the knack of seeming interested. Noblesse oblige and all that. Feed the horses first, then look after the troops.

'Oh yes. I'm down here on an interview for a Flying Instructor's job abroad.'

'Jolly Good,' breezed Tommy, 'Best of Luck, I Do Hope it Goes Well.'

Somehow they always seem to be able to speak with capital letters.

'Me too, Sir, me too.' I replied with a fervour that I really felt.

'Well, I really must dash, see you around.'

Tommy drifted off from whence he came, back into the anonymity of the crowd around the bar. I didn't realise until much later, but my military background had just been checked out and confirmed. I had been 'cleared' by the simple expedient of bringing in a serving officer who knew me by sight.

Another grey-suited chap joined us at lunch, apparently from the Ministry of Defence. He was, of course, 'very discreet' and seemed to spend the whole of the meal talking in riddles about some prospective security contract for the company abroad but letting nothing slip in front of me, a stranger, except perhaps that he wouldn't let anything slip in front of a stranger.

Obviously the company had some sort of Government blessing, and a tenuous connection with the Ministry of Defence.

Some of Greg's excited chatter about 'AirTran' and 'government jobs' on the phone was now beginning to slip into place. I was about to become some of Maggie's invisible earnings. I was suitably hushed and deferential, not wanting to appear a complete and utterly uncomprehending prat in amongst all these awfully good chaps and gung-ho types.

Already I could see myself. Tanned, in tropical lightweights, with a tall glass of beer on a veranda at sunset, and a succession of sunny days with bright-eyed students to teach how to fly. Wonderful. 'Don't rock the boat, bonny lad,' I thought, 'no sense in buggering it up.'

The short ride back to the office after lunch gave me a few moments to myself to reflect on the morning's progress. It seemed quite clear to me that the company definitely had some sort of Government approval and connections with the MOD. That being the case, it just couldn't be a bad deal.

As we crept through the lunch-hour traffic thoughts of a sunnier future drifted gently through my mind. My earlier flippant thoughts of being one of Maggie's invisible earnings would probably result in some pompous Treasury type standing up in the House in the not too distant future to declare that 'invisible earnings over the last financial period had increased dramatically.' Sleepy Tom would nod knowingly from the Front Bench and continue to snooze.

And then there was the meeting with the man from the Ministry; it had all been very guarded, but the tone of the conversation had been such that the less said the better. 'Ho hum,' I thought, 'there's enough to think about during the run back up to Carlisle this evening. For the time being let's see what they have to offer ... nice to have met old Tommy again.'

If the morning's interview could have been likened to an interrogation, then the afternoon's session was more like a full-scale military briefing. Tables and chairs were moved around to make some space in the waiting room. An overhead projector with one of those portable screens was set up and the lights were turned down.

Slides were shown of Sri Lankan police officers marching around a very pre-war camp. You know the ones I mean, all wooden huts with verandas and wriggly tin roofs. There were more slides of men in olive drab fatigues banging away with rifles on the ranges. It appeared to be all very well organised. Well, all the arms and legs seemed to be going the right way at the same time. Mike, or maybe was it David, made some brief, offhanded apologies for the lack of slides showing the training staff. 'We really haven't had time to get around to it, they've been awfully busy,' and, 'oh! Here's one of our Local Team Leaders.' A head of greying wavy hair over a tanned, fit-looking face appeared on the screen. He struck me right away as being an ex-ranker of some sort. Maybe ex-infantry or Parachute Regiment. I thought; a Drill Sergeant or Small Arms Instructor that had made good with a Quartermasters Commission.

Some recent clippings from *Newsweek* and the *Telegraph* were produced to provide a bit of background to the local situation. References in the cuttings to KMS and British mercenaries were carefully glossed over and claims of Israeli military advisers were poo-pooed with a muttered, 'We're a security and training organisation.'

Note: I don't know who works from those offices today, they are, however, still *very* security-conscious.

It was all so very plausible, so very much like our own training operation with the Iraqis had been up in Carlisle. They had obviously accepted me, and I was most definitely hooked. Back into military harness, well almost, with shoulder-length hair and a beard, now that couldn't be bad.

A security organisation

Yes, there was certainly a lot to think about during the train journey north that evening but, truth to tell, my mind was already made up.

Several weeks later I was invited down to Kensington again for a final interview. It was patently obvious that I'd been discreetly checked out at very close quarters. Dave, or was it Mike, casually dropped in the question of my pregnant wife being all right during my absence. I hadn't even mentioned the fact that she was pregnant. They had obviously got someone to ask a few questions about us in the local shops and pubs at home, but still the warning bells were silent. What the hell, with a company in that sort of business they doubtless had to keep some sort of internal security going.

There wasn't a single tiny 'ting' of a warning bell as I signed the contract according to the Law of the Cayman Islands and opened a bank account with Morgan Grenfell in the Channel Islands. Adventurous stuff this, *Boys Own Annual* with a whiff of politics.

Anyway I had a pregnant wife, a 14-year-old son to look out for and, on top of it all, there was a £3000 hole in my roof where the rain came in.

In retrospect, the whole KMS setup was beautifully choreographed. Either they weren't aware, or they didn't care about the rights or wrongs of the deal.

KMS was in it for the money and, whether they wanted to or not, they provided an excellent firewall between themselves, the contract and the British Government.

2

The First Ten Days

Out of the crooked timber of humanity
no straight thing can ever be made.

Immanuel Kant

The timing of the whole thing was a little less than perfect. The baby was due in about a week and there was the matter of the hole in the roof, for which the go-ahead for repair had already given, and if I wasn't careful there'd very soon be a bigger hole in my bank account. I was totally committed to going.

Never being one for weepy farewells on railway station platforms, my goodbyes were said at home. Just the matter of a taxi into town to catch the night sleeper to London for a final visit to the office.

Since my early days in the Army, railway stations late at night had always held a strange attraction for me, and it was with an odd, somehow uncertain, sense of freedom and adventure that I walked into the echoing emptiness of Carlisle Station that night. One late arriving passenger was scurrying away from the dimly lit platforms out into the bright lights of town, leaving me on my own to savour the sense of freedom and the feeling of imminent change.

Looking around me in the half-light I noticed a small figure some distance away swathed in a fur coat, stamping small booted feet to keep warm. There was something familiar about her. Coppery red hair tumbled over the top of her fur collar. Spray-on blue jeans and an excellent arse inside them. To finish the job a pair of calf-length high-heeled boots. I knew who it was long before she turned to face me, but even that was not enough to keep the look of surprise from my face. It was Carol.

We'd lived together for one riotous and turbulent year before she left me, for a bloody horse and a bet that she had made with JR (the publican) in the Sportsman's Arms some 18 months before. She stepped forward into a pool of light and, even at that distance, I could see the wicked gleam in her eyes and the dull gleam of her nicotine stained teeth in a 'got you, you bastard' grin.

'Hiyah, what the hell are you doing here?' I asked, trying to be casual but knowing full well that she was up to something.

'I've come to see you off,' she replied waving a ticket at me.

'Not like you to buy a platform ticket,' I said hopefully, thinking, 'I do hope to hell that is a platform ticket.'

'Nah,' she said, walking towards me with the wicked glint still in her eye. 'I'm coming with you to London. I haven't been down for a while and thought that you'd like a bit of company on the way.'

She pushed up close to me and put an arm through mine. Still the same old smell of horses and leather overlaid with soap.

'I've never done it on a train,' she murmured, smiling wickedly up at me. Carol was going to be harder to shrug off than she had been in the past. She'd already had five grand out of me when we'd split. Maybe it was time to get some sort of return on the outlay. 'What the hell,' I thought, 'you're a long time dead.'

We took the underground across town the next morning. Emerging from the tube at Kensington High Street we window-shopped our way to the office, where she waited across the road whilst I went in. Tweedledum presented me with my ticket, 'Any final questions, no? ... good.' Tweedledee produced a bundle of letters for the company's Colombo office.

'Ken Whyte will meet you at the airport,' explained Tweedledee, and in no time at all they had me bundled out of the door, to spend the night at the company's expense in the Heathrow Penta, with head-spinning speed and efficiency.

I hardly had time to think, let alone ask any last-minute questions. What the hell, I was in the globetrotting mood and it would have taken wild horses to have stopped me going. Aye, I had one last day of poling around town and one last night to say farewell to Scotch and water, good food, and a good frolic between the sheets. What is it about the human mind that will never let me forget a seemingly inconsequential detail, like the large spot on her back, just beneath her bra strap?

The following morning I showered and shaved as quietly as

possible. Leaving Carol sleeping, I boarded the hotel's courtesy bus for the airport.

The International terminal was in a state of absolute bloody chaos. Some knucklehead had left an unattended suitcase near gate 7 and a full-scale bomb alert was in progress. Just what everyone needs to go with a hangover and 40 pounds of excess baggage.

Time, ill-concealed impatience and the dextrous, if somewhat carefree, use of my Barclaycard eventually relieved me of my bags and excess baggage and got me into the appropriate gaggle of shuffling sweating and cursing humanity to check in for the flight to Colombo, Sri Lanka, via Dubai.

Already armed with a good book and with an ex-Squaddie's ability to ignore the world around him at such times I boarded the plane and fell into a light hangover-induced sleep.

Dubai came and went sometime during the night, just as it had at other times during my earlier khaki-coloured career. After many hours of sleeping, waking, reading, drinking, eating and occasionally chatting to the very smart young German female tour guide in the seat across the aisle, I drifted out of sleep for the last time.

I woke to find myself peering deeply into the cleavage of the same young tour guide as she leaned across me to watch the sun rise over the edge of the world from my window. Personally I thought it preferable to watch the twin golden orbs just under my nose to the one outside. Idly I wondered what it would be like to watch them rise over the bed sheets in the morning. Dream on, lover boy.

'Women,' I thought then, 'are like buses, when you want one there are none around, and when you don't they turn up in convoys.'

The plane descended through rose-coloured clouds into daylight, and on down towards the eye-searing whiteness of Colombo's concrete strip. The palm trees surrounding the airfield seemed to creep slowly up the window until the sudden thump and screech of the tyres announced that the ballache of a journey was over. God alive, but I hate the roaring, jerking, landing part of plane journeys almost as much as the thundering and shuddering take-off part. It is not at all genteel, as it is with helicopters.

Although it was still only early morning, the heat was already shimmering off the ground. We shuffled away from the aircraft like so many weary and wartorn refugees. My globetrotting mood had noticeably waned. The build up of sweat under my rumpled suit made me feel like a bloody tourist and positively out of place. It reminded me of my arrival in Hong Kong in 1975. That was equally as hot and smelly, only this time it was daylight.

In the Arrivals Hall a few minutes later, the temperature climbed another couple of notches and frantic took on a whole new meaning as a couple of hundred travel-stained passengers rushed about like headless chickens in a manic search for their baggage. Presumably before they forgot what their bags looked like.

Standing back, I waited stoically until the stampede around the baggage conveyor belt had subsided somewhat before gathering my own bags about me, and looked around for a baggage trolley and the exit to Customs and Immigration. There were no bloody trolleys left. So much for enduring British patience.

There were police absolutely everywhere. They were all armed to the teeth and looked as furtive and bloody dangerous as only the under-trained and under-confident can. I decided not to ask for directions.

'Mr Smith ... I'm Ken Whyte.' a quiet voice came from behind me. Like a wraith the local Team Leader had appeared out of the woodwork. He looked just like the photo that I'd seen of him in London, a Regimental Quartermaster in civvies, which was just as well, for I must have looked like a bag lady or the wreck of the *Hesperus*.

'Welcome' he said briefly, and gathering the rest of my bags, he escorted me totally unchallenged straight out through Customs, Immigration, and Security. I could so easily have taken a few thousand cigarettes and a crate of Scotch with me. I would have, had I known what was in store for me over the next five months.

Out in front of the airport a car was waved up and my bags were loaded into the boot. We clambered in and shut the doors. Within seconds I was wishing for the comparative cool of the Arrivals Hall again. The heat was awful, and the car's ancient air-conditioning just couldn't cope with it.

We ground away from the curb into what seemed an endless stream of ancient Morris Minor taxis. In the futile hope of some respite from the cloying heat I wound the window down and used a cupped hand to deflect some cooling air into my face. The smell of decaying vegetation, rotting fish and stagnant water was like a

Airport Road on a quiet day

solid, physical blow to my senses. I quickly wound the window up and decided to sweat.

Once on the main road we turned right, away from town, and followed the airfield boundary for a few miles. We stopped for a few minutes at an ungated railway crossing and waited for an ancient steam train as it pulled an enormous string of carriages across the road. It was absolutely festooned with people hanging from the doors, standing on the steps, and sitting on the roofs. Eventually it disappeared into the jungle. It was certainly picturesque.

Half a mile further on the road came to a sudden end at a security gate set in a chain link fence. A large sign in squiggly Sinhalese and English proclaimed it to be

SRI LANKA AIR FORCE
4 SQUADRON
KATUNAYAKA

The security gate was a mere formality. After a brief pause to show some ID at the guardroom we were grandly saluted by the sergeant, the corporal, the man at the gate and waved on through.

I waited briefly for massed bands to appear, but was disappointed. Ken Whyte obviously had some impressive documentation.

Coconut trees surrounded the camp and its buildings, like the airport. Totally surrounded. Every space that could take a tree had one in it. Everywhere coconut trees. A short winding drive through the camp brought us to a car park behind some old, but fairly standard, British-style aircraft hangars and offices, obviously the remnants of the country's colonial past.

Leaving my bags in the boot of the car, we went inside. The air in the hangar swirled about us, cloying, warm, invisible, like the locker room at the sauna.

A brief wait in an outer office brought some respite from the heat but provided me with little time to gather my scattered wits. The journey had been about four miles, and was just long enough for me to come to the conclusion that I should get out of my sweat-soaked European clothes at the earliest opportunity.

Minutes later, and well within an hour of arriving in Sri Lanka I was being presented to the Sri Lankan Air Force's Helicopter Squadron Commander.

'Squadron Leader Oliver, this is Mr Smith, your new pilot. He's just arrived from the UK,' said Ken as he introduced me.

'Good morning, welcome to Sri Lanka, Mr Smith, I do hope that your journey was not too wearing. Please take a seat.'

The Squadron Leader's voice was pleasant, well modulated, and very, very, English. The highly lacquered wooden sign on his desk said Squadron Leader Oliver Ranasinghe. He was tall and slim, almost elegant, the very picture of a well tanned British cavalry officer. I was shocked and tried not to look too surprised but probably didn't succeed. I had expected at least a little bit of 'Oh, golly gosh' in his voice.

'During your time with us you will hold the honorary rank of Captain and may live in the Officers Mess if you wish, or you may stay at the bungalow in the camp with the others.' He paused for a moment and I nodded my understanding. I didn't mind instant promotion. Well, it fitted with what Greg had said on the phone.

'For the time being you will not be required as there is an operation going on in the North and all our personnel are being utilised.'

'Thank you, Sir. If there is anything I can do I would be more than pleased to help.' I heard a voice that sounded very much like my own. Did I really say that! Fool, buffoon, complete and utter prat. I'd been there for barely an hour and already I was volunteering. So much for instant promotion. It must have been jet lag. Fortunately for me, there were other matters to attend to first and my offer was politely refused.

Ten minutes later we were back in the mobile Turkish bath that the company called a car, but this time thankfully for only a few minutes. We wound our way through the coconut groves again to a bungalow at the edge of the camp. With hardly time to realise that the ramshackle heap of wood and wriggly tin in front of me was to be my future home, my gear was unloaded from the car and was dumped in the hallway.

The place was a wreck, a complete and utter bloody shambles. I lugged my gear through into a dusty lounge half full of furniture that had seen better days. A broken door led off into a couple of bedrooms, one of which showed remote signs of recent occupancy. I dumped my bags on the bed and took a few minutes out to unpack and clamber into some wrinkled but lighter and fresher clothes. Quickly I stuffed my money, passport and travel documents into my pockets before we were off again, downtown to the company's offices to get my documentation and passes sorted out.

'Bloody hectic life,' I thought, 'Mother would just love the bougainvillea.'

The journey into Colombo was a revelation. The company, Ken explained on the way, were not in favour of us driving the company's cars. Should we require a car, the police sergeant attached to the company's office would chauffeur us around. I could see why. The roads and traffic were total bloody chaos. There were two lanes of traffic going each way on a two-lane road, and still some clowns were trying to overtake down the middle.

There were all manner of vehicles. Pushbikes and trishaws, clapped-out tractors with trailers loaded to the point of collapse, minibuses with the latest passenger to board still hanging from the door, buses with most of the passengers hanging out of the windows, and cows pulling wooden-wheeled carts. Ye Gods!

From the squalor of atap-roofed, corrugated tin shanties held together with string and wire on the outskirts we passed through an area of well appointed houses set back in spacious grounds, surrounded by well kept lawns with water sprinklers on them. This had doubtless been the domain of the white rulers in years gone by, but now housed the rich and powerful of Colombo.

Airport Road

We drove on through the overcrowded slums of the Pettah district that only served to underline the divide between the indecently rich and the extremely poor in the third world. Slums that were so redolent of lapsed colonial rule.

Eventually we struggled free of traffic into the relative calm of the old town centre. The Fort, with its beautiful old buildings that had once housed the foreign banks and companies in a much grander past. Beautiful old buildings that were now the premises of much lesser concerns, cheap jewellers and pawnshops, shady goldsmiths and tourist traps selling ethnic clothing and wooden bloody elephants.

We edged our way carefully through the mass of pedestrians and left the faded splendour of the Fort and continued along Galle Face, back into the suburbs of Kollupitiya. We eventually pulled up in front of what had once been a pleasant suburban house but now, with its untended front garden and electronic gizmos at the door had obviously been turned into the Sri Lankan equivalent of the London office. Inside was quite a different matter. It was wonderfully cool, the storm shutters were closed, the lights were on, and the air-con worked.

The female secretary, a Portuguese Sri Lankan as I found out later, was as pleasant as her Kensington counterpart and produced an excellent cup of coffee for me. We chatted briefly whilst Ken got the paperwork together. It transpired that she had relatives in Cumbria somewhere. Did one of her relatives ask the questions about me at home? Maybe, who knows, it's a small enough world?

Relaxing with a cigarette a short time later, I was briefed on the company's role in Sri Lanka.

The company, so Ken said, were originally contracted to train the police force in anti-terrorist operations. For this there was a staff of ex-military instructors who worked in a training camp some distance to the south-east of town.

Lately they had been tasked with the training of an elite force of the Sri Lankan Army's finest. I didn't know it then, but I was to work with the Trackers in the future and find out just how good a job the company had really done.

The aviation side had been tacked on later at the Sri Lankan Government's request, and was just a small part of the contract. The general tone of the briefing led me to think that I should have been grateful for having been met and looked after at all. Once again, as in London, there was no mention of KMS or British mercenaries. Oh no. Heaven forbid!

The company was always a little conservative with their information, with the truth. Like any good quartermaster, they kept something back to issue later, for emergencies, to be produced like baksheesh surreptitiously from a box under the counter.

Out of idle interest I asked about the British High Commission's position regarding our presence in the country, and got my first minor shock.

'As far as the British High Commission is concerned, we do not exist. They have washed their hands of us,' Ken replied blandly. Shock, it was a full-scale tremor. About four on the Richter scale, and nothing to what I would get later.

To wind up the visit some forms were produced to record my bank details, next of kin and suchlike. One of those portable security-pass photo machines was produced from somewhere and was set up in a small side office. Standing with my back pressed firmly against the wall, some spot-the-criminal photos were taken. Yet another form was quickly filled out and signed to provide me with a police pass that I was assured would get me into and out of all the places that I was ever likely to use. I never did get that pass issued, but that didn't seem to stop me going anywhere, particularly to the nastier places.

Our salary would be paid into our nominated bank account one month in arrears. We would also receive a local allowance of 3000 rupees a month in cash that we could collect from the office personally or have delivered by the company's internal mail system. That turned out to mean by the hand of whoever was going your way.

'Unfortunately, we've run out of petty cash at the moment, would you mind waiting for a few days' Ken explained.

'Yeh, okay, no problem,' I said, being the trusting sort that I was. 'Bollocks,' I thought, 'I'm not too flush for funds. It will have to be the old plastic card again.'

The moral of that story is never trust officers with cheque books or organisations that pretend to be based on the British Military.

An hour and a half later I found myself back in the sweatbox of a car being treated to a drive-by tour of the local hotels and watering holes that were used by the other aviators as and when they were in town. There was the Oberoi, noted for its swimming pool and prawn salads, the Ramada, the Galle Face and its faded colonial splendour, the Taj Samudra with its massive pillars and wooden floors, the Meridian and the International.

On the way we stopped by at the company's off-duty house in town. It was a very pleasant Mediterranean-style bungalow in a clean and quiet suburb. Not a bit like the ramshackle heap of a hut back at Katunayaka. There was even a cleaning lady tidying the place up. Very nice it was, too, but I had the distinct feeling that it was for the groundhogs only. What the hell, I never saw the place again. I must admit that I'd hoped to meet some of the 'boys on the ground'; it would have provided me with a good insight as to what was going on. Perhaps that was why I never met them.

As it turned out later we, the aviators, preferred to use places closer to the airfield at Katunayaka. The Blue Oceanic with its tatty mosquito nets and groaning ceiling fans, Browns Bar for happy hour, and the cheaper delights of the bars, restaurants and whorehouses of Negombo. When we did get time off it was used to the full, with no unnecessary trips to Colombo and Kollupitiya.

Later that morning we arrived back in the camp at Katunayaka and I moved into the 'instructors' bungalow'. It was an awful place, a ramshackle shed with peeling paint and a sagging roof of wriggly tin, busted locks on the doors and torn mosquito netting at the windows. Not exactly a pleasant Mediterranean bungalow in a quiet suburb, and no sign whatever of a cleaning lady.

I unpacked my gear and stowed it in a busted steel locker. From a collection of sagging wreckage I cobbled together a fairly serviceable steel-framed army-style bed in the second bedroom. Somehow, eventually, I managed to make the shower work, but with little effect, for the cold water was tepid and the hot water nonexistent. Nevertheless, carefully dodging the cockroaches scuttling around the bottom, I showered and got changed into something more comfortable. In the very best of military traditions, I decided to tidy the place up at the earliest opportunity.

Showered and dressed, with my gear neatly stowed, I felt more like the confident, globetrotting man of the world that I knew I should be. I took a stroll up to the Squadron to find out what the long-term plan was. It was going on lunchtime by then, and the young Sri Lankan soldiers on their way to and from the cookhouse found time to stop and gawk and chatter at the passing of a new Whiteface in their camp.

The hangars and attendant offices were so very much like those that I had worked in during my service life in the UK, Europe and the Far East, that I found the Squadron Clerk's office at the first attempt. Like most military establishments at lunchtime, the place was virtually empty and all that I could gather from the Squadron Clerk was that there was no plan and that I wouldn't be needed for a few days.

It was then, as I was walking out of the hangar, that I had the good fortune to meet the American. A stocky, cheerful chap with an open, friendly face and a pleasant smile.

'Howdy, you the new guy?' he hollered as he ambled along a gap between the aircraft and stuck out a paw. 'Mah name's Dwayne, Dwayne Speers, Ah'm the Bell rep, Bell Helicopters representative for Seer Lonka.'

'Hiyah, Tim Smith, just arrived this mornin',' I replied, shaking his hand. 'I've been trying to find out what's going on around here. Seems remarkably quiet.'

I didn't know that a man could smile so much, talk, and shake hands all at the same time.

'Pleased to meet yah, Tim. Uhhm, well. It seems that they got themselves sorta caught up for a few days. Mah advice to you is to disappear down town for a while, come back in a couple a days,' he explained right off. ‘Get yourself a decent bed, some good grub an’ a few beers. Just pitch up here on Monday.’

Hell, it was only Thursday, but such good advice coming so confidently could hardly be turned down. Anyway, I needed to make a phone call home and let them know that I had arrived in one piece.

‘Sounds good to me,’ I agreed, and we carried on walking out of the hangar towards the car park.

‘I’ll give you a lift down if you like, we can stop by your rooms to pick up an overnight bag. This here is Lionel, mah driver,’ he went on as we arrived at his car.

‘Thanks very much.’ Nodding ‘hello’ to Lionel. ‘I’ll take you up on that, I’m up at the bungalow.’ ‘Yeh, no problem. Get in.’

It took no time at all to grab an overnight bag and stuff it with a change of clothes and my shaving gear. I felt like a schoolchild playing truant. We stopped by at his place on the way, the Airport Garden Hotel, just down the road from the airport, and had a beer or two at the poolside before we finally left to go on into town.

There was no doubt about it, Dwayne was on to a really good number as the Bell rep for South East Asia. An air-conditioned room in a first class hotel right next to the airport and a company car complete with a driver. I wondered if I would ever pull such a cushy number. Idly I thought of my own job and hoped to spend many more lazy afternoons sitting in the sun with an ice-cold beer. Much later it came to me that if the CIA had a man in Sri Lanka it just had to be Dwayne, an opinion that was shared by us all.

I really wasn’t too flush for funds and knew that much of my cash would be used on phoning home over the next few days. When I explained the situation to Dwayne, he advised me to use the Taj Samudra, which was one of the cheaper hotels and had also been recommended by ‘the local Team Leader’ as providing a good discount to the company.

It was going on four o’clock by time I waved farewell to Dwayne from the steps of the Taj. Grabbing my overnight bag, I strode inside like a conquering hero. That feeling didn’t last long. The place itself had been designed and built on someone’s disjointed idea of the ‘Splendour of the Raj’.

The reception and bar areas were cavernous with ceilings that were almost nonexistent in the gloom. Huge arches supported on enormous marble pillars that rose like monoliths from acres of tiles, in a forest of dark hardwood panelling.

An enormous set of stairs rose in brooding majesty towards the upper levels. Unfortunately, the place was staffed by mere mortals who were totally unaware of my heroic dreams.

When I explained to the receptionist that I was with the Special Training Force and would like a room for a few days at the company's discounted price, I was greeted with blank stares. I tried again using KMS and got more blank stares.

'Bollocks,' I thought, 'just what I need right now.'

I tried not to lose my conquering hero's cool and was trying very hard to explain for the third time to yet another receptionist just who I was and who I worked for, and could I please have a room at a discount, when the woman waiting next to me at the reception desk turned and asked if she could help.

It was the blond bombshell with the twin golden orbs that I had met on the plane.

'Hello, how nice to see you again,' she said in an incredibly sexy German accent. 'I am the Kuoni Tours Guide here at the Taj and may be able to get you a room with a good discount.'

With that she unfolded a string of discount cards a yard long from her bag. Hey, who was I to argue at a time like that, and 40 per cent off was not to be sneezed at, particularly when it came from a good-looking young woman. So I took her up on her offer, and in next to no time was booked into a room. Out of pure courtesy, and you can believe that if you like, I agreed to keep her company at supper that evening, and 'Ja, I would meet her in the foyer at seven-sirty, punktlich'.

The evening was interesting, to say the least. Not for her the bars and restaurants in the hotels at the tourist end of town, she'd probably had enough of that anyway, but downtown to the Pettah district. To a cheap and cheerful local diner with a dirty floor and steamy windows.

Locked in lust, with my eyeballs firmly fixed on that wonderful cleavage, I sat across from her at a Melamine-topped table on a rickety chair and chattered like an adolescent. We ordered some curried chicken that was as hot as sin and swam in oil the colour of brick dust. Maybe it was Sri Lankan Duck, how should I know, and with a woman as gorgeous as she was why should I care. I'd been in tidier NAAFI canteens, but never with a woman like that.

Pettah District Colombo

After supper we strolled hand in hand through the litter-strewn and unlit streets of the Pettah district slums. It was hardly what you would call romantic, she was fully three inches taller than me and wore high heels.

Actually, we were hanging on to each other for mutual support as we felt our way through the darkened streets and alleyways, stumbling on rubble, stepping over litter and around puddles of dirty stagnant water. Some ten minutes later we came upon a dimly lit square. I wouldn't have admitted it to her, but I was more than a little concerned for our safety as we groped through the shadows.

We stopped there for a while to gather our composure and were persuaded to have our fortunes told by an old hag who squatted in the dirt and cast her runes in the filth of the gutter.

The old harridan had a scraggy parrot that tottered from its cage and selected one of her laid-out cards, which was then interpreted as our fortune. Erika was to have a good life full of love and happiness. I hoped so, and really soon.

When the old hag took my card from the parrot, she paused for a moment before she turned and screeched at an old man on the edge of the small crowd that had gathered to watch. There was much shaking of heads as a short argument followed. After a few moments the old man spat on the ground at his feet and turned away. Looking up from under her eyebrows, the old hag grudgingly handed me back my money.

'So, I don't get kissed by the princess tonight,' I thought.

A real confidence-booster, that. I've always wondered what the old bat saw in her cards that night.

The same thing had happened several times in the past when people had wanted to read my palm or teacup. None of them had ever deigned to tell me what it was they saw and didn't like.

We eventually picked our way out of the Pettah district back into the brighter lights of the Fort and took a trishaw ride back to the Taj. After a nightcap at the bar she took her leave and went to her bed, alone. I never saw her again after that evening, I supposed that she was guiding tourists around the sights.

During those first three days I spent much of my time investigating Colombo on foot. I looked in on all the hotels that had been mentioned on the drive-by tour, to see what they had to offer. I bought a street map and located the main banks and the British High Commission, just in case I needed them in the future.

I walked miles in search of the shops that might provide me with day-to-day European necessities at a reasonable price, cigarettes, writing material, corned beef, breakfast cereal, booze and so on. The standard creature comforts.

Hours were spent being pestered by pimps offering me their sisters, daughters, mothers and brothers, one at a time or all together for a short time. It took me a long time to stop chucking coppers into outstretched hands and even longer to stop telling the pimps to bugger off. In the end I found the only way was to ignore them completely and walk on by.

My evenings were spent in the bar of the Taj, waiting until it was time to phone home. It also saved my food bill, for the bar was laden with free nibbles. By the night of 18 May I had spent £200 on phone bills. Things were getting desperate all round. Back at home my wife, Eileen, had been taken into hospital on 16 May and had been having difficulties with the birth ever since.

Getting a line through to the hospital had proven to be difficult enough, it took me some time to convince the Sister in charge that

I really was the husband and prospective father and had a right to know what the hell was going on.

On 18 May, after 12 hours in labour, Eileen managed to produce a son. At the end they were both fortunate to be alive. As little respect as I had for my latest mother-in-law, I was grateful that the old clucking hen was there to fuss over my wife and our newborn son.

After three days in the Taj I used the last of my cash to take a taxi back to 4 Squadron at Katunayaka. Virtually broke, I walked into the shed that my friend, Greg had chosen to call a bungalow, to find him sat in a dilapidated armchair with a glass of whisky in his hand. He looked very much the old colonial planter in his safari suit and desert boots.

'Welcome old buddy,' says he, full of bonhomie, 'fancy a drink?'

'Hiyah Greg, how are you? A beer will be fine for me,' I replied, knowing that my own bottle of Grouse was pretty low. 'Well, Greg me old lad, Eileen's just produced a son after a really difficult labour. They're both OK now, but the phone calls back home have almost cleaned me out,' I told him straight off.

'Well, congratulations old chap, just sit down, relax and have a beer,' he said, pulling a bottle of the local beer from a clanking contraption in the corner that passed for a fridge. 'I can lend you some cash until we get some money sent up from the office. Now, is there anything that Jan can do to help?'

Taking the beer, I slumped back into one of the sagging chairs. Good old Greg, as laid-back as he ever was, with everything at his fingertips. Back home Greg and Jan and their family lived just 15 or so miles up the road, and we had been friends for several years.

Several beers later we were still talking, or at least he was, explaining the situation 'up north' and the effect that it would have on my nice little number down here in the south.

The 'op' in the north had been designed by the Sri Lankan forces to redress the balance of power on the Jaffna Peninsula before the start of the next round of peace talks. It had been planned to give the Tamils a bloody nose and reduce their bargaining power at future peace talks. The combined might of the Army and the Air Force were to have pushed 10 kilometres west from the Army base at Elephant Pass, on the eastern neck of the peninsula, towards Jaffna City. Unfortunately the column had come across 22 culvert bombs and land mines in the first six kilometres. The advance had ground to a shuddering halt, as one might well expect, and many of the demoralised young soldiers had just sat on the roadside crying, and refused to go another step further.

The resulting chaos had required the use of all the air support that they could muster to cover the withdrawal of the column to Elephant Pass. All of which had left me with nothing to do for the present and a much different future in store than I could possibly have imagined.

Over the next few days I drew up my flying gear and some military clothing from a Quartermaster's Department that took me straight back to joining the Army at Bovington in 1958: Vests PT, red, one; Vests PT, white, one; Shorts PT, blue, down to the knee, pairs, two. It was just like being back in the mob. Plimsolls, black, size 7, pairs one, complete with laces. Bloody wonderful!

Carting the lot back to the bungalow, I tried to find at least one more serviceable locker to store it all in. It seemed to me that those who used the place didn't bother too much about such things.

Most of the lockers contained a selection of suitcases and bags, much of it just piled in haphazardly with no nametags. Were it not for the odd jacket or shirt on a wire clothes hanger, I would have taken it for junk left by the previous occupiers.

There were only two beds made up. Mine, and Greg's in the next room. In the best of military traditions, I tidied the lot up and made the best of a bad job. If I had to live in it, it would at least be orderly.

Pigsty or not, I quickly got used to the place. The evenings were really quite pleasant. With someone to talk to over a beer and the gentle rustling of the warm evening breeze through the coconut trees, it was easy to slip into a 'who gives a shit about the future' attitude. Greg had rung the office downtown and got some local allowances sent up for me. It all seemed so easy.

Greg drifted in and out of Katunayaka a couple of times over the next few days, sometimes staying the night, but always going back up north. During those brief visits he was full of praises for the gentle lifestyle that he had led before and would lead again when the operation up north was over. Neither of us could know that he would be Medevaced back to UK within the year.

All in all it was ten days before I started any flying duties. Ten days to mull over what I had let myself in for. Ten days to think about the job I had chucked in to get this one. The hole in the roof at home that was being repaired with money that I didn't yet have. The Tax Inspectors who would have a field day if I returned to the UK before the year was up. I was fairly stuck with it, but we really needed the money at home. I should have left right then, but it all seemed to be going as planned.

Suddenly the waiting was over. One morning on my daily ramble up to the Squadron in search of info, I noticed that there were rather more vehicles than usual around the place. In the hangars brown skinned technicians were working on a couple of Bell 212 helicopters. On the pans outside sat another 212 fitted out as a Gunship with rocket and machine gun pods, and over to the side sat a Jet Ranger.

The Squadron Clerk, my only source of military contact over the past week, greeted me with some interest for a change and showed me straight into Squadron Leader Oliver Ranasinghe's office. The Squadron Leader stood to greet me as I entered. His uniform was immaculate. Tall and slim with an intelligent face, he was indeed the very picture of a British Cavalry Officer, if somewhat tanned.

Bell 212

He elegantly waved his hand to a chair and in his pleasant and well modulated English asked that I take a seat and make myself comfortable. Without preamble he explained that my 212 conversion course was to start the very next day and that the Squadron Clerk would take all the relevant details to cover it as soon as we were finished there. 'Great stuff,' I thought, 'just the job, twin engine conversion before I even start work.' The Squadron Instructor would issue me with all the necessary books, and Ground School would start the next morning at eight o'clock sharp.

'The course will take three days,' he concluded, 'following which we are sending you to KKS for a short while so that you may develop an understanding and appreciate more fully the conditions under which our young pilots have to operate.'

It was just as well that I was seated. I was astounded. KKS was the main airstrip on the Jaffna Peninsula, Kankesanturai. A stream of questions tumbled from my lips, 'How long for?' and 'What about doing some instruction on the Jet Ranger?' and 'What am I supposed to do in KKS?'

In my mind were a few less professional queries, regarding cold beers in tall glasses beaded with condensation in the Taj, Pimms in the Galle Face or prawn cocktails in the Oberoi, what about the easy life of the well-paid expatriate in cloudless climes under star-filled skies?

Soon, I was told. As soon as the situation called for my skills as an instructor I would have my chance, meanwhile I would have to learn to fly the Bell 212.

'Well,' I thought, 'that was something at least.'

I had done my time in the Army, all 22 years of it, and I'd been around a bit. As a Tankie I'd spent most of my time between UK and Germany and had seen some fairly grisly accidents. I had escaped from the Tank Regiment into the Air Corps. I'd done my bit in Northern Ireland and had been shot at by the IRA many times on border patrols around Fermanagh and Tyrone. Having flown helicopter top cover on several culvert and car bomb disposals, I had witnessed for myself the destruction that a couple of hundred pounds of Co-op Mix stuffed into a beer keg could bring; that or a few ounces of plastic explosive in the wrong place.

Indeed, my first posting to NI had been to replace the helicopter pilots lost in the Birches car bombing in Omagh during 1973. I'd seen and done enough in the Army to know that I didn't really want to get too involved in the shit that was going on with the Tamils on the Jaffna Peninsula. Yet there I was, up the bloody Jaffna creek without a paddle.

Even today I still cannot fathom out why I elected to stay. Perhaps I thought it would all turn out right in the end, maybe I just wanted the dosh. Was it face or pride? Whatever it was that convinced me to stay there, it was just one more step along an uncharted and decidedly rocky road; a financial cripple led by the morally blind.

The next three days passed all too quickly, but not without some wry humour. Ground School the following morning had me shaking with silent laughter as I found out that the Sinhalese have difficulty with pronouncing their V's and a lever became a lewer. It took me some time to work out what a 'collectew lewer' was. I thought that maybe I had missed something in my years of flying in the Army and was keenly alert to discover what it was. In the end it turned out to be the bit that makes a helicopter go up and down. They did not nod their heads in agreement but rather shook the head and nodded at the same time, a sort of figure of eight with the nose. 'So that was why they had all seemed so uncertain whenever they spoke to me,' I thought, 'that was why they called them Jinglies.' I was on a really steep learning curve.

The flying was no problem. After all, a helicopter is pretty much a helicopter, big or small. I also had the good fortune to spend the first afternoon doing engine runs with Dwayne, the Bell sales rep. His knowledge of the aircraft was unsurpassed, and I was happy to pick his brains while I could.

My flying instructor was Roger Weerasinghe, a pleasant if somewhat amateurish Sri Lankan Air Force Flight Lieutenant. We scooted through the programme of take-offs, circuits and landings and confined areas operations at the gallop. The standard drills for engine failures and emergencies were all taken at a fast clip, after all I had been an A2 category QHI with my name on the Birthday Honours List for Valuable Service in the Air. I was no slouch. By lunchtime on the third day the course was all but complete. Instrument flying had been given the brush on the strength that I'd been an Instrument Rating Examiner in the Army Air Corps. There was only the night flying bit to complete.

Roger

That afternoon Roger turned me over to the one of the door gunners who, he explained, would take me to draw up some extra equipment that would be needed in KKS. I couldn't think for the life of me what that extra equipment might be until we arrived at the Armoury, and there I found out.

Ah, yes, those oh so vital accessories that are a must in such places. A T56, the Chinese equivalent of the AK47 assault rifle, and 120 rounds of ammo in four magazines, and the absolute end in *News at Ten* fashion statements, a flak jacket.

I should have been a bit pissed off if only by the fact that it wasn't a nice blue one. Khaki had never been one of my favourite colours.

Night flying on the last evening of the course was a mere formality, I was rather more skilful at it than Roger, and he was glad to sign me off as fully qualified and send me back to my quarters for the night. The bungalow was empty when I got back.

Dumping my newly acquired T56 and flak jacket in a corner, I scuffed about the kitchen knocking some grub together from my meagre stock of tinned European food. I was seriously considering going down to the Airport Garden Hotel for one of their blood-drained, cardboard steaks and a few cold beers.

I couldn't guess at what I was supposed to do with my weapon at such times, and presumed that the Sri Lankans took them to bed with them.

The sound of wheels crunching on the gravel drive out front interrupted my bemused train of thought for a moment, and I idly wondered who could be visiting me at this time of night. I stepped onto the veranda to find out. An Air Force Jeep finished one more circuit of the drive and pulled up in front of the veranda steps.

In halting English and that, by now familiar, rolling figure of eight with his nose, the driver slowly explained that he would pick me up the next morning at five-thirty and take me to 2 Squadron at Ratmalana, the military airstrip on the southern edge of Colombo, where I would get the plane for Jaffna.

Bloody hell, I'd been in the Squadron office only five hours earlier, and nothing had been said about this at all.

It seemed to me that it was the local custom to drop things on you at the last moment, and wherever possible, by some innocent third party. I rang the Squadron Office to find out what the hell was going on, only to be told by the Duty Engineer that 'Everyone had gone away' and he did not know where they were. Chaotic bloody place.

Resigned to my fate, I packed my gear and assembled as much as possible in the way of creature comforts for a short stay.

Two hundred cigarettes, some paperback books from the put-and-take library. The few tins of food that were left over from my visits to the local shops down by the railway crossing, and anything else that I could lay my hands on that might make life bearable in what I knew for sure would be a bloody awful spot.

With my bags bulging beside my bed, I packed my remaining clothes and instruction manuals into an empty and busted steel locker. I took a tepid shower and, after a final shot of medicinal whisky, tucked my newly repaired mosquito net around the rickety cot and tried to sleep.

3

Kankesanturai

It's evening time and across the Straits of Palk
the length'ning shadows of night-time stalk,
whilst South and Eastward 'neath the gathering cloak of night
the Tigers stretch and snarl their might.
Smithy, Jaffna 1986

It was a bloody awful night. Sticky hot with mosquitoes buzzing in and out of earshot. My feet stuck out from under the off-white sheet offering juicy pickings to the little airborne bastards. I was glad when my alarm clock put an end to it.

It was not that I was concerned about going to Jaffna. I felt sure that the company wouldn't think of sending me into the thick of it. Of course I'd just spend some time up there as an observer. Then I'd return to Katunayaka and teach bright-eyed and bushy-tailed students how to fly. Brilliant.

After all I was there to be employed as an instructor, and the Squadron Leader had been quite emphatic when he told me that it was a semi-operational area. Surely the idea was for me to gain a mere insight on the operational situation so that I could teach those same bright-eyed and bushy-tailed students the tactics and techniques that would serve them best. Yes, of course, that was it, what else could there be in a place where the coconut trees sighed gently on a jacaranda-scented breeze, where bougainvillea bushes spread their scarlet blossoms over the lawn.?

The eternal bloody ex-military optimist. And, quite naturally, I didn't want to be late for parade on my first day.

Having showered and shaved I was dressed, as smart as a button stick, waiting on the veranda with my gear at the ready by five-twenty-five. I waited, inwardly fuming, for three-quarters of an hour until the driver eventually turned up.

'Some bloody army this,' I muttered to myself as I smiled

pleasantly at the driver and tossed him a hearty 'Good morning', like a hand grenade with the pin pulled out.

I was beginning to form the opinion that these people weren't laid-back, they were totally bloody incompetent, they just didn't bloody care. 'Nil desperandum,' I thought, and climbed into the front seat.

Ratmalana, an hour later, was like a chicken run with the fox on the inside. Collaring a chap in an Air Force uniform I explained who I was. He in turn found an Army sergeant and passed on the news. The Army seemed to treat flyers with some respect, and when it had sunk in that here was a Professional Flyer going to KKS doors opened. The sergeant proudly escorted me to the officers' waiting room, where a chair was made instantly vacant for me to park my butt.

In no time at all I was surrounded by bright-eyed young officers introducing themselves, and they in turn were replaced by older, brown-faced officers, Lieutenants, Captains and Majors, all looking for a safe seat out of it when the time came it seemed. Awfully jolly.

The 748, when it was ready, was packed to the roof, and only the fact that I was escorted to the plane by a young Airman assured me of getting on board without being trampled underfoot.

Wriggling about, an effort was made to fasten my seat belt only to find that the general idea was to keep the seat cushion down with it. Presumably clenching the buckle firmly between the cheeks of your arse kept one from sliding off the seat in moments of extreme terror.

Peering keenly through a side window, I saw my gear go aboard and breathed a sigh of relief. All of my creature comforts, the rest of my life was in those bags.

The engines were fired up and the fully laden plane taxied out on to the runway. They backtracked the plane as far as they possibly could before turning it around and lining it up on the runway. Without pausing, the throttles were then thrown wide open, and the roaring, shuddering beast thundered down the strip. I really did have my doubts about the coconut trees at the end of the strip and gently, unobtrusively braced myself for the impact, but the trees stayed firmly in the ground and the plane groaned and staggered over them and into the air.

The aircraft eventually levelled off and we droned northwards

Avro YP748 airborne for Colombo

above the clouds. I relaxed and dozed a little, listening to the chatter of the young Sinhalese soldiers going back to Jaffna. They seemed happy enough, so it couldn't be that bad.

The ever-present coconut trees slid up the windows once again, but somehow this time the screech and thump of the tyres on tarmac was not so reassuring. Maybe it was something to do with the sudden dive for the treetops and the last minute sliding turn to line up with the runway, maybe.

A short while later, when the doors were thrown open, the passengers disembarked with what seemed like a rush of relief. Calmly I remained in my seat until the rush had cleared before leaving the aircraft, I paused at the top of the steps for a moment to pose and take in the scene. 'S'truth, but it was bare-arsed.

Laid out before me, surrounded by a chain-link wire fence in various states of disrepair, was an airstrip that looked like it had not been touched since the fall of Singapore. There were sandbagged walls wherever my gaze stopped. Sangars (watch-towers) built of tree trunks, perforated steel planking (PSP) and sandbags were sited at every corner and vantagepoint.

Beneath and behind the steps a horde of sweating soldiery was already carting away a mountain of gear from the cargo hold to the sheds and Nissen huts beside the control tower. Suddenly I felt very exposed standing up there and made my way with a forced casualness down the steps.

Control building

Glancing further afield, I noticed a white face at the edge of the crowd and felt a little less out of place, but not for long. The face seemed somehow wrong, too young, sallow and spotty. The spotty face eased through the crush followed by another white face with a camera hung around its neck. At arm's length I positively disliked them both.

Spotty thrust out his hand, with a list of names in it. I noticed Mark Burrows' near the bottom.

'Do you know any of these chaps? . . .' he asked.

'Do you know where any of them are?' asked the cameraman.

'. . . we're from *Soldier of Fortune*,' continued Spotty.

'Piss off,' I replied, 'and don't try using that camera on me or I'll push it into a very dark place.'

Shouldering my way roughly past them I pushed into the throng and headed towards the buildings. Bloody *Soldier of* bloody *Fortune*, inside the camp, whatever next.

Breaking clear of the crush, I found a young Sri Lankan Flying Officer walking towards me.

'You are Smeeth?' he asked.

'Yes,' I nodded.

'Come with me, please,' he went on and, without waiting for an answer, turned and led off towards a very new-looking Isuzu Trooper on the edge of the dispersal.

'Very slick,' I thought, as I bundled my gear in the back and climbed into the front beside him.

A 300-metre drive brought us to the Squadron lines, another collection of sandbagged walls, tree-trunk sangars, and PSP rocket and mortar fences. Huge blast walls of sandbags, earth and rocks masked the entrance to the helicopter hangar.

'To prewent damage to the helicopters from rockets and mortars,' explained the young Flying Officer, as he drove on through a manned gate into a chain-link and barbed-wire fenced compound which a sign proclaimed to be Airforce Officers Mess Kankesanturai.

We pulled up in front of a long brick building with a red pantiled roof. There were flowerbeds out front with a gravel drive and bougainvillea bushes dotted around a small lawn. Very laid-back. With hardly a word spoken I was shown to a room in a breezeblock extension at one end of the bungalow and told that I should unpack and relax for a while, he would be back to show me around in about an hour.

The room was less awful than the ramshackle bungalow at Katunayaka, if only because there was a lot less of it. There was no broken furniture. Indeed, there was very little furniture at all. Just two cot beds with coir-filled palliasses on them and the ever-present mosquito nets. A hardwood wardrobe stood between them in a 12 × 12 room in a breezeblock hut with an asbestos sheet ceiling and a corrugated tin roof. A shower-cum-toilet cubicle with two doors linked the room with its mirror image next door.

Airforce compound and hangar KKS

Namal

One mosquito-netted window looked out to the rear of the building onto a PSP anti-rocket fence some 15 yards away. Eight yards away was an open cesspool. Later it was to become known as Froggy Pond. The next couple of hours were spent unpacking and settling in.

I was lounging on my bed some two hours later when the young Flying Officer eventually returned to show me around the Mess. Very politely, and quite formally he introduced himself.

'I am Flying Officer Namal, you are Smeeth?' he asked.

'I am Tim Smith', I replied firmly, not entirely sure that I liked the tone of his voice when he said 'Smeeth'.

'Good, Smeeth, I will show you around the Mess,' and he turned to walk out.

'One moment …' I called after him, determined not to leave the room until I had this uppity little bugger sorted out.

'… I am Captain Tim Smith. You may call me Tim if you want to be friends, or Captain Smith if you don't, but if you call me Smith in that tone of voice ever again I'll be extremely angry with you.'

He looked flustered for a moment and then, taking a breath,

said, 'Please, follow me, Captain Smeeth, and I will show you around the Mess and explain what we do here.'

'Cocksure little sod,' I thought, and followed him out.

How should I have known that surnames were used as the standard form of address?

The Mess was basically a small bungalow containing a lounge, part of which was used as an 'operations room', a dining room and a couple of bedrooms. Tacked onto the back was the most disgusting hovel that they proudly called 'the kitchen', beyond which was an equally disgusting hovel, which were 'the boys quarters'. It contained six bunk beds stacked three high with filthy palliasses on them.

To accommodate the increased numbers of aircrew, four breeze-block rooms had been tacked on to the end of the bungalow, one of which was to be Chez-moi. Spartan it certainly was, and would be my home for a while.

Stopping in front of a wall map in the 'ops room' Namal paused to give me a brief outline of the operational area and the Squadron's role within it. I'll give the uppity little sod his due, his briefing was good.

Officers Mess KKS

Jaffna is a seasonal peninsula cut off in the monsoon season by salt-water lagoons which are crossed by three causeways and a ferry, all of which were controlled by army outposts. In the dry season it was possible to cross the lagoons in many places on the firmer stretches of sand. Each outpost was virtually cut off from surface support by the LTTE, the Liberation Tigers of Tamil Eelam, who prowled the scrubby jungle. Many of the outstations were not accessible from the sea. (The LTTE had virtually wiped out the TELO in a recent and bloody internecine power struggle.)

The primary task of the Squadron was to support and re-supply all the outstations from Mullaittivu and Kilinochchi on the mainland at the east and south-eastern end of the peninsula to Karainagar, the naval base to the south-west of Jaffna Town.

We would carry coconuts, cabbages, chillies, cartridges, conscripts and constables. cannons, casualties, correspondents and cameramen, some of whom I'd already met. Anything and everything, particularly if its initial letter was 'C', day or night, week in and week out.

The next couple of weeks would be spent learning the ropes. Locations, routes, heights to fly, frequencies and call signs and so on. A couple of weeks, what were they talking about?

'It shouldn't take that long,' were my thoughts at the time; but then I hadn't been properly introduced to the Sri Lankan concept of 'if, perhaps and maybe.'

Whilst stationed at KKS our meals would be provided by the Army from their cookhouse some 200 metres away along the rocket fence to the rear of my room. Our food would be collected in containers by the Mess boys, reheated in the 'kitchen', plated up and served in the Mess dining room.

Breakfast was normally 'bulls-eyes' (fried eggs) on toast, proudly prepared by the boys themselves in the dungheap they called a kitchen.

Returning to my room, there was enough to think about for a while. It was a good job that an ample supply of Diocalm had been brought along.

That first lunch wasn't a tremendous shock, for I'd spent some time with the Ghurkas in Hong Kong and Brunei, but it did make me appreciate Ghurka cooking a little more. Even reheated, the food was only lukewarm and, like the curried chicken in the Pettah

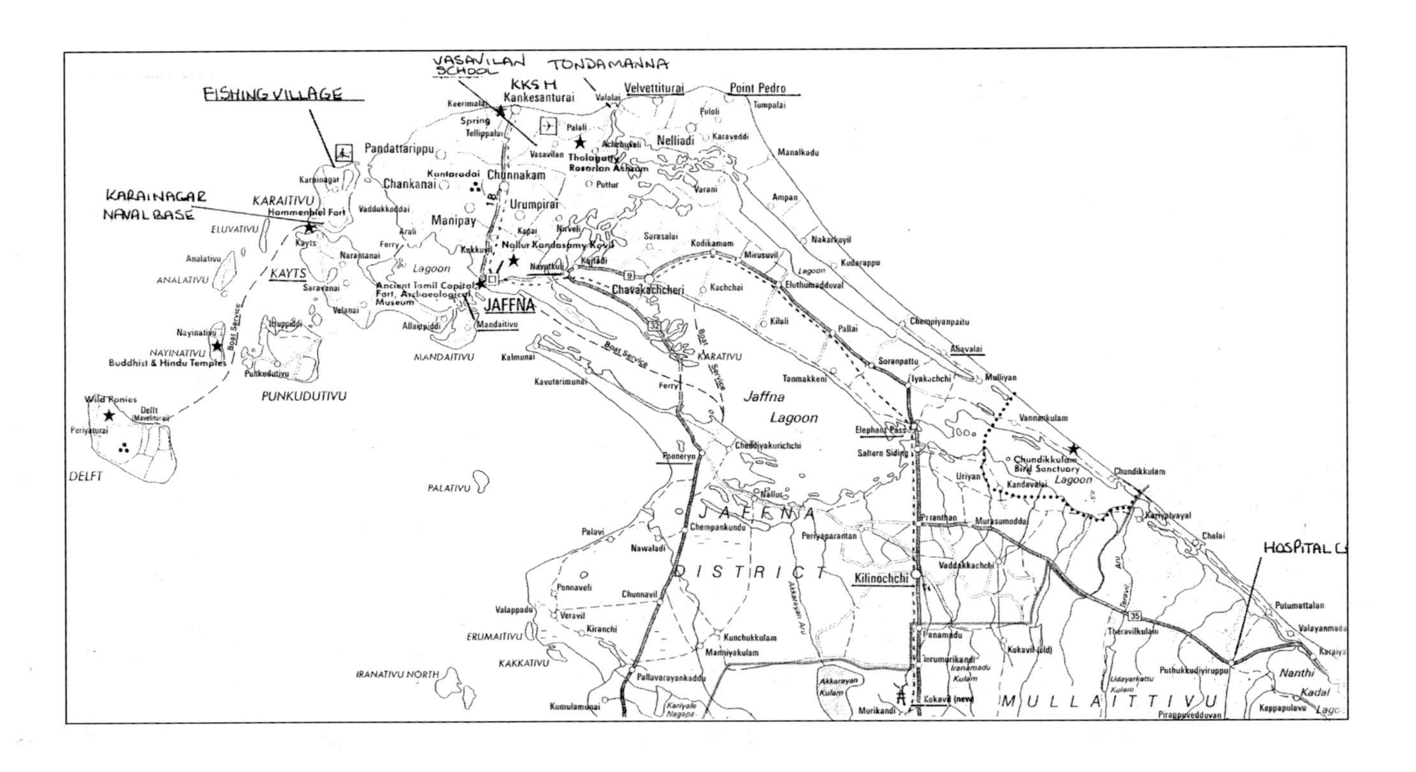

Jaffna area map

restaurant, it swam in oil the colour of brickdust. That's not to say that the curried cabbage wasn't as hot as sin and tasted like something out of a cattle trough.

That afternoon brought an unexpected and pleasant surprise. Looking out from the door of my room towards the helicopter landing pads, I noticed a lone figure trudging towards the Mess festooned with gear and a T56 slung over his shoulder, was a 'Whiteface' complete with a droopy moustache. He came on with a sense of purpose in his stride that said 'I belong'. Barely pausing at the door of the room, he strode right on in and dumped his gear on my bed.

'See you've cleaned it out a bit,' he declared in a pronounced Rhodesian accent and stuck out a well-tanned hairy hand.

'I'm Dave Warton,' he went on, 'how long y' stayin'?'

'Hiyah, I'm Tim Smith,' I replied taking his hand. Oh, how I wished then that little turd Namal could have been there to see how it was done properly.

'As for how long,' I went on, 'who knows? It's supposed to be for a couple of weeks from all that anybody has seen fit to tell me, I'm the new Flying Instructor.'

Dave sniffed expressively and sat on the edge of the bed. Dragging his boots and socks off, he explained that he'd been away to Anuradhapura for a few days and had just got back. We chatted away like old friends. Very soon I had a better idea of what I had let myself in for.

For the next couple of days Dave was away with a Trooper on day trips to Kilinochchi. He returned in the evenings bringing with him bags of fruit that he'd scrounged from the roadblock on the northern end of the causeway at Elephant Pass. Meanwhile my time was spent flying as co-pilot to Namal on Coconut Runs to the outstations.

The Army called on the Air Force for help on a regular basis, at least twice daily it seemed. On the third day of learning the ropes, I had my first glimpse of another Namal, a glimpse of something other than Coconut Runs.

Lounging on my bed, I was waiting for lunch when Namal came by in a hurry with his flying gear.

'There is some trouble at Mandaitivu,' he said, 'come on.'

I grabbed my flak jacket, helmet and T56. Running towards the heli-pads I noticed that he was cranking up the 212 Gunship.

'Trouble,' I mused, as I clambered in to the left seat of the Gunship and slid the seat armour forwards.

Plugging in my helmet's pigtail connector, I switched on the radios and navigation aids. I called the control tower for a radio check, checked out the intercom with the door gunners and the .50in gunner in the cabin. The post-start checks were completed in double-quick time, and we hover-taxied slowly to the take-off strip.

The Bell 212, fitted with weapons pods, sideways-firing cabin-mounted .50in heavy machine gun and 7.62mm sideguns, was one heavy and ponderous beast in the hover. Like an overloaded shopping trolley, it tended to go pretty much where it liked. The heat was shimmering off the tarmac, which didn't improve things at all. Namal nosed the Gunship forward, and we wobbled off down the strip and into the air towards Jaffna.

We climbed away southwards, the door gunners lounging back in their seats in the main rotor gearbox recesses and enjoying the view. At 3000 feet we levelled off and flew over Jaffna Town. It was my

Jaffna fort

first view of an old Portuguese fort, and I was impressed with its moated star shape.

'We do not fly lower than three thousand feet here,' Namal explained to me, 'they have a 12.7mm machine gun somewhere in the town.' I nodded in agreement.

'Suits me,' I thought. 12.7mm rounds make big holes in flak jackets.

Clearing the town to the south-west, we descended to 1500 feet and turned east again towards Mandaitivu. Checking in on the tactical radio, I asked the Army what their problem was. The outpost reported that some boats had been seen on the lagoon close to the road some 1500 metres from their check-point on the causeway south of Jaffna Fort. The Army at Mandaitivu were getting twitchy and feared that a culvert bomb was being laid, or that an attack on their roadblock was imminent.

We flew a big lazy orbit on the area, but saw nothing except for an old man on a pushbike about two kilometres away, pedalling slowly towards the roadblock. Namal called for guns. Without thinking, I set the circuit breakers and selected the pod gun on the weapons control panel. Pulling the sight down from the roof and locking it into place, Namal gently rolled the aircraft out of the orbit and set up a shallow attack dive towards the old man.

'Where are you going, what have you seen?' I asked.

'I think he is maybe a bad guy, if I shoot at him and he runs

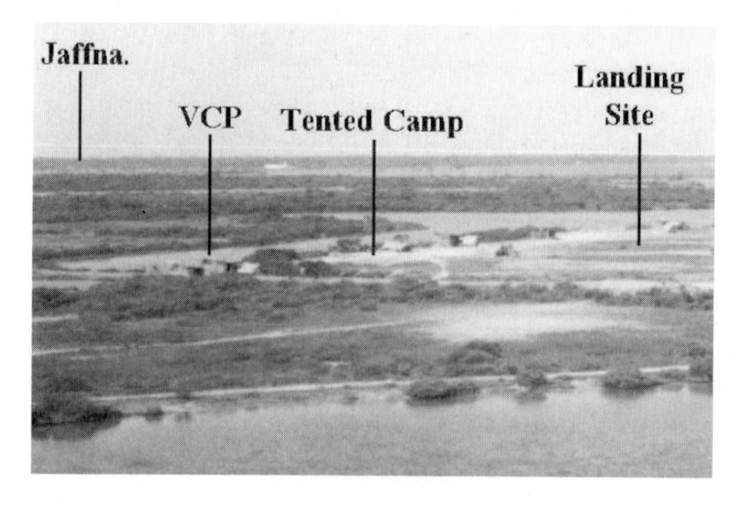

Mandaitivu camp

away, it will prove that he is,' Namal replied with a childlike innocence that was totally confounding. With that he sent a stream of .50 bullets stitching along the road. The old man fell from his bike and lay very still. I was stunned. He didn't run away. Maybe that meant he was a good guy.

As we pulled out of the dive another call came from the outpost at the Jaffna end of the causeway. They reported that two motorcycles had been seen leaving the area of the jetty near the Fort at high speed, and they wanted us to take a look at them.

Due to the nearness of the town, and the threat of 12.7mm hidden in there, we first flew north-eastwards parallel to the edge of town. The port door gunner soon spotted the two bikes racing along the north side of the lagoon.

Another gentle dive brought us down to 1000 feet as we closed rapidly on the bikes. We crossed the causeway to the Fort and Jaffna, and passed the tented camp that was Mandaitivu before turning eastward to run on down the middle of the lagoon. The two bikes were now racing neck and neck less than 800 metres away and parallel to us. Namal slowed down, virtually matching speed with them and, edging a bit closer, gave the order to fire.

A withering stream of 7.62mm rounds from the doorgun engulfed both bikes and riders. They tumbled to the ground amongst small fountains of dust and lay still. We pulled away and climbed to 3000 feet heading back to KKS. I was numbed, a hollow, empty feeling filled my stomach. Without thinking I switched the weapons to safe and pulled the circuit breakers. I should have done that 20 minutes before. The pair on the motorbikes I wouldn't care to guess about, but perhaps the harmless old man on his push bike would still have been alive. I was learning all right, I didn't like it, but was learning.

The following day a daylight attack on the Army gate to the airfield at KKS brought the same response that the old man on the pushbike had got, and I discovered that anything that moves following an attack was 'in season'. By day six I knew that trucks and buses were also on the 'list'.

Returning from a coconut run to Elephant Pass, we flew over a truck standing at the road junction at Nelliadi a couple of klicks (kilometres) to the south-west of Point Pedro. As we passed overhead it turned away from us and sped off along the road to Karaveddi in a cloud of dust.

Namal swung the Trooper around in a blade thumping tight turn and brought the port doorgun to bear. He gave a brief order to the gunner, and a stream of 7.62mm machine gun fire raised dust across the road and rattled its way across the cab, shattering the windscreen and killing the passenger. The truck came to a sliding halt in a cloud of dust and steam from the radiator.

The driver left the cab at a blind run and almost made it into the coconut groves before the creeping fingers of tracer stroked across his back. He stumbled, staggered a few more paces and fell. He twitched for a second or two and finally lay still. It seemed to me that good guys and bad guys all lie down when they're dead.

The 5th of June had been a special day, a glimpse into the murky crystal ball of the future. In one week I had watched at least five people die, supposedly in the cause of peace. This Namal chap was really uptight. I was certainly getting a feel for the conditions under which the young Sri Lankan pilots operated.

At the end of a week's flying with Namal I thought that I'd seen it all. From Pooneryn, to the south of the Jaffna Lagoon, north over the causeway to Elephant Pass with it's sunny, sandy lagoon and blindingly white salt pans. Westwards along the thin, scrub covered strip of the Peninsula to Point Pedro and Velvettiturai, the real hardcore places, bandit country. On again to Valalai and the army's outstation at Tondamanna, facing each other across a hundred yards of a sandy river estuary in a Sri Lankan stand-off.

Further west to the Kankesanturai Hotel (KKSH) on the beach to the north of the Airfield. The troops stationed there were the best accommodated on the peninsula. They lived in a purpose-built tourist hotel at Kankesanturai which had been taken over by the Armed Forces for the duration.

Going south from the airfield at Kankesanturai (KKS) the army had more outstations, covering the northern and eastern approaches to Jaffna Town, Kodavil and Navatkuli. In Jaffna Town itself the Army held only the Fort and the television and radio broadcasting station to the west of it on the south edge of the town.

The islands and the southern approaches to Jaffna were covered by a tented camp on the causeway-linked island of Mandaitivu and the Naval Base at Karainagar on Karaitivu. All of them had their own hotspots, places to fly and places to avoid.

KKSH

Each had its own heli-pad, and all of them were different. I gained a whole new insight into heli-pad construction. They used everything, from trampled earth to PSP, concrete blocks and coconut palm logs. Anything that came to hand.

One outstation, on Delft Island I seem to remember, had an enormous pad of interlocking paving blocks, the sort that would make your average millionaire in West Sussex turn green with envy. Somehow I didn't think that the legal owners of the blocks would have been too happy about it, but then they probably didn't visit too often.

During that first week in KKS a routine was quickly developed. I think perhaps it was to keep my mind off what was going on during the day. A rigorous daily programme of flying and housework during the day, and in the cool of the evening a three-mile run around the northern half of perimeter track.

The southern portion of the perimeter track was definitely bandit country. Out of respect for the local Tigers the army patrolled it by armoured car, on the inside of the fence.

Sometimes my new roommate, Dave, came along with me, but

Run for your life with a T56

more often than not I was alone except for my constant companion of the last week, my trusty T56 with two 30-round magazines taped back to back.

Carrying the T56 was a must, for it wasn't unknown for the Tigers to pop off a round or two at the perimeter guards from time to time. An unarmed Whiteface jogging by would have been an irresistible target. So carry it I did.

Unfortunately a T56 with two magazines and a sling weighs in at about 12 pounds. Carry it on your back with the sling, and it will beat you full of bruises whilst you're running. The only answer was to carry it in your hand at the trail with the stock folded. That way the only real snag was that the cocking lever and the magazine housing dug into my hand something bloody awful, rapidly forming blisters around my thumb and forefinger.

It was a local variation on 'ninety-nine change hands'.

Those runs were a masterpiece of timing. You had to set out while it was still light enough to get back before the tropical darkness set in, but cool enough to be able to complete the course without completely knackering yourself.

Go too early and the sweat ran in streams from every pore on your body, and I didn't dare to set off too late for to go running around the place with a loaded weapon in the dark was asking for trouble. The young conscripts on guard duty were twitchy enough during daylight, and I didn't really fancy getting shot at in the cause of fitness.

Nosing around the camp during the daytime, I came across some old hardwood carver chairs on a rubbish tip and I immediately claimed them for the Whiteface mess. During a couple of evenings I re-wove the seats with some D10, Field Telephone wire, that I'd liberated from the Signals Section, and installed them on our patio, an area of concrete outside the door.

I had also come across a semicircular sheet of rusting mild steel lying against a nearby PSP rocket fence and purloined it. I placed it across a couple of old tyres that were borrowed from the top of the Mess' Bunker. We now had a table and two chairs on our patio. Yes, civilisation. Eat your heart out, MFI.

After my daily gallop around the airfield I generally spent ten minutes cooling down in a wrap-around towel or sarong whilst I washed out my sweat-soaked shorts and T-shirt. Following a shower and a change into something cool, the rest of the evening would be devoted to eating and relaxing.

With our meagre supper finished we sat out on our patio under those star-filled skies with a coffee or sometimes a beer. We listened to the gentle rustling of the evening breeze through the palmyras and the squawking of the mynah birds arguing amongst themselves as they settled to roost there for the night.

In low, murmured tones we discussed the how and the why of our presence there, the morality of what we and the SLAF pilots were doing. Flying Gunships had never been mentioned when we had signed our contracts for this trip, and we had no intention of doing so. The mention of 'western mercenaries flying Gunships' in the *Newsweek* article had been specifically denied by the company.

We asked ourselves why was there never any follow-up to the almost daily air-to-ground skirmishes. Why didn't anyone go and find out who had been killed or wounded? Did anyone actually get brought in for questioning, did anyone want to know the answers? It seemed to me that so much military intelligence was lost at the pressing of a trigger.

Each evening, at about half-past nine or maybe ten o'clock, the

Liberation Tigers of Tamil Eelam gave the Army a nightly salute, a few rounds of mortar and machine gun fire from the area immediately to the south of the airfield towards Jaffna.

The first time it happened I was half out of my chair to get my gun before I realised that Dave had not even budged. The Army would reply in kind as we talked on into the night, sipping sparingly at our warm beer and trying to identify the rounds as they riffled through the night sky over the camp.

On 6 June I flew four coconut runs into Velvettiturai (VVT) with Namal. On the second run in there was the by-now familiar crack and slap of passing 7.62mm rounds. Namal, lounging back behind his seat armour in the left seat, as I flew in the right, casually reached over and turned up Radio Australia, which he had tuned in on the AutoDirectionFinder (ADF).

We continued on into the landing site to the strains of Jeff Beck singing 'Hi Ho Silver Lining'. I suppose that if you can't hear it, it ain't happening. I suppose it was a case of 'if a tree falls in the jungle and there's no one there to hear it, did it really fall?' It seemed to me that no one cared that the Tamils were challenging the Sri Lankan Forces' right to operate into the landing sites.

VVT

On that very same day Kapila, one of the Squadron's Flying Instructors from Katunayaka, arrived during the afternoon. That evening, in an apparently casual conversation, he asked me if I would object to flying the Gunship as Captain.

That selfsame subject had already been discussed at length during our evening talks on the patio, and the answer was already on my lips when thoughts of the hole in the roof at home and the unpaid £3000 bill flashed through my head. I'd been there a month and would have to stay longer to cover the outlay on the roof, and then I would have to stay even longer to pay the taxman if I decided to leave before the tax year was up.

Dave and me had both flown as co-pilot in the left seat of the Gunship with Namal, and were united in our opinion that he was a bloodthirsty, murderous little bastard. The Gunship seemed to be used as a morale booster for the ground troops. Blow away anything that popped up and frightened the Army, regardless of its validity as a target, seemed to be the unspoken rule for engagement with the Gunship. Under those terms neither of us had any inclination to Captain the Gunship, and up until then we hadn't been asked. Now here it was. I made the fine distinction that I would go along in the capacity of Safety Pilot.

How easy it had been to arrive in a tropical paradise as a flying instructor in search of some good money, to be diverted to Jaffna for a while for expediencies' sake and a Bell 212 conversion course. Then to take the next step along the path in the belief that I wouldn't get my hands dirty in the Gunship by being there in the capacity of Safety Pilot. Money before morality, step two down the rocky road. Gutless wimp.

Looking back on that moment, my feelings are that if the Sri Lankan Air Force had faced the truth and had the guts to ask us to Captain the Gunship as a means of reducing the chances of opening fire on innocent bystanders, we may well have agreed to their request.

The same could be said of our local Team Leader who could only express his feelings on the matter by later declaring to all and sundry that we lacked moral fibre. This from a 'training and security organisation'. A company that implied or lied that they had, however tenuous, contact with and approval of our glorious Government's Foreign and Defence Departments.

Lack of moral fibre? Complete and utter bollocks. They didn't know what they were talking about. Passengers had often sat in the back and praised their pilots for stoically pressing on into a hot LS without flinching as the bullets slapped and rattled past the windows.

The truth of the matter is that we were sat in the front of airborne six-ton trucks without brakes, doing 80 miles an hour and only the gearbox to stop us.

In front of us there is only a glass reinforced plastic radome, some electric wiring, and a few instruments, none of which were designed to stop bullets.

Lack of moral fibre? You had better believe that the decision to go in had already been made and implemented a thousand yards away, before the bullets started to fly.

Heroism? Complete and utter bollocks. Pragmatism, pure bloody pragmatism.

Tell me about moral fibre when you've flown in the face of fire day in and day out for five months knowing that the bullets are certainly going to fly, knowing that the troops on the ground don't give a shit about the safety of the incoming helicopter; unless they happen to be sat in it.

The day following Kapila's visit and his 'casual chat' started as they always did, with a pre-breakfast flight as top cover for the Avro 748 re-supply plane from 2 Squadron at Ratmalana, followed by a morning of distributing cabbages and coconuts (C&C) to the outstations.

That day it was mainly C&C to Mandaitivu, south of Jaffna Fort. We finished well before midday, and the rest of the morning had been spent mending the mosquito nets at the back window.

Just before lunchtime the Gunship was called for. Namal and me were scrambled to go and look for a green bus just outside the fence on the Army's side of the airfield camp, heading east along the road towards Achchuveli. A couple of local heavies had shot up the main gate yet again and then legged it on the local bus. Some heavies, eh?

As before, Namal fired up the engines whilst I checked out the systems. Quickly taking off, we swung left-hand down around the camp perimeter and caught up with the bus in no time at all. We chased after it as it raced eastward along the road towards Achchuveli at a furious pace, rocking and weaving from side to side across the road while the doorguns hammered and hastened its flight.

On the edge of Achchuveli it careered off the road into some bushes, and I seriously thought that the chase would end there. I had some sort of misguided idea that the Army would send out a patrol to take over on the ground. More fool me.

The passengers, men, women and children, leapt from the bus and scrambled madly through the bushes for the safety of the houses on the edge of the village. The doorgunner just kept on firing.

'Bloody hell, Namal, there are people in those houses, the bloody main street is full of innocent people, you can't keep on with this,' I was almost shouting by then. Namal ordered the gunner to cease firing as he reluctantly called off the attack. Sulky little bastard.

What I didn't know then was that there was very little military presence on the ground anywhere on the peninsula. Hearts and minds patrols did not exist. If a foot patrol went more than a kilometre from its base it was considered a resounding military success.

In situations such as we had just been in you couldn't call on a local patrol to back up an airborne stand-off. However, I didn't see that as a good reason to blow away a busload of villagers or pepper the main street on market day. Jaffna really was one great big bucket of shit.

That evening brought a call for a casualty evacuation from Mandaitivu, just one klick across the causeway from the Fort. I legged it down to the Trooper on standby at the hangar and got it ready to fly.

Kapila, the instructor pilot from Kat, appeared at a stroll. He climbed in, fired it up and off we went. By then it was full dark and, quite unusually, it was getting misty. Out on the end of the causeway at Mandaitivu it was as dark as the inside of a monk's habit, and foggy. The troops out there were head-down and arse-up in their trenches, and wouldn't show more than a single torch light for us to land on.

Kapila started an approach to the LS but got himself really screwed up, tight on the controls to the point where he couldn't hack using the landing lamp with any accuracy. Finally he got himself a dose of the leans. Totally disorientated, Kapila had lost all sense of pitch and roll. It happens.

Slipping quickly into instructor mode with a quiet but firm 'I have control', turning the landing lamp off, I immediately went on to the flying instruments. First things first. Getting us straight and level, I then used the radio-altimeter to get us going down to where the torch had glimmered in the dark.

'Forward and down, forward and down.' A quiet and wilful chant; like teaching rookies to night-fly back at Middle Wallop.

With 100 feet showing on the rad-alt, the landing lamp was switched briefly on and off again. Through the mist I could just make out the dark shapes of tents and trucks ahead of us, with a lighter, sandy open space in front of them. With my eyes glued firmly on the landing pad I flared the aircraft quickly, washing off the forward speed and the rate of descent. At 20 feet I nosed the Trooper forward again and dumped it firmly on the ground, obliterating the LS in a self-made storm of dust and sand.

The casualty was suffering from gunshot wounds. It was an own goal scored on a returning foot patrol that had forgotten the password. By time we had dumped him off at the Casualty Receiving Station at KKS it was going on bedtime, and as I walked back to my room the Tigers were playing Lights Out with a combination of mortars, AK47s and their mobile 12.7mm. Hey, don't get the wrong idea. It wasn't an all-out battle, they just sent a couple over every few minutes for about half an hour. Dave lay snoring on his bed.

4

Dust-off and Dust Off

> ... and Western mercenaries from KMS were sighted last week commanding helicopter Gunships.
>
> *Newsweek,* 19 May 1986

A few more days were spent flying with Namal before I was rostered to fly with a chap that I had not seen or met before. I was glad to see the back of Namal for a while.

The new chap was a different kettle of fish altogether. Married with two kids, Flt Lt Roshan Goonatilike was quiet-spoken and thoughtful, an altogether pleasant chap. A quiet Sri Lankan Rowdy Yates lookalike; I took an instant liking to him.

During a run down to the eastern end of the peninsula together we heard an Army patrol calling on the tactical radio asking for a casualty evacuation, a Cas-evac, a dust-off in American terms. From 3000 feet it looked so peaceful down there, Serendib, the jewel in the Indian Ocean – sweeping palm-fringed beaches, fishing villages sleeping in the sunshine and sandy lagoons skirted with lazy coconut palms leaning on the prevailing wind. Absolutely bloody lovely I could hardly believe that people were fighting down there.

The casualty was already in the grounds of the hospital on the outskirts of Puthukkudiyiruppu awaiting our arrival. I hadn't been that far down the peninsula before and wasn't sure of the local situation, but thought that a casualty in the grounds of a hospital couldn't be that much trouble, now could it?

Roshan, however, was flying big circles and seemed to be very undecided. I couldn't understand why, so I asked him where the LS was and to describe the layout on the ground. From the anxious and halting reply I gathered that the foot patrol had withdrawn to the hospital under fire and that their casualty was in a bad way.

'Uh huh, now that's a bit of a bastard,' I thought, carefully studying the ground around the hospital. A plan formed rapidly in my mind. A piece of cake. This would be no worse than flying into St Angelo in Northern Ireland.

'I have control,' I murmured. Roshan grunted but said nothing and let me take it. 'Ohh shit, here comes the instructor again'.

There was a track through the coconut groves; a long dark line that led straight in to the rear of the hospital. Nosing the 212 down we accelerated away from the hospital towards the far end of the track about four or five klicks distant, way out of sight of the local Tigers.

Turning low over the treetops, we followed the track back in towards the hospital, lickety spit. In essence it was a bog-standard Army Air Corps low-level concealed approach and take off (CATO), as taught at the School of Army Aviation.

The LS came up sooner than expected, and suddenly we were clear of the covering trees and rocketing out into the open.

'Wires.' A brief call on the intercom and the Trooper was quickly poled up and over a set of low-slung power lines that threatened to take the skids off. Then, flaring the aircraft hard, we dropped into the clearing.

With my heart thudding in my chest, the 212 Trooper was dumped on the ground behind some rubbish bins near the side entrance to the hospital. Those wires had been so bloody close that they had looked like drainpipes stretched across the flight path.

No sooner had we landed than the place erupted into seething activity. Brown-skinned soldiers in scruffy olive drab overalls scuttled out from cover with their wounded and unceremoniously dumped them on board.

The rattle of small arms fire and the slap of bullets as they passed close around the cockpit were plain to the ear. Then again another, much closer, rattle of fire as more soldiers raced into the hospital grounds. Zigzagging for cover behind the walls and dustbins, they squeezed off long bursts of fire over their shoulders as they ran.

'Ohh shit, this is a hot one. You've really done it this time, Smithy.'

Roshan, though, was somewhere else, slouched back in his seat behind his side armour in some private little world of his own. He was jabbering away heatedly in Sinhalese to the young subaltern who was supposedly in charge of this scrummage, but who was in reality using the Trooper as some sort of magnificent high-tech body armour.

Shouting over my shoulder to the starboard door-gunner sat just behind me, I told him to keep his eyes and his gun trained on the area beyond the side entrance to the hospital. Screwing round in my seat, I shouted across at the port doorgunner to get back to his weapon and leave the loading of the wounded to the troops and keep his eyes on our rear. I was more than a bit pissed off with Roshan for not keeping control of the crew.

The tricky bit was yet to come: getting out of there without seriously getting shot up the arse. We would have to pull up into a hover above the rubbish bins and the covering wall, completely exposing ourselves to the Tigers. There was nothing more for it but to get on with it. As soon as the wounded were on board, I pulled pitch.

The rattle of fire increased as we rose clear of the wall. Without pausing to think, the Trooper was swung around on its tail, presenting the narrowest target to the Tamils, and poled away; away, back down that lovely track through the coconut groves with bullets still slapping past the windows as we went.

Oh yes, I was certainly very glad to get out of there.

Back at 3000 feet I was trying to decide between Kilinochchi and KKS for the nearest fuel and medical services, when another call came from the beleaguered patrol at the hospital. They had some more wounded and wanted us to return to fetch them out. Really, I didn't want to go back in there. I was still trying to control my breathing and heart rate. Truth to tell, I had just scared myself shitless. A quick glance at the fuel gauges confirmed what I already knew, that we were way down on fuel.

'We must get fuel first, we'll be back in about an hour.' Came my reply, with some relief.

Seconds later a quiet voice came on the radio: 'We have enough fuel, where do you want me?' Dave, flying out of Kilinochchi that day, went in for the rest.

Rest! Huh! I had no peace of mind until he was safe out of there. That question still lurks at the back of my mind, just how much fuel did I have left? Could we have gone back for a few minutes to finish what I had started? My suspicions are that we could have gone back. However, I'll never really know the answer to that and have learned to live with it. So much for my first Dust-off!

Somewhat chastened in my attitude, we returned to KKS that day totally unprepared for the evening's entertainment. The houseboys were setting up another cot in our room, it was going to be full in the shed tonight.

Our visitor turned out to be a Whiteface fixed-wing pilot known as Spike. One of the Roughy Toughy Pilots (RTPs), with Cocopalm and Bar. Yes, that's right: we presented ourselves with make-believe medals no other bugger would.

Spike was due to finish his contract in a few days and was night-stopping at KKS for one last time. Spike was a prophet of doom, he carried his own personal weapon as well as the standard issue and, I suspect, was not unhappy to be leaving.

The night passed in a haze of VSOA and apocalyptic foresight. His opinion of the local Team Leader, the company and the suits in London was something else.

Ken Whyte, it turned out, was not Ken Whyte at all but Brian somebody or other. A Major or Lt Colonel in the SAS. The one that had hit the headlines with a letter bomb through his letterbox in Hereford. Ken, so Spike explained, had little time for the aviators and would do as little as possible to make our lot any better.

Our local Team Leader's attitude towards us, explained Spike, may have had something to do with one of the ex-Rhodesian helicopter pilots asking the Australian Consul's daughter at a downtown party his three standard questions. 'Did she like blecks, did she have a car, and did she screw?' When she had answered 'Yes, yes, no,' he poured his beer down her cleavage and ambled off.

By all accounts Mark'd had a rough time of it back home in Rhodesia. He'd lost his fiancée and her family to the guerrillas and undergone a fairly traumatic experience during the aftermath. It was said that he'd got captured by the bastards that had done it while out on a deep penetration raid.

It sounded to me like the story of one of the raids on the Tembue or Chimoio guerrilla training camps in the late 70s. Maybe it was just bullshit. Who knows?

Whatever the truth of the matter, Mark practised a fairly basic philosophy which came down to his three standard questions. Apparently he was thrown out of the party. Rumour had it that the company sent him off to fly in Nicaragua. Whatever the truth of it might have been, our local Team Leader left the aviators to shift for themselves.

The company was apparently of the opinion that if we were forced to land (shot down) in Bandit Country we would have no trouble in getting back to base safely. Bandit Country was anywhere outside the wire. From where we were sat right then, it was something less than half a mile away.

What should we do, we wondered in our drunken and owlish philosophy? Flag down a passing bus and ask for 'Four singles to the nearest outstation,' and 'Can we put our sideguns and ammo on the luggage rack?'

Spike was of the opinion that the Liberation Tigers of Tamil Eelam would be rather more interested in our teeth, toenails, kneecaps and finger joints than the fact that we were only there as part of a 'training and security organisation'.

I liked Spike, but was glad to see him go. He made my teeth itch.

It didn't take long for Spike's foresight to become hindsight. The following day saw the arrival at KKS of the company's local man, Ken Whyte, and the big man from the UK, Bill Walker, both of them resplendent in tropical lightweights, like a couple of white planters. The pair of them spouted an endless stream of high flown and meaningless phrases. Company loyalty, a job to be done, a lack of moral fibre and so on. Inanities, bullshit really, about our refusal to captain the gunships.

They didn't realise that they were speaking to two of Spike's disciples, two ordinary chaps who felt that they'd been well and truly rubber-dicked by the company. Get rid of one wart and two grow in its place. Shit, we'd been hired as instructors, not gunship pilots. We didn't even know the game plan let alone whose team we were on.

Those two people didn't have a clue anyway. They just sat in their air-conditioned offices, hundreds or thousands of miles from the action and counted the cash. Who were they trying to kid?

Anyway, I'd been into VVT twice that morning to deliver just three bloody constables and two hundredweight of cabbages. Both times we came under heavy fire from the Hindu Kovil, a temple that is, about 300 metres along the beach to the east, and where was the Army? Head-down and arse-up in their bloody bunkers.

Huh, if the Army couldn't secure and defend their own landing sites, they could stuff it. What did the company want us to do, fight the whole bloody war on our own?

So, here we are again at that seeming British Military impasse. Trained to fight, you fight and get bollocked for it. Get hired to train the fighters, and when you complain that you aren't being allowed to do it you still get bollocked.

The confrontation with Ken and Bill brought only one thought to my mind. As long as we were in Sri Lanka we were on our own. Only one person was ultimately responsible for my safety, me. Right then I decided that if it ever came down to a forced landing in Bandit Country the only way out was to leg it, hot foot, for the nearest outstation and to hell with the rest of the crew.

My evening runs took on a new importance, and the old maxim of 'Run for your life' took on a very real meaning. My fitness training would have to be altered to include some form of weight training for shoulders and chest to improve my breathing. Although we were at sea level the density altitude was somewhere closer to 7000 feet, and breathing during any sustained exercise like the evening run soon became an effort.

Certainly the Sri Lankans weren't worth so much heartache.

When a Navy Commander realised that the morning's route would take him to the Naval Base at Karainagar via Mandaitivu, close to Jaffna Fort, he refused to get on. Only when he was told that the route would not change and that he would be charged with cowardice if he did not get aboard, did he condescend to join us. Lack of moral fibre, tell me about it.

Shit! On the return trip from Karainagar we had to put a Naval Rating off the chopper because it was overloaded. He stood at my window and burst into tears as he pleaded with us to take him along. He thought that he would have to stay another night and listen to another sunset serenade from Praburakan's finest, the Liberation Tigers of Tamil Eelam. We took him out on the next trip.

I wished to God that I was working three weeks on and one off. Anyway I was there to observe and learn the ropes ready to instruct, not to fly Gunships; the Sri Lankans could do that. Hell, if Tweedledum and Tweedledee had told me about all this crap back in the UK, I'd have found some other way to get the roof fixed. I'd had enough crap that day without having to take bullshit from Ken Whyte and Bill Walker.

That night I lay awake for some time listening to lights out; trying to organise my thoughts on the day. That crap about 'moral fibre' had really got my goat.

It struck me that there are many sides to fear, each to be faced and handled separately. Fear of losing face. Fear of being shot. Fear of pain. Fear of being wounded or maimed. Fear of death. Fear of just getting it wrong, and everyone was different when it came down to handling their fear.

Namal always rushed headlong at things. I wondered if it was some sort of device for overcoming his fear. Don't think, just do it! Press in close with a mental shout at some inner devil. Namal didn't give himself time to think about it. Like the first time you dived off the high board.

Roshan refused to face his fear. He was afraid of fear. He sat back and did nothing in the blind hope that all would turn out right in the end. He succumbed to it.

Kapila was different again and put on a brave face and an air of nonchalance. He was afraid of losing face. He sauntered on through situations, hoping that he was getting it right and actually going further than his ability could carry him. He bit off more than he could chew just to save face.

Courage is a matter of facing your fear and overcoming it.

Yes, I know something about it. How many times my fear was faced and overcome from 1000 metres out I don't know. It wasn't by some magical ingredient like Bill Walker's moral fibre, but by pure bloody-minded determination to get the job done, backed up with flying skill, military training and experience.

Oh yes, there came a time when my fear of being blown out of the sky over the water and drowning became greater than my fear of being hit. After that my flak jacket was left in the room rather than risk drowning with it on. The breastplate went under my seat to cover my balls, and the back plate went behind it. I never wore it again, and somehow the knowledge that if the Tigers finally got our range the job would be completely buggered seemed to put an edge on life. It certainly kept me on my toes.

After Ken Whyte and Bill Walker's 'morale boosting' visit there followed a brief respite in the daily grind with two days of airtesting on a Trooper, while the SLAF pilots and armourers zeroed and tested the Gunship's sights.

It seemed that they would never learn that to get a rocket to fly straight they really must keep the dirt and dust off the springs and fins that keep them stable in flight. It was no wonder that they couldn't hit any bloody thing when those teeny little fins fail to extend properly when the rocket left the pod.

As for the .50in pod gun, they insisted on using cheap Indian ammo. We'd had some of it for training ammunition when I was in the Army. When fired at a target 200 metres away the rounds were hitting the ground anywhere from 80 to 300 metres away and 20 metres to the left or right. It was bloody curry powder not gunpowder, and then they wondered why they had to press in so close to hit the target?

For a while, following Ken's visit, the evenings discussions on our patio were concerned primarily with what would happen if we *really were* brought down in Bandit Country?

The British High Commissioner had openly declared to the company that he wasn't aware of, and would deny, any knowledge of our presence in the country. We couldn't expect any diplomatic moves to get us back if we were captured following a forced landing, and it wasn't as if we were gung-ho Paras or SAS types to fight our way back. Oh, the ground training staff were OK. They paraded around their Police Training Camp and taught them how to march and fire their weapons, but they didn't get involved in anti-social things like killing Tamils.

We, on the other hand, did on a daily basis, and we did not even exist. It didn't bear too much thinking about. When it came down to it, we were very much on our own, and it would be a case of look out for yourself and run for your life. It was hard to believe that our Government was up to their nuts in it.

Hell, at KKS we had other, more pressing, problems to resolve, and rationalising the Company's attitude towards us was low on our list of priorities.

Food, or rather the lack of it, was a frequent and recurring problem. Our stock of grub was getting low, and some sort of plan for replenishment had to be devised. Shit, just think of that. We even had to scrounge about for some decent grub. Trips to Elephant Pass were becoming less frequent for us, and we were having to eat more and more of the Curried Something that was brought over from the Army cookhouse for us and reheated on a gas stove by the houseboys. It really was some awful stuff. Stuff that would take barnacles from off the bottom of boats.

Dave had a stock of tinned cheese that we shared. He solemnly declared that there was an art to opening the can so that the minimum amount of cheese was wasted. The last few days had been spent very carefully under dual instruction on cheese can opening. I expected to go solo very soon.

The morning of 10 June 1986 brought a fresh culinary disaster. Getting up at four-thirty a.m. to provide top-cover for the infantry Company changeover at KKSH, I found that my electric water heating element was bust. I had it mended by four-forty-five only to discover that there was no water in the bloody tap. God, but I was really pissed off! So up and away on top-cover with no coffee. So okay, it's in the Gunship. It's top-cover, it's a preventative measure. I'm the safety man, there to put the brakes on Namal if something soft should take his fancy.

The column of 80 troops marched from KKS to the Hotel on the beach about four kilometres away, KKSH. It was hailed as a military success.

No small wonder that there was no trouble, for the Navy were carrying out beach landings on the south side of Mandaitivu Island at the same time and had a firm grip on the Tigers' attention. Equally it was no small wonder that on our return to KKS for fuel, we got a call from the Army on the southern beach of Mandaitivu Island to say they needed help.

Reports came in as we flew southwards over Jaffna Fort that people had been seen running out of the fishing village that the beach landings had been aimed at. Arriving on the north side of the village, it was plain to see that those fleeing the area were in fact women and children with a scattering of old men. Namal immediately started manoeuvring the Gunship to set it up for an attack. There seemed to be no stopping the bloodthirsty little fool, so I casually reminded him that it wouldn't look too good on his military record if he were charged for massacring the fleeing villagers. He shuffled visibly in his seat but took the tip and continued towards the beach and left the villagers to escape the attentions of landing troops.

On the west side of the village, however, the situation was somewhat different. A group of young men were easily seen zigzagging through the village from hut to hut, taking cover where they could, heading towards the fishing boats tied up at the jetty.

Namal called for weapons and once more I selected and armed

the pod gun. Climbing rapidly to 2000 feet, we turned towards the jetty and set the nose down to adjust the aim. By 1500 feet nothing had happened. The group of young men had already reached the boats.

'Fifteen hundred feet.' I called quietly into the intercom, expecting him to open fire. Namal pressed on.

'Twelve hundred.' Still no response, nothing. Not a flicker.

By then the young men were scrambling across the moored boats to get at those tied up on the outside.

'One thousand feet, Namal.'

We had less than 800 metres to run, and still he pressed on without opening fire. Some of those young Tamils had realised that they were not going to make it and dived into the water between the boats in a last futile attempt to hide, but .50s make holes in brick walls; wooden jetties and boats had no chance.

At 800 feet and about 700 metres out came the first short burst, which fell short. Namal made a small adjustment and then loosed a constant stream of fire until the pod gun jammed.

The sea seethed, bodies jerked, twitched and fell in untidy heaps, like puppets with the strings cut. Splinters, lumps of wood, flew from the boats and the jetty. The beautiful blue-green sea had turned to muddy brown, and shadowy forms bumped on the sea bed; in seconds it was all over.

We broke off so low that I could see the ragged holes in the woodwork as we overflew the target. Making the weapons system safe, we climbed away and returned to KKS.

Hell yes, they were probably bad guys. But no effort was made to pin them down or turn them back. No effort was made to co-ordinate with the ground troops to take them in alive for interrogation. No effort was made to contact the ground troops and get them over to the jetty to search the boats and the bodies for information and military intelligence. It was just a matter of kill 'em all and to hell with the future. What a complete waste of life.

Back at the shack I made myself a coffee and lit up a much-needed cigarette. Dave was away somewhere in the Trooper.

'Must be somewhere down Elephant Pass way,' I thought, for I had noticed that there was no activity down at the loading area near the heli-pad. A second Trooper stood idle on the pan. Odd that, a second Trooper, but not so unusual that it made me think too hard.

Shortly after lunch Roshan came wandering slowly past our door.

'We have some casualties to fetch from VVT,' he called quietly, almost sadly. Grabbing my gear, I followed him down to the Trooper. It then occurred to me that this second Trooper was there for a purpose, and this might well be it, but no one had said anything about any local operations today. We cranked it up, and checking in with the sidegunners and the tower, we left for VVT.

As ever with Roshan he let me do the flying. We scooted into VVT in the normal way, bobbing and weaving, fast and low. Surprise, surprise, there was no hostile fire. Intriguing, so many casualties and no welcome from Velvettiturai's social committee. Something was definitely afoot. Pessimist. Or maybe my luck had changed, optimist. Ah well, the shit will probably hit the fan later, pragmatist. But what in hell had they been up to that they had so many casualties? Perhaps I would find out later.

The next day was take it easy day. Lounge in the sun day. Tan time. Of course all those chaps with brown skin couldn't understand the Whiteface's desire to get brown, so they spent a lot of their time walking past on the way to do 'something' just to check if I was dead or not.

Around mid-morning I woke with a jerk. I thought that it must be going to rain, the thunder that woke me had seemed so very close. I sat and looked around me, listening for the next roll of thunder. Strange, there wasn't a cloud in the sky. And there it was again, a rumbling roll of sound to the east, out towards Point Pedro and VVT. It was followed several seconds later by the crump of impacting shells.

'That's it,' I thought, 'the buggers had been having a ball with the Tigers, and I haven't been given an invite.'

Wandering into the Mess to find out what was going on, I found Roshan and Namal glued to the television set, watching blue movies on video.

'Hi chaps, what's going on over at Tondamanna?' I asked cheerily.

Without taking his eyes off of the naked, writhing bodies on the screen, Namal explained offhandedly that the Army had sent out foot patrols from Point Pedro and Velvettiturai the previous day and had received a jolly good thrashing.

Well, that explained yesterday's casualties, but what about today? They were now redressing the balance by giving the area a dose of medicinal 105mm Pack Howitzer fire from Tondamanna, about ten klicks to the east of the airfield, and were combining that with Navy beach landings to supplement the troops already stationed there.

Staying nosey, I found out from a casual visit to the Intelligence Section that afternoon that the assault and insertion of troops had failed. Inaccurate artillery fire had flattened a large area of housing and killed 70 civilians. The Navy had backed up the operation with a gunboat, but had little or no success in their efforts to dislodge the Tamils from their fortified bungalow up the beach from VVT. All they had managed to do was knock a few holes in the roof of the house and leave half a dozen pockmarks in the sea wall with their 25mm cannon.

That night I went to bed wondering what the hell I was doing there mixed up with a bunch of people that couldn't police a small coastal strip with all the resources they had to hand. It was Fred Karno's Army.

They, the Sri Lankan Officer Corps, wore the uniforms and affected the attitudes of the British Army Officer, but when it came down to it they knew little or nothing of order and organisation. In times of stress they displayed a distinct lack of control over their own actions and behaviour, and seemed to have little interest in or control over their subordinates.

A bunch of frightened and selfish bastards, I found them to be a grotesque parody of the British Officer: opinionated, self-seeking, two-faced bastards without wit, grace or manners. I fell asleep thinking that there must be one hell of a strong leader out there holding those Tigers together. I thought maybe it was Gunga Din.

The following day started quietly enough, no coconut runs, nothing until lunchtime, when a Gunship and a Trooper arrived from Batticaloa. Wonder of wonders, Dave had returned from Anuradhapura, getting picked up in the Trooper on the way. With him were two more Whitefaces, Stan 'the Man' and Don Burton, over from the east coast, Batticaloa, Trincomalee and China Bay.

The afternoon brought a brief flurry of excitement as the two Gunships and two Troopers were used for an airborne insertion. We put 35 troops into VVT. Two trips each covered by the

Gunships, who had a whale of a time rocketing the shit out of the surrounding jungle and empty houses.

Returning to KKS to re-arm the Gunship, Kapila, so he said later, hit the wrong button by mistake and dropped a full rocket pod on the heli-pad. The engineering staff, led by the armourer who was closest, broke the standing quarter-mile record and Kapila's head didn't stop its sheepish rolling for ages.

We laughed like hell at that and wondered if he'd maybe jettisoned it on purpose so that he wouldn't have to go back to the hornets nest that they'd just stirred up.

The local news broadcast that evening told of the re-taking of VVT. No mention was made of the pasting they'd taken to get there, the 70 civilians that had died for it, the flattened houses, the cock-ups or of the Whitefaces who did most of the work. Still, we had a bloody good natter about it that night.

The days rapidly became weeks, and still I was there. My questions about my instructional role were deftly sidestepped or totally ignored. Oliver Ranasinghe had the footwork skills of a Fred Astaire. He suggested that I should be used to provide practical advice and training in the tactical aspects of heli-ops, a sort of operational training unit instructor.

Perhaps my restraining influence on Namal and my practical help with Roshan had not gone un-noticed. The obvious but unasked question was 'Where?'; maybe I already knew the answer and didn't like it.

It was during those first few weeks that I perfected my re-supply system. With the aid of the Mess boys who travelled to and from Colombo on a 'three weeks on duty, one week off' basis, I was able to build and maintain a small stock of tinned food, coffee, cigarettes and various other bits of household equipment. I had put up a washing line out the back between the mango tree just at the rear of my room and the window frame, and had also organised some polish for the floor of the room. A few old sacks liberated from the Army cookhouse had been washed and then frayed at the ends. With a bit of careful stitching they made some half-decent rugs for the floor. I was making life bearable in a veritable shithole.

During my almost daily wanderings around the camp I made a habit of dropping in for a chat at the little-used Intelligence

Section, the Int Cell, and had a constant source of information on our own progress and that of Gunga Din.

Both sides monitored each others' radio frequencies and gleaned as much as they could about each others' daily movements and the success or otherwise of the various skirmishes and confrontations. Local and national radio news broadcasts as well as broadcasts from Tamil Nadu brought information of the various political moves that were being made in the effort to put an end to the fighting.

It seemed that radio traffic increased as soon as a European voice, mine, or Dave's, was heard on the radio. Ground activity, theirs, also increased shortly after. An earlier radio intercept had already identified the re-supply Avro 748 as a target. The buggers were after a Whiteface for sure. Now it seemed they were after Dave and me.

Dave had been away at Vavuniya for some time, but the evenings, as ever, were spent in much the same way. As soon as it was cool enough, and well before dark, I changed into my running shoes and shorts and, carting my T56, dragged myself around the airfield for three miles. Afterwards a tepid shower and rinsing out my sweat-soaked shorts, T-shirt and socks, then scratching together some sort of meal and finally sitting with a glass or two of shandy to mull over the results of my Int Cell visits, until the Tigers played Lights Out.

Oh, it was relaxed enough, and never got to be totally depressing. Sometimes a bit of loneliness crept in as I jogged around the peri-track or sat on my own in the evenings with a shandy or a coffee on the patio. Aye, and sometimes a bit of despair.

Hell, the company didn't want to know us, the British High Commission wouldn't recognise us, and the SLAF didn't care. Bloody pariahs, whether we liked it or not, we were considered by everyone to be Dogs of War. We were in truth, and more than somewhat, Reluctant Mercenaries.

People have often asked me about the things we did out there but don't wish to talk about. They have wanted to hear about Western Mercenaries in Gunships. They want to know if it really is like *Apocalypse Now*. They have never wanted to know how we survived the social upheaval or the emotional turmoil of being uprooted from home and family and chucked into a situation like that. They didn't want to know how we overcame being unwanted and unsung Whitefaces among so many unhappy people.

By the middle of June we were well into the dry season, and the Tigers had moved with the times. Like all good farmers, they understood the seasons and had started moving stuff across the sands to the east of Elephant Pass.

They were stocking up for the monsoon season, making the best of the opportunity to move fuel and ammunition, explosives and the trade goods that provided the hard cash for their operations to and from the Peninsula over the sands under the cover of the darkness. More and more time was spent on stand-by at Elephant Pass in the hope of catching the Tigers out on the sands in the middle of the dried-up lagoon.

I always wondered why they had called it Elephant Pass when most of the time the Tigers used it; I supposed that in the past, before the causeway was built, it was dry enough there for elephants to cross. Certainly it was a bit damp for tractors.

One afternoon a report came in from the roadblock on the Elephant Pass Causeway that four tractors had been seen making their way towards the southern edge of the lagoon to the east of the Pass. We got airborne with the Gunship in time to catch them halfway across.

There was no doubt that they were up to no good, but I still felt happy about the fact that the drivers and their helpers had started legging it to safety as soon as they saw us on our way. They left their tractors and trailers loaded to the gunnels with 45-gallon drums of fuel out there on the sand. It was a glorious chance for a bit of target practice.

Roshan was more than a little taken aback when it was put to him, but I could see that he was pleased to take the opportunity for some practice. We stood off about three-quarters of a mile and started an attack run with the .50in pod-gun, but the bloody thing jammed after half a dozen rounds.

'Bloody hell, this thing is no good at all.' Roshan had already spent too long in my company.

'It's all right. Don't worry about it, we can have a try with the rockets.' Expense was the least of my concerns. Maybe the Sri Lankan Airforce Commander would have viewed it differently, but he was in an air-conditioned office at Headquarters in Colombo.

Quickly orbiting for a re-strike and switching to rockets, we continued with our efforts to destroy them, and failed miserably. The rockets went all ways but straight. The only way we could get the rockets to perform at all well was to shallow out the attack dive. Finally we ended up coming to the hover at about three hundred yards and used the doorguns to finish the job.

Roshan had doubtless reported my practical approach to the situation to the Squadron Leader at Katunayaka, for more and more pressure was put on both me and Dave to captain the Gunships. Still we refused, agreeing only to fly as co-pilots.

Apart from anything else, there were the problems of the pod-guns jamming after a few rounds and the rockets flying all over the place.

We didn't want to be charged with any claims of killing innocent bystanders, and it was obvious to us that any suggestions we made to improve the accuracy of the equipment would be taken with a pinch of salt.

It seemed that they would never learn that there is no replacement for good maintenance. The most reliable weapons we had were the 7.62mm side-guns, but their capacity for protection or destruction was limited to a great extent by the skill of the gunners, who rarely got the chance to improve those skills.

On a later occasion, when we caught a tractor out in the middle with six drums of fuel on it, we were able to wave the driver off before we used the doorguns to give the gunners some more badly needed static firing practice. The drums went up with an explosive 'Wumph', like some clip from a movie.

One good thing that could be said for the standby duties at Elephant Pass was the availability of fresh fruit. On reflection it may have been too good a thing. Dave was passing grape seeds at mach two, and an attack of wind during the night had almost resulted in a sheet change.

As the dry season went on, the pressure was stepped up by the ground troops. The Tigers got really pissed off with the restrictions on their operations and, snarling their defiance, they severely clawed a foot patrol near Mullaittivu.

That day I had again been rostered to fly with Roshan, and we legged it down the coast to Mullaitivu with the Trooper to go and hook their casualties out. It was very much like my first Dust-off with Roshan, and pretty much the same area. Roshan froze again and left it for me to take it in.

This time, when Dave came to pick up the remainder I wouldn't

Elephant Pass

let him near the place until we had some top cover on station in the form of a Siai Marchete, a Light Ground Attack aircraft from Ratmalana with rockets and guns that actually worked.

I didn't mind doing those Dust-off trips. Yes, of course we got shot at. Yes, it was dangerous, but we did save lives, I could teach someone flying skills without killing people. I could hold my head up when some arsehole in a fine suit talked about moral fibre. I could, in some way, justify my continued presence in Sri Lanka.

Thinking back to my first Dust-off, I felt that the balance had in some way been redressed, but there was a price. Having been sent there to observe, I was getting more and more involved in trying to improve the tactical flying abilities of the SLAF pilots and in trying to keep the fight clean.

That night I dreamt that the wall was falling on me. I woke up rolling across the floor with my T56 clutched in my hands. I'd been there a month by then, learning the ropes.

5

First Blood

At Tondamanna beside the road soldiers from their sangar strode;
the Tiger bloodied from the air had slunk defeated to his lair
Smithy, KKS, June 1986

It was June 20, and after a strange night's sleep it was a good day. I had been in KKS for 24 days with just one day off. The HouseBoy, elevated to capital letters due to his success, had got back from leave the day before, bringing my shopping. The re-supply system was working.

Georgius Maximus

By six o'clock that morning I was up for a coffee before doing two hours of coconut and cabbage runs. Back at nine-thirty for a breakfast of 'bullseyes' and beans, and then a stand-easy until the afternoon, when the whole process was repeated again. In the ups and downs of this life I was on a high point. Yes, 20 June was a good day. After lunch I even took a shower before pulling on my flying gear for the afternoon's grocery deliveries.

That afternoon Roshan sat in the left seat as laid-back as ever, the side gunners were the usual crew. I was beginning to like those runs. I don't know why I was so relaxed. The first hour of deliveries had gone well, and we were onto the north coast part. Point Pedro had been unusually quiet, and the run into Velvettiturai had gone like a dream.

Returning to KKS for yet another load for somewhere else, I suggested to Roshan that we could take a short cut to KKS by flying cross-country to the south of Tondamanna.

'No problem,' replied Roshan, as laid-back as ever, 'it's quiet enough down there.'

As soon as we were high enough and clear of Velvettiturai we swung, left hand down, inland on a direct track to KKS.

Tondamanna, Valalai

The vehicle checkpoint (VCP) just south of the outstation was in place. What appeared to be small puffs of smoke were coming from the small sandbag emplacements on either side of it. As we passed alongside it the tactical radio crackled intermittently into life,

'... and we are ...' burrp '... under ...' crackle '... from the south ...' ping, '... terrorists in black ...' burrp '... the village.'

From 1500 feet it was so easy to see it all: the black-clad figures of the Tigers as they dashed from one piece of cover to the next along the northern edge of the village. The puffs of smoke as they fired at the soldiers trapped in their outpost.

'... some of our ...' ping '... are hit.'

'On a day like this,' I thought. 'How dare they ruin a bloody good day like this.' They had some bloody nerve, though, to take on Tondamanna in the open like that.

Roshan, suddenly not so laid-back, and decidedly agitated, was fidgeting in his seat.

'Roshan, can we call up the Gunship?'

Roshan looked up with the most hangdog of expressions on his face as he replied, 'Unfortunately it has gone back to Vavuniya'. He rolled a figure of eight with his nose.

'Roshan, talk to Tondamanna, tell them what we are doing. Come on, I'll show you how to put down a sustained covering fire while the army withdraw or reinforce their roadblock.'

'Do you think we should? I am not so sure.' Roshan replied, as nervous as ever.

'Roshan, we have to help them to get out of there, they have no cover to get back to their camp.' Roshan rocked his head, totally undecided.

'I have control.' The bloody Flying Instructor was at it again. 'Action,' hollering in my best Tank Commander's voice. 'Number two gunner standby.'

I put the Trooper into a steady right-hand orbit at 1500 feet over the village. Roshan was at last on the radio to Tondamanna.

'Number one gunner ready, Captain.'

'Number two gunner ready, Captain,'

'Do you see the men in black clothes?'

'Yes, Captain.'

'Twenty round bursts, please, and take your time. Fire when ready.'

Round and round we went, holding our height, speed and angle of bank. First this way and then the other. From number two gunner to number one and back again. The gunners reloading whilst on the outside of the turn. Lovely figures of eight, laying down an almost constant stream of 7.62mm covering fire.

Once the gunners had got the idea I handed over to Roshan and coached him into keeping the height, speed and angle constant, warning the gunners as we were about to change direction and allowing them the best opportunity of hitting their targets in this very one-sided gunfight.

It was like firing down a funnel with the target in the middle at the bottom. It was almost impossible to miss.

The gunners rapidly improved their aim and quickly learned to control their bursts of fire to 15 to 20 rounds at a time. Roshan improved his flying and for a brief time overcame his fear. The Tigers were shooting back by then, but the soldiery at the roadblock had actually got their heads up above the parapet and were starting to withdraw to their camp at Tondamanna, 800 metres away, laying down their own covering fire as they went.

The Tigers were getting it from both sides now, and they decided to head for cover. That was a bad move, as we could see behind walls from up there and 7.62mm bullets go through corrugated tin and asbestos roofs with ease.

Black-clad figures, looking like matchstick men from 500 yards up, dashed between the bougainvillea bushes and the jacaranda trees. They ran from bush to wall to tree in an effort to save themselves from the withering hail of fire. Some didn't make it. On the way they seemed to trip over the odd root or branch from the tree of life and lie still, huddled figurines sprawled in death on the ground.

We put four boxes of ammo down on those Tigers that afternoon, about 1000 rounds, before the Army had successfully completed their withdrawal to Tondamanna with no further casualties.

Real hearts and minds stuff. To give them their due, those Tigers at Tondamanna sent a few back at us, but somehow the fact that we could see them for a change and were laying it down on them made all the difference. Roshan had learned to control his fear for a bit and to fly under fire, and the side-gunners had got some more well-needed mobile gunnery practice.

Me, well I suppose I'd had enough of being shot at and had

decided bollocks to them all, to Gunga fucking Din, Oliver Ranasinghe, Ken bloody Who, KMS, the sodding taxman, Melinda Liu and *Newsweek*, and anybody else that I could think of.

We made safe and trundled off to KKS for some fuel, ammunition and some more coconuts and cabbages. A first successful engagement. I was on a cordite high, and yet another step down the rocky road. I had picked up King Etzel's sword. It would swing of its own volition.

A casual visit to the Int Cell the following day gave the result as 12 dead Tigers at Tondamanna. There had been 50 Tigers involved with the attack and they had obviously intended to do some damage. I didn't start counting heads until some time later.

By Sunday afternoon Gunga Din had got his boys back together to give the Army roadblock at the school in Vasivilan a going-over. Hell! That was just down the road, just outside the wire.

At a range of only 500 metres from the Mess we were able to watch the proceedings in some comfort and safety. For openers they put over three 40mm Grenades that airburst about 100 yards short of the school. They shifted their firing point and the fourth one, a short while later, landed in the school grounds. One and a half hours after the start, the Army called for Air Support.

Making myself comfortable on a camp bed, I lay back and listened as the Tigers brought up reinforcements.

There was the unmistakable sound of a home-made Mortar, and over there the familiar thump of the real thing. A short while later the same thump from a different place. The beat of the helicopter's blades and the occasional solid rattle of the .50in pod-gun or side gun could be heard between it all, but still the Tigers kept it up. They must have been really pissed off with their losses at Tondamanna. I smiled and giggled maniacally to myself.

It was obvious that they were moving their best gear around on the back of an open truck and on foot, but still they were dropping mortar bombs and grenades very close to the schoolyard.

At the beginning the 40mm grenades and their home-made mortars were airbursting short of the target, but as time went on they were getting them on the ground inside the Army's perimeter. It was obvious that they had an observer somewhere close in, calling the fall of shot. They really were quite good.

Deciding to watch Command and Control of the whole thing

from inside, I wandered into the 'ops room'. Strangely enough, it was unmanned. The Squadron Leader was actually busy playing space invaders on the TV. It seemed that I really was fighting the whole bloody war on my own.

Another week passed whilst I learned *the ropes*. Dave was about to leave for the last time, and I was happy for him. He was going home to South Africa, to buy the place down on the south-west coast for his Mum and Dad that we'd so often spoken about during our evenings on the patio.

I was at once both sad and glad to see him go. We had formed a loose and easygoing friendship during our short time together, and I felt that I would never experience anything like it again. It was the sort of relationship that can only develop in times of danger and stress, the sort of relationship that women seem incapable of understanding and makes them instantly jealous.

Stan the Man turned up for an overnight stop, delivering a Gunship. Before he left I found out that he too would shortly be on his way.

'Come and visit me on Alderney some time,' he said, 'any time.'

'How about next week' I thought. 'Yeh, sure, Stan. Take care.'

Such firm friends, such bloody good friends, both suddenly gone.

Some bastard had eaten the last of my cornflakes. It just had to be Namal, bloody Buddhist vegetarian, I'd give him bloody ommm!

The same Mess boy that last week had chucked away the last dregs of my coffee powder so that he could have the empty jar had just served up my cornflakes to Namal.

'I want some cornflakes,' he had demanded in that haughty tone of voice of his.

The HouseBoy had quaked for a moment and then served them up. I was so bloody angry.

Up and down, like some bloody emotional yo-yo. One day high, the next so bloody low. I'd been in KKS for four weeks without a break. No problem, they're bound to change me out soon.

It was nine o'clock in the evening of 25 June 1986.

A call had just come in from the Medical Station on the airfield for a Cas-evac to Colombo. This had to be a bad one. It was also dark and the boys don't like night flying, so they volunteered me to go.

'You can stay overnight at Katunayaka,' said Kapila. Big bloody deal. I also had Namal for company. There was a huge storm brewing to the south, and the night sky was full of rumbling thunderclouds. Going to Colombo was going to be bloody awful. The Trooper had its sliding doors refitted for the trip.

We fired up at about nine-thirty and hover-taxied along to the Hospital helipad at the north-eastern end of the runway. We loaded up with the casualty and a brace of medics and got under way. Back there in the cabin the storm light cast an eerie glow over the casualty and the medics who attended to the weird array of drips and tubes that were festooned about him.

At 5000 feet the whole world was totally black as we flew on a dead reckoning heading for Colombo. The Weather Radar screen was covered in big red spots like a severe dose of the measles. Cumulo-nimbus cells, thunderstorms. We carefully threaded our way between them as we thumped and bumped our way through turbulence and torrential rain southwards.

There are some big mountains to south east of Anuradhapura, the Central Highlands, and I was more than a little worried about our heading in the strong westerly wind; especially worried since the Non-Directional Beacon (NDB) at Polunnaruwa was blotted out by the weather. I sweated cobs for a bit, flicking an ever-anxious eye to the Rad-alt for any large or sudden changes in altitude. It was no time to fly into cumulo granite.

We eventually picked up the Colombo NDB and a short time later, with a great sigh of relief, made our way out of the storms into the bright lights over the city.

Finding the Military Hospital was no problem. There were so many security lights around it that it looked like the circus had come to town. The Hospital's heli-pad was on a cricket pitch a short distance away. It too was lit up like a fairground. Thankfully we flopped the Trooper onto the heli-pad and left the ground crew from Airforce Headquarters and the Military Hospital's medics to take care of the casualty.

Once we had disposed of our casualty and the medics, the short trip to Katunayaka was nothing more than a quick 'I don't give a shit' trip over the rooftops.

The hangar doors were already open and the engineering night shift was ready to roll the Trooper into the hangar as soon as the blades stopped turning.

The Trooper, with its side doors fitted, had no side-guns to dismount and it took no time at all to sign the aircraft down and hand it over to the technicians. Slinging my T56 over my shoulder, I walked out into the humid darkness and headed for the Sri Lankan Officers Mess.

Less than an hour after landing I ordered a large whisky and downed it fairly quick, just in case some complete prat expected me to go flying again that night.

The Mess was surprisingly full, was it a weekend? I didn't even know what day it was. There was only one Whiteface in the place, me. Unshaven, dirty and looking dog-tired, I stood there in my oil-covered, sweat-stained and dusty flying suit, feeling like a pig in a palace. I looked around at faces I didn't know and felt their stares back at me. Haughty shower of bastards, posers, walking uniforms.

'Bollocks to you' I thought and, ordering another whisky, buggered off to bed. I had been up since four-thirty that morning for a full day's work and then flown two hours on instruments through the most appalling rain and thunderstorms. Totally knackered, I slept like a log.

Breakfast the next morning was a feast. Coffee, orange juice, cornflakes. I had two 'bullseyes' on toast and slipped two fresh eggs into my pocket to take back with me to KKS. Yee-ha.

Up at the Squadron an hour later, I wasn't so wildly happy. I'd marched in to Oliver's office with the intention of finding out just when I was getting out of Jaffna. His answer to my questions was a real stunner.

'With the departure of Mark, Spike, Dave and Stan, we have a shortage of experienced pilots like yourself. Greg is instructing on the Jet Ranger and our own instructors are doing the conversions to the 212 and 412s,' he explained in that oh! so sincere English voice of his.

'I would be very happy if you could bring some practical experience to the people at KKS. I would like you to stay at KKS a little longer, until we have some more contract pilots ready to take over from you. I'll try to give you some time off in about a fortnight.'

Silver-tongued, smooth-talking, two-faced, lah-dee-dah, lying bastard.

I went back to Jaffna with as many creature comfort goodies as could be raised in the short time available to me. The small shop outside the main gate must have thought me totally mad. I bought out their entire stock of frankfurters, all four tins.

The next few weeks passed in a constant round of activity. What in KKS passed for normality. The Top Cover Gunship was constantly late on station for the daily 748's re-supply run. Namal got more and more gun-happy and shot at anything that moved, he also got more and more twitched-up with his flying and constantly overshot the landing sites, which basically put him and his crew in Bandit Country on every approach.

On the days when I flew we went around at 2000 or 3000 feet plus. When Namal flew we went around at 1500 feet and often a lot less. I constantly chided him for his stupidity in unnecessarily exposing himself to small arms fire and risking damage and injury to the aircraft and crew.

On the day he landed with yet another bullet hole in the aircraft I asked him if he thought that he was bulletproof.

Later that day he cried off from flying with me, claiming that he had a bad back.

The Army continued to call for Cas-evacs on a daily basis. Gunshot wounds to the hand? Inside the camp! The unfortunate victims regarded home goals as acts of personal heroism.

Every trip we took to the outstations, whether it was for C&C, casualties or troop changes, brought us into the firing line.

Whilst out delivering groceries Namal caught a LTTE Jeep in the open on the Nawatkuli causeway to the north-east of Jaffna Town and worked it over with the side-guns.

'It blew up just like on TV,' he said with a figure of eight roll of his nose and a huge grin. Unfortunately he also blew a damn great hole in the causeway and cut off the only all-season route from Nawatkuli to Jaffna. The Army wasn't sure if that was a good thing or not.

Squadron Leader Perez declared that 'You cannot possibly hear the bullets going past the cockpit,' and in almost the same breath commanded that we 'don't use more than thirty degrees of bank in case the passengers fall out,' and this man was the Commanding Officer of the KKS Helicopter Squadron. Mind you, he'd never flown on active service, he'd never been fired at in his life. But I didn't know that at the time.

The Sri Lankan Government felt at that time that they had sufficient control on the Jaffna Peninsula to go to the next round of peace talks with some authority. However, if those talks fell through because the LTTE didn't get what they wanted, there was going to be all hell let loose. Even I had noticed that the Tigers had not been as active of late, and there was no real reason for that except the impending peace talks.

I feared for the future safety of the poor unfortunate outstation that would get it in the chest when they started again in earnest. Nothing sucks as bad as a chest wound.

For some time I'd been on my own in the room and had really got it quite tidy. There were some home-made sacking rugs on the washed and polished floor. The mosquito nets at the windows had been repaired, and I'd got the door handle fixed. A light shade had been found and the fly shit cleaned off the lightbulb. Really quite civilised. I'd covered my disgust with what I was doing at work in personal cleanliness.

Then a new Officer Cadet was bunked in with me.

'Ee ... Smith, I am Officer Cadet Priantha,' he said as he introduced himself. I wondered, 'Who put you up to that,' and knew that it had to be Namal.

'I am Captain Smith or Tim. Take your pick,' I replied, taking his proffered hand and looking him square in the eyes. He backed off. He moved out after a week. The scruffy little shit wouldn't keep his bedspace clean, and one night he puked all over the floor after a drunken session in the Mess. Worse still, the dirty little bugger left it there for the Mess boys to clean up.

My link with the shops of Colombo had been going well until the HouseBoy, then known as Georgius Maximus, was medevaced with a hernia after trying to push-start the Squadron's Jeep. Just as well, really, for I had caught him smoking my cigarettes. He was lucky not to have his skinny little throat bitten out. I would have to recruit someone else to take his place.

It's 3 July and I'm sat on the mid-morning 748 with a weekend bag. I'm over the moon with bonhomie. Oliver had kept his word and had given me a whole weekend off. Every man was my friend. Up and down like a bloody yo-yo. I had the emotional stability of a liverish alligator.

That night was spent in the Taj Samudra, where I met Stan the

Man at the bar, having his final fling before leaving that evening. We'd got ourselves absolutely blitzed before teatime. Swaying on the steps of the Taj, I waved good-bye to him as he left for the airport in a taxi.

The next morning I woke at four-thirty a.m. as usual. What a load of shite, even on my days off I woke up in time for the early morning top-cover. Ah, well, at least I was able to get all my shopping done down at the Fort and on Main Street and still get back to the bar in time to get drunk again before teatime. What an existence.

That evening was spent over a quiet supper with Greg in the Oberoi. I'd met him somewhere in town that day. Having completed the training of the latest batch of pilots, he'd been on R&R for a month in the UK.

On his return he'd brought some letters from home for me and the gift of a camera from a professional photographer who I'd taught to fly some time before. I was having a wonderful time, enjoying every minute of my break, and tomorrow would be even better.

I got back to the Taj just before midnight to find a note on my door from the Squadron telling me to be back in Ratmalana for the seven-fifteen flight to KKS the next morning. So much for the long weekend. What the hell, I had some letters from home to read and an old Nikon camera to play with. That old Nikon was to prove invaluable later, particularly the 400 mm, elephant's-dick, fixed-length lens that had been sent along with it.

After less than 48 hours I was back in KKS. Burrp, burrp, bup ... bup ... bup in the distance. Cabbages and coconuts. The occasional dull thump of landing mortars. Nobody moves. Operations normal.

At dusk we were called out to Karainagar, the naval base south-west of Jaffna City. They were under fire and needed help. They confused south with north, and as a result we flew straight into the heavy end of it.

We saw the twinkle of gunfire in the gloom and heard the slap of bullets as they passed close by. The radios crackled with interference and were next to useless. The number one gunner was a new boy and was as good as the radios, next to useless. The bloody side-guns jammed one after the other. I was angry and frustrated and totally pissed off.

The bloody Navy had called us into their fight and then put us right on top of the bad guys, and to cap it all the bloody guns didn't work. Strange how you can see the ground fire flashing below you in the dusk and, knowing that both guns are jammed, just feel mildly frustrated. No, nothing had changed in 48 hours. Yes, ops were still very normal.

The Navy had some casualties to shift and wanted them out of their hair. I pondered for a moment or two on how to get in there without any side-guns for protection and no knowledge of the Tigers' positions.

Back in 1968 my basic helicopter flying instructor had briefly demonstrated how to get from the top of a jebel to the bottom in quick time to avoid coming under fire from the ragheads on the way down. There were no bloody jebels here, but yes, a good idea that would do very nicely in our present situation. Now how did it go ...?

From 4000 feet I dumped the lever, eased the speed back to forty knots, and rolled right into a fairly tight orbit. We were in a low-airspeed spiral auto-rotation. We went down like an express lift.

Karainagar navy base

The rate of descent went off the clock. I was bloody shocked, for I'd never tried this manoeuvre in such a large helicopter before.

On the third orbit we had less than 1000 feet to go and the ground was coming up remarkably fast. Rolling out of the fourth turn, I lined us up with a gap in the coconut trees surrounding the camp. Pulling the power gently back in again, I brought the machine back under control as we swept between the coconut trees around the perimeter fence and flared hard into the LS.

'Follow that, you Tiger bastards,' I sniggered into the intercom. Namal sat in the left seat with his mouth open and said nothing. Looking back on it I was, even then, decidedly flaky.

We had just covered 4000 feet vertically in about one minute in the dark. If the recovery had been left a second later, we would have taken the perimeter fence with us into the LS. It was real smokey hole stuff. Bloody impressive, though.

Olive-drab figures carrying stretchers scurried through the veil of dust that we'd created with our arrival. The casualties were quickly transferred onto the seats and cabin floor. In a new storm of dust we struggled into the air.

Hover-taxiing to the far end of the cricket pitch, I knew that the take-off would be touch and go. There were far more wounded than we'd expected, and we were more than somewhat overloaded with fuel.

Some makeshift washing lines at the end of the strip were either ripped off with the main rotor or blown away as we backed as tight into the corner as I could get us. Frankly, I didn't give a shit for their washing lines.

Sat in the left seat with nothing to do but watch, Namal had also twigged to the fact that we weren't too well off for power in hand. There was nothing left for it but to put the nose down towards the Junior Officers accommodation and go for it.

We shuffled forward with the front of the skids bouncing on the ground as I pulled all the torque available and then a bit more. By time we got to first slip we were still bouncing. At the wicket keeper's position we were airborne but still struggling. Over the crease and down the pitch, two feet off the ground and accelerating. The umpire would have had to duck, but by then we were too far gone to stop. We were totally committed to take-off.

At the far boundary I gave the yaw-pedals a quick kick to release a small amount of power to the main rotor, and gave the cyclic stick a quick tug backwards and then forwards again.

We went over the boundary and the Junior Officers accommodation in a sort of high jumper's roll, taking their TV aerial with us as we left low level between the trees, taking the shortest route out to sea.

We climbed away slowly, praying that there were no Tigers out that way to take advantage of our lumbering departure. 'Follow that, Namal,' I thought.

The days followed one after another, they merged one into the other. There was only one certainty: the Tigers of Tamil Eelam were constantly probing, testing the outstations and us.

Flights into Point Pedro were being met with what was becoming a standard welcome, three or four brief taps of automatic fire as we flared into the LS somewhere near the fourth wave out. Three or four more as we lunged seawards on departure.

There was little time to think about anything too hard, though, for I had developed a dose of the trots and even my evening run was taken carefully. Timing was now even more crucial: if I spent too long out running I'd get caught short and have to spend the last half mile back to the Mess at a mincing gait with my buttocks clenched firmly together.

Roshan appeared on the perimeter track that evening with Namal and Royce as I went mincing by on my third mile. After 400 metres he collapsed from heat exhaustion and was taken to the hospital to recover. I would have loved to have laughed, but didn't dare in case I farted and filled my running shorts. No, nothing had changed; ops normal.

The Tigers had also increased their activity across the still-dry lagoon to the east of Elephant Pass and across the channel north of Pooneryn. Coconut and cabbage trips to Elephant Pass or Kilinochichi provided us with an opportunity to check the sand for vehicle tracks.

Roshan and me were out one day collecting conscripts from Elephant Pass for R&R when we came across a tractor and trailer out on the sands. Obviously they were avoiding the roadblock on the Elephant Pass causeway, and they needed investigating. Closing on the tractor from the west, I called on the starboard side-gunner to put a short warning burst across the track in front of the tractor and to wave the driver off. As soon as the driver and his mate were clear, I landed us alongside and asked Roshan to direct the soldiery in the back to get out and check the trailer over.

Unbelievably, the soldiers didn't want to go, for they had no weapons with them. I was amazed, I couldn't believe it. We had ten soldiers back there in the cabin without a single weapon between them, and Roshan was ready to let the whole thing drop.

'Roshan, if we let this go now the Tigers will think they can get away with this all the time, we have to finish the job,' I explained earnestly and quietly. Roshan just shrugged his shoulders and looked at me with a hangdog expression on his face.

'Bollocks,' I thought, 'there has to be something we can do about this.'

'Roshan, get your T56 out,' I said quietly, reaching round to get my own off the back of my seat, 'and detail two of the soldiers to take our weapons and check that trailer out.'

My tone of voice didn't permit any argument, it was the very best of quiet Sergeant Major's orders to his senior officer. Polite but firm.

Two minutes later, a couple of very anxious-looking conscripts were turning the trailer over in their frantic haste to get the job done and get back in the cabin.

Roshan looked pleased with himself, I think that ordering the soldiery about was something new for him and he was getting the job done. As it turned out there was little of worth on board, nothing that we could positively identify as being contraband and therefore fit for setting on fire.

A day or so later we tried the same sweep again and came up with another tractor and trailer stuck out there in the sand. This time the trailer had thrown a wheel some 400 yards short of the northern edge of the lagoon and was resting on its left axle. Following our earlier success, Roshan was beginning to feel his boots.

Rolling into a left-handed orbit he rattled off a string of fire orders in Sinhalese and proceeded to give it a once-over with the side-guns. Two men upped and ran for the cover of a nearby clump of trees; what would be an island when the rains came. They were decidedly bad guys; they were waving Kalashnikovs, so we gave them a fair dusting with the side-guns before turning our attention back to the tractor and trailer.

The lines of tracer stretched out, curving through the air, disappearing into the belly of the tractor; feeling, groping for life, they scratched their way over the trailer knocking lumps of wood into the air as it went.

The chatter of the side-gunners' first burst at the tractor was still ringing in my ears when a woman stepped out from beneath the trailer. Dressed in a vibrant blue-green sari, with a child on her hip, she walked away.

Even when the side-gunner opened fire again she continued; with her shoulders back and her head erect she just kept walking away from it.

'Stop, stop, for God's sake stop. Are you bloody blind, do you kill women and children?' I shouted.

The gunner stopped. The woman walked on. She sure had some guts, that woman. She was brave, so very brave, she deserved to live, if only for that.

On yet another trip from Kilinochichi to Elephant Pass with Namal, the sandy surface of the dried-out lagoon showed no signs of movement. I suggested that we take a trip back to KKS by the pretty route along the beach.

As we approached the coast near Mulliyan Namal spotted a fast-boat about half a mile offshore heading west. Off he went. 'Tally ho,' I thought, 'let's see what the boy wonder gets up to now.'

'Gunners ready.' I called on the intercom. The metallic sound of side-guns being made ready came clearly over the noise in the cabin.

The crew of the boat had already seen us. One of them was already stood in the back, frantically starting up the other two engines. In no time at all they had all three engines running and were going flat out, heading for the open sea.

Namal raced after it and managed to get alongside them fairly quickly. The port side-gunner opened fire as soon as we were in range and was able to put a fairly accurate burst in front of it.

The boat's crew realised at once that they weren't going to make it out to sea, and in a racking turn they flung the boat about, heading back for the beach.

Caught by surprise, Namal was late in following them round and we overshot the target quite badly. By the time that we had caught up with them again they were fairly close in to the beach and

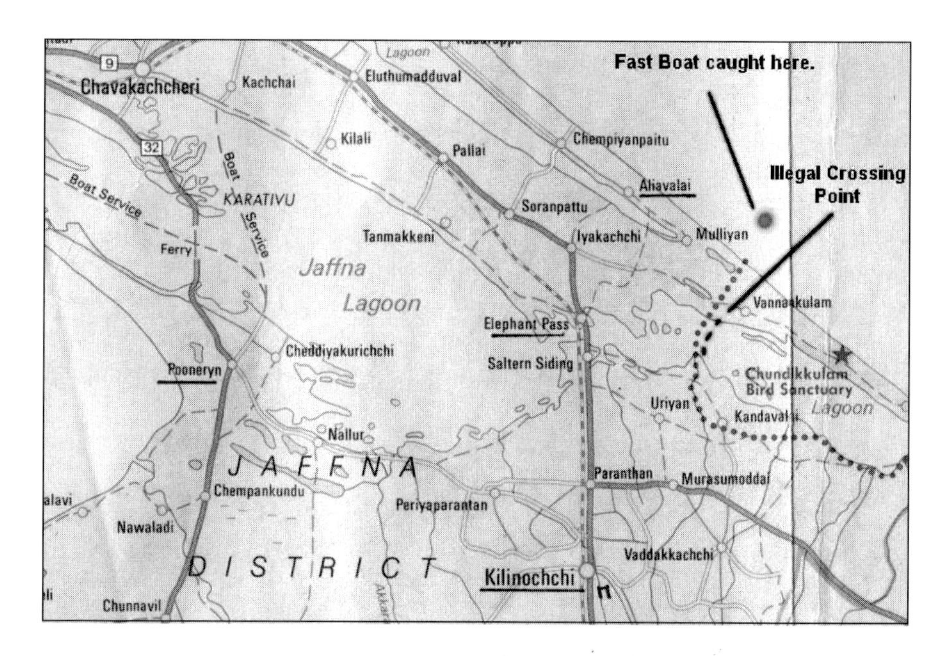

Elephant pass illegal crossing track

closing it fast. With about half a mile to go Namal brought us back alongside again.

The cabin filled with the smell of cordite as the side-guns rattled and hammered again. The port gunner put a long burst straight into the boat, hitting the driver hard and toppling him overboard.

Without his hand on the throttle the boat suddenly slowed, and again we overshot the mark. Throwing the Trooper around in a pedal turn, Namal raced back to the boat, which was again getting under way; the gunners were firing wildly now and missing badly.

The whole thing was turning to ratshit. The next thing that I knew, we were racking around on the pedals again, this time at low speed with a high rate of descent. Namal was trying to round on the man who was struggling with death in the water.

The aircraft started to wallow, and I knew that if I wasn't quick the next thing to happen would be our last. Helicopters do not like very low airspeeds with a high rate of descent. It's called the Vortex Ring State, the helicopter's version of an aeroplane stalling. In any language it is a case of flick, spin, crash and burn.

'I have control,' I shouted. Quickly grabbing the controls, I shoved the cyclic stick forward, pushing the Trooper's nose down for more airspeed and prayed that we would get some before we fell into the water. With about 20 feet to go the machine began to feel more comfortable. I pulled in all the collective lever that it could take to get us away from the water. With no more than a few feet to go, we staggered back into the air.

Back in the boat the two surviving crew-members had grabbed their weapons and were giving us all they had, bless 'em.

In the Trooper Namal was complaining that I was over-torquing the engines.

'Fucking shut up, you clown,' I hollered angrily back at him, 'those fucking Tigers want to kill us and all you want to do is throw us into the sea in front of their boat. I'm saving your fucking life. Sit the fuck still and shut the hell up.'

Coldly, angrily in charge of myself, I swung the Trooper round in a flying school low-level steep turn. Someone was going to die for this.

'Number one gunner, man in the water, short bursts, fire when ready.'

The fire orders came out crisp and clear and brooked no argument.

We swept around the wounded boatman like some clattering, chattering and thumping Angel of Death. The driver had already been badly wounded during the first pass, but still he struggled to swim away from us.

The body nodded and twitched as the bullets struck him again and again. The water around him filled with grotesque swirling patterns of blood. After a few seconds he stopped his struggling and was still.

'Gunner, stop firing, he's dead. Namal, you have control, now see if you can finish the job properly.' My voice was savage, full of controlled anger.

Rolling out of the turn, we came alongside the boat again and opened fire on it. With 100 metres left to run to the beach, the boat started to burn and seconds later, under a constant stream of fire, it burst into a fireball of red and yellow flame as it ran up onto the beach.

One man lay dead, hanging by one leg over the side of the burning boat. The one remaining Tiger leapt from the boat and landed on the sand at a dead run, with his arms and legs pumping like an Olympic sprinter. He raced up the beach, running for the cover of an abandoned fishing boat.

Screaming at the gunners to keep on firing, Namal pursued him. The sand leapt in fountains around his feet, the tracer rounds seemed to caress his back; he staggered as the bullets hit him. His shattered body was thrown in a convulsing heap as he dived for cover behind the abandoned boat, and still the hacking rattle of the machine guns filled my ears. Splinters flew from the sides of the fishing boat.

'Gunner, cease firing,' I screamed, 'for God's sake stop. Leave his mother something fit to bury.' The fast boat continued to burn as we turned away for KKS. A plume of black smoke climbed into the sky. A funeral pyre.

The days wore on and VVT took its turn with the Tigers. The Army tried their best to push the LTTE out of the village area with foot patrols and some heavy support in the form of a Navy Fast Patrol Boat with a 25mm deck gun just offshore. Using poorly trained conscripts to carry out a professional's job could only result in one thing.

We fetched their casualties out later with the Gunship along for top cover while VVT burned, and still the Tigers rattled off a few shots at us as we went in and out. They were some hard-nosed buggers, those Liberation Tigers of Tamil Eelam. 'Aye,' I thought, ' . . . you are a better man than I am, Gunga Din.'

And so the Tigers went on, chipping away at morale and constantly eroding the Army's authority in the area. I felt sure it would be Point Pedro when the time came.

The Army had developed a sort of siege mentality in the outstations and barely showed their heads above the parapet. Although the Tigers had not shown themselves in any strength, they continued to nibble away at the Army's morale. There was nothing like their earlier abortive 50-man attack on the VCP at Tondamanna. A 'one-shot' sniper at Navatkuli, a culvert bomb on a convoy to Kilinochichi, a hit-and-run attack on the outstation at Pooneryn.

Surprisingly, Navatkuli, on the eastern approach to Jaffna Town, the one outstation that was more open to an attack on an arriving helicopter than any other, remained reasonably untroubled. A simple land mine on the unguarded approach would have been so easy to set and would have taken out a chopper with no problem.

The thought had crossed my mind to get the hell out of the Sri

Lankan Air Force and join the opposition. As it was, I was extremely grateful that the Tigers didn't have any paid help.

Throughout it all the Air Force kept up a never-ending flow of coconuts and cabbages, cartridges and conscripts. One trip the 106mm recoilless rifle, the next a cabin load of ammunition. Every day a Cas-evac from somewhere.

Back in the Mess at KKS, a prolonged bout of sickness seemed to be going the rounds amongst the Sri Lankan pilots. Well, at least amongst the more senior officers, for I was constantly rostered to fly with the junior pilots. I thought maybe a dose of moral fibre needed to be administered.

Quite who would do it I didn't know, for the only thing that the CO had found worthy of note was the fact that Froggy Pond posed a health hazard. Huffing and puffing through his walrus moustache, he called up some minions and had it doused with five gallons of aviation fuel. Having ceremonially struck the match, he then buggered off into the Mess to play space invaders and left it to burn.

The Army, 500 metres downwind of it, was not amused. Nor was I, come to that, for the Whiteface's quarters were only eight metres away.

There seemed to be no sense or reason in the attitude of the powers that be. The Jaffna commanders appeared to be hiding their collective head in the sand. They couldn't see that very soon all hell would break loose somewhere there on the Peninsula.

Maybe they thought that if they didn't annoy the Tiger he would go away. Bullshit, he was getting ready to eat an outstation. So what did they do? They didn't send us Bob Hope. Oh, no, they sent us an ABC film crew. The crew wanted to go and film life in an outstation. They bloody well wanted to film Point Pedro.

The film crew turned up on the heli-pad in a state of barely controlled excitement, like it was a school outing or something. Nobody actually said 'I want to sit next to the driver' but that was the distinct feeling they gave me.

Because they were whitefaces who spoke the English language, albeit with a Canadian drawl, the task of taking them into Point Pedro was given to me. It probably had nothing to do with losing a foreign reporter to the Tigers and blotting their military copybook.

'Good morning chaps, if you'll just gather round I'll fill you in on the trip today. Before we start let's get one thing straight, if you as much as point that camera at me while we're flying I'll stuff it up your arse so far you'll be able to film your own fillings, OK.' I started in on their flight briefing.

'Yeah, OK, yeah, no sweat, all we want is some film of Point Pedro,' said their head honcho.

'These people cannot be for real,' I thought, 'We risk our neck day in and day out for coconuts and cabbages, and these guys want a film of it. Very interesting.'

'Now look,' I went on, 'there is some slight risk with going into Point Pedro.'

'Risk. Risk of what?' queried their head man.

'Getting shot.'

'Ah, I see,' murmured the head honcho. I hoped that he did.

The trip in and out was, as expected, not without some attention from the black pyjama gang, Gunga Din's boys.

Taking off from KKS, we left directly north-bound, straight for the coast. There was no way that I wanted to prolong the trip. No sooner were we airborne than I sensed someone over my left shoulder. The stills photographer grinned sheepishly and pointedly tucked his camera into his shirt out of the way. My scowl turned into less of a scowl as I shouted back at him over the noise of the blades and the gearboxes.

'You'll have enough pictures to take in a few minutes.' He nodded as though he understood.

'In a few minutes we'll turn in again towards the beach,' I hollered, 'after that anything can happen, so get back in the cabin and wait for the shit to hit the fan.'

The stills man nodded again and turned back to a shouted conversation with the rest of the crew. Suddenly they were taking the whole thing a little more seriously, perhaps they realised that my pre-flight briefing was for real and I really didn't want my photograph taken.

As we passed north abeam of VVT I shouted back to them again, explaining where we were and how long it would take until we started our approach to Point Pedro. The crew nodded, like so many nodding dogs in the back window of a car.

They tried hard to look professional and cool as they prepared their cameras and light meters and played with the assorted junk that camera teams cart about with them. I suspect they were hiding a last-minute bout of nerves. Headquarters in Colombo had probably told them it was a semi-operational area.

With a mile to run we descended to about 100 feet off the water and rolled right, heading in for the beach and the sea wall behind it at Point Pedro. I could feel the tension building in the cabin behind me, but nobody said, 'Don't do it, let's go back.' Half a mile to run and closing fast.

What do you look for when you're running in to a hot landing site? Muzzle flashes, smoke in the bushes, guerrillas in the trees? I don't know. What I do know is that you look everywhere at once and still see nothing, but you're finely tuned to life.

Fourth wave out from the beach, just about to flare off the speed for the landing. Crack crackle crack, half a dozen waterspouts leap out of the sea to the right of us. Gunga Din's boys are early today.

Flaring the Trooper hard for landing, I briefly look over my shoulder to the left. The side gunner is looking hard but has seen nothing for he is still half-sat, half-crouched, poised behind his gun peering intently along the beach.

The Tigers hidden out there along the treeline gave us one last burst to hurry us on our way. The familiar slap and crack of passing bullets had the film crew climbing all over the cabin to get out of the way.

The return trip later that day was no different. Gunga Din had no respect for the world's media.

Later, back in the relative safety of KKS, their head man asked me for some comment on the trip. He doubtless needed the comments of a Dog of War to underline the hardship and dangers that they had just gone through for their viewing public committed to film. He tried hard to conceal his tape recorder as he casually ambled up to me.

'Ahh, Captain, as we were going into Point Pedro, would you say "We were taking fire" or "Coming under fire" or what?' he naïvely asked.

'Taking fire is an Americanism, we were getting fucking shot at,' I replied.

'Oh, umm, yes. Well, that's an accurate statement' he said as I walked away.

I hoped that the viewing public liked his film.

The sense of unreality continued. Perez tended his garden. The film

Point Pedro Approach

crews and reporters came and went, as did the Cas-evacs. The number of bullet holes in the aircraft was increasing. The engineers covered them with blade tape, a sort of heavy sellotape used for protecting the leading edge on the main rotor blades.

The evening serenades went on. Each evening around about ten o'clock a symphony for Mortars and Machine Gun, composed by Praburakan, directed by Gunga Din.

One evening, though, there was a change in the tune. Someone in the percussion section dropped a really heavy one. The silence following the explosion was deafening, even I stopped and looked southwards.

'Was this it, then,' I thought, 'the big one?' Not Point Pedro, but maybe Nawatkuli on Route 9, or even Mandaitivu.

'Dear God,' I thought, 'that's only a tented camp with sandbag walls, it'll be near murder.' I waited with my heart thumping in my chest. There were no thoughts in my head of 'I'm an instructor,' or 'It's dark, so it'll be bloody me again.'

When the call for Cas-evac came I was already dressed and waiting to go. Only it wasn't Mandaitivu, it was Jaffna Fort itself.

The Tigers had launched a mortar attack on the Fort from the suburbs to the west of the town. This time the mortar team had waited around for the second and third shot and had scored a direct hit on the Officers Mess at suppertime. Three Mess waiters had been killed outright, two officers were badly wounded.

There was no landing site at the Fort, it was too risky getting in and out with the amount of firepower that the Tigers could muster from the town at a moment's notice. The casualties would be carried on stretchers to the Mandaitivu LS. We would pick them up from there.

As before, the LS at Mandaitivu was as black as the inside of a witch's hat, and the possibility of the Tigers still being in the area was high, but I was something more than a disenchanted Whiteface flying instructor that night. Suddenly I had become the Jaffna Dust-off pilot. I was angry with myself for not realising that it would be somewhere as high profile as Jaffna Fort that got it in the neck and not Point Pedro. With their sniping and hit-and-run tactics they had been diverting our attention away from the obvious all the time.

The subsequent trip to the hospital at Anuradhapura wasn't easy. There was no natural horizon and visibility was bloody awful. On top of all that the main artificial horizon had a lazy wander in it, but I was determined that the two young Sinhalese officers on stretchers back there in the darkened cabin were going to get to a hospital that night. I strained my eyes as never before to make out the murky horizon. I steeled myself not to believe in the wandering instrument in front of me, but to use airspeed and heading as an assurance that we were straight and level.

Standing between 200 and 300 feet high the enormous white domes of the Buddhist shrines at Anuradhapura loomed out of the darkness as they had done for near a thousand years. We descended towards the lights of the town. Following the glistening strip of the Malavatu River, we slipped along the western edge of the Nuwara Wewa reservoir before turning right to land at the heli-pad across the road from the hospital.

Even at midnight the heli-pad was lit up like a nighttime street market and was thronged with people out for a good gawp at the wounded that were being brought in. That place always gave me the heebie-jeebies.

Security for the site was absolutely zero. All it needed was for

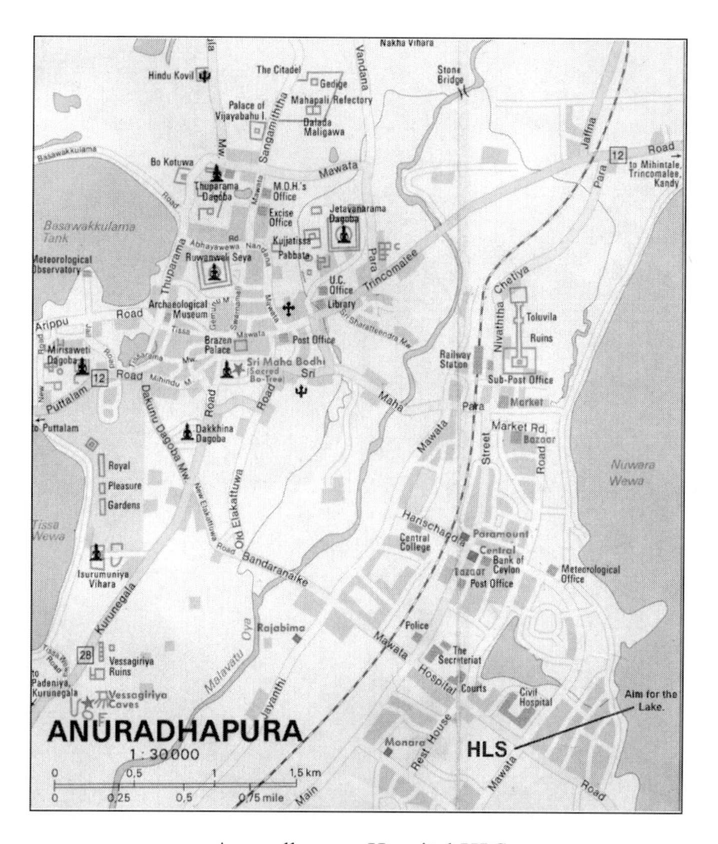

Anuradhapura Hospital HLS

one bad-tempered Tiger to gently lob a hand grenade out of the darkness and the hospital would have more casualties than they could handle.

I was tired and resigned myself to the fact that if it happened, we wouldn't stand a chance. Lifting out of there a few minutes later, I almost succumbed to the possibility of just a quick hop across the Nuwara Wewa reservoir to the military airstrip on the southern edge of the town and spending a night in the relative comfort of the Air Force Mess.

Still feeling some of the resolve that had earlier prepared me for the trip, I pointed the Trooper northward for KKS. I finally got to bed at two a.m. feeling like a dishrag. There was, however, a subtle difference, I was one step further along the road. I had suddenly joined the team.

Anuradhapura Airstrip

At six-thirty a.m. I was up again, flying back to Mandaitivu. This time, though, to pick up the dead. With hardly a pause to deliver the bodies to the Casualty Receiving Station on the airfield, we went on to Point Pedro to collect a Medevac.

Some time later in the morning the daily Avro 748 re-supply crew called for top-cover for their landing. I told them to get stuffed, I was going for breakfast, anyway I had a copy of the signal in my pocket that stated quite categorically that we were not to cover every arrival of the 748, as it created a pattern for the Tigers to respond to. Somebody, somewhere, was getting the right idea. Anyway I was completely and utterly shagged.

The end of July was upon us, and with it the beginning of the monsoon season. I felt that the Tigers were almost ready for a really big push, but still they only probed and feinted. The attack on Jaffna Fort had been a show of strength and determination following their two abortive attacks on Tondamanna and KKS.

Yesterday it had been Vasivilan school and Mankulam to the south of Kilinochchi. Every day was shoot-out day at Point Pedro, but still our newly appointed Wing Commander, Perez, insisted that we continue going into Point Pedro without the Gunship, even though the Troops there refused to go out and secure the LS for us. Tomorrow, well who knew where they would strike next?

The Joint Officer Commanding (JOC) decided to visit Jaffna. He wanted to see for himself what the hell was going on. He wanted to report back to the politicians that all was under control and going well before the next peace talks meeting.

He wanted to go to Mullaittivu and VVT. He wanted to see the troops at Point Pedro. 'No problem,' said Perez, 'take the Gunship.' Shit, a foreign film crew hadn't got that much. There is something to be said for social climbing, if it's only that it's great watching them scrambling on the lower slopes.

Naturally the Tigers saw the Gunship and kept their heads well down, and the JOC was dropped off in relative calm at Point Pedro.

The shit really hit the fan a few hours later when we went back to collect him. The Gunship had gone unserviceable with a Chip Light during start up. Chips of metal floating around in the engine oil had gathered on the magnetic Chip Detector in large enough pieces to bring on a warning light in the cockpit during start-up.

Nobody keeps their JOC waiting, just nobody, so we used the Bell 412 Trooper to pick him up. As ever, I took us in low and some distance out to sea before turning sharply in for the final approach.

The plan, as ever, was to go balls out towards the sea wall at Point Pedro until we were over the fourth wave out, and then flare like hell to wash the speed off before dumping it on the heli-pad just behind the sea wall. The idea was to expose ourselves to hostile fire for as short a time as possible and even then to give them an oblique, fast-moving target.

This time they were ready for us. Somehow they already knew that the Gunship was out of commission. Well, either that or they had their firing point manned up 24 hours a day. Gunga Din's boys along the beach to the east gave us a good rattling with machine gun fire from their toilets bunker on our way in. Now that really pissed me off no end. The port-side doorgunner was Ariyaratna, one of the better gunners, and he reacted immediately when I called for a return of fire.

We rattled our way into the camp with the port-side gun blazing away, streaming smoke and empty cases. The sea beneath us was whipped to a frenzy in the storm of return fire from the Tigers in the toilets. What a jolly way to run a taxi service.

As the cloud of dust that we'd created with our arrival settled about us, conscripts scuttled from the cover of the makeshift buildings that made up much of Point Pedro to offload the supplies that we'd brought along. From one of the sheds appeared a small kowtowing group of junior officers and God himself, the Joint Officer Commanding. The JOC stepped calmly aboard. He had to, for there was only one way out of PPO, by air.

Take-offs from PPO and VVT were almost always downwind, resulting in a deficit in power to accommodate the slight tailwind. Add to that the heat and the inevitable full load, and you had little left for acceleration and manoeuvring. We generally staggered over the seawall with precious little to spare and then dived towards the wave tops to pick up some much-needed speed to remain airborne and struggle seawards.

Film crews or Joint Officers Commanding made no difference; no matter how close to God they were, they didn't give you any more lift.

Pulling into a low hover, I backed the Trooper up to the far corner of the compound, all 50 metres of it. Young officers keen to see their careers furthered braced themselves into our downwash and gladly suffered the sandblasting they took to salute smartly.

Pulling in more power, I eased the cyclic stick forward and went like hell for the sea wall with 100 per cent torque on the clock. The young officers breathed a sigh of relief and scuttled back to their bunkers. Their bit was finished, it was now time for my bit.

I thought that I'd beaten them until about 200 metres out, low over the water, there came the all too familiar slap and crack of passing hardware. The sea beyond and beneath us leapt again in a copper-cased frenzy of bullets. I flung the Trooper hard right going directly out to sea, changing direction, speed and height, trying to confuse the unknown machine-gunner back beneath the coconut trees.

Head-down and ass-up in their bunkers, they couldn't even secure their own LS for the Joint Officer Commanding. Shit, the LS was inside their camp and they still did not dare to man their own walls for fear of getting shot at.

Perez had his promotion and his pension to think of, and so he still expected us to go in.

'If you come under fire, then overshoot,' he had said. Overshoot was Bandit Country. Overshoot was the village of Point Pedro,

Praburakan's home village. To overshoot there was asking for more than just bullet holes in the tailboom. Only this time the JOC had been on board, and the last that I'd seen of him he was clinging for dear life to the vertical cabin post.

It was 3 August and the rainy season had started during the night. Namal was still claiming that he was sick, and refused to fly.

Roshan was, quite unnaturally for him, getting badly drunk in the evenings. He even offered to throw a bottle at me one night. I had thought him to be a friend. I had even had some tomato and flower seeds sent out from the UK for him to plant in the garden of his quarters in Katunayaka.

Ranil did the easy stuff, like pamphlet drops over Jaffna Town and top-cover on the Avro. And Smithy? Well, Smithy remained on flying duty with the Junior Officers every day. Everyone was tired and irritable. Hell, the casualties that we took into the Receiving Station that day had looked fitter than I did.

The Tigers had been nibbling away for 23 days, and the Army were beginning to lose their cool. They were getting angry and afraid, which was bad news, for they had no control over their

Ranil, chief pamphlet dropper

anger and didn't know how to face their fear. What more could you expect, though, the soldiers were poorly trained conscripts and their young officers had little or no experience.

The Sinhalese are basically a peaceable lot with no great ability or desire for either work or war. They would much prefer that someone else did the dirty work, which was probably why the industrious Tamils had been so successful under British rule. Many of the people that I met and talked to on my occasional days of freedom in town would have been quite happy to see the return of British rule. 'At least the roads and water works would be fixed, and I don't think we would have all this trouble,' said one old chap in Negombo.

Getting back to it, the pilots at KKS were expected to perform miracles for the Army without ground support out there in the sticks, and no moral support back in the Mess. The Army stayed head-down and ass-up in their bunkers, whilst our CO pruned his roses and played space invaders on the TV.

Left to their own devices then, the chaps didn't know what to do when confronted with their fear, which often resulted in rash and uncontrolled reactions.

Namal mentally yahooed and pressed in far too close, which gave him instant results but left him mentally washed out.

Roshan curled up in some snug corner of his mind and hid from the stark reality of death and destruction, letting fate or someone else make the decisions.

Ranil volunteered for the easy stuff and kept his face while keeping reasonably safe.

Perez pruned his roses as the mortars and bullets riffled overhead. He knew the Tigers had a healthy respect for the Gunships and wouldn't risk a direct attack on the Squadron lines.

They didn't seem to realise that I too got frightened, but was able to overcome my fear by making quick off-the-cuff plans of action to follow, something to carry me through. It was about that time, though, that I succumbed to my fear of drowning just off the beach and gave up wearing the ceramic plated flak jackets we were issued. Not wearing the jacket gave me the edge that I needed to get in and out of Point Pedro and VVT without getting hit. Rather than giving in to fear, I worked on it.

It also gave the Sri Lankan pilots a reason to dislike me. I flew well under fire, and didn't show my fear when the shit was hitting the fan.

6

Gunga Din

Out along the Ham Bone's shank
Tigers prowled the seaward flank,
and soldiers in their forts of tin
lived in fear of Gunga Din
Smithy, Jaffna 1986

The idea that 'Gunga Din' was determined to take out a helicopter had long since been accepted, certainly by me. Any helicopter would do. One with a Whiteface in it would be better. Equally, I was determined that he wouldn't get anywhere near me.

Gone now were all thoughts of the Taxman and a hole in the roof. Gone too were any thoughts of who flew the Gunships, the company, and Ken Who. The Tigers were some hard-nosed bastards that were taking a pop at me. They'd learn a thing or two about helicopters.

The one overriding thought in my mind was that before going home for some hard earned R&R, 'Gunga Din' would be where I wanted him, on a slab.

My determination to come to grips with the shadowy monster of my waking life was not that easy, however, and the next two weeks were spent in one frustrated attempt after another. Nietzsche said something about 'the snake becoming a dragon in order that the hero should have a proper enemy'. No hero me, but my shadowy monster had certainly become a dragon.

Following several confrontations with the newly promoted Wing Commander Perez, our daily trips into PPO and VVT were supposed to be cut to two or three a week. In truth the Quarter masters department took three flights for delivering coconuts and cabbages whilst Administration took another three to rotate constables and conscripts on R&R.

Added to that, every effort was made to keep me away from the northern flank and any further embarrassment to the weak and ineffectual Army Commanders, both in the outstations and in Headquarters at KKS.

On the few occasions that I did manage to get into Point Pedro and Velvettiturai I was more than ready to come to grips with the Tiger. On crossing the beach outbound the gunners were ordered to test their weapons, in that way there would be no hesitation when it came to them pulling the trigger in earnest.

Inbound to Point Pedro or Velvettiturai, our gunners were briefed on likely firing positions and were ordered to open fire as soon as they had a recognisable target. Essentially I was creating my own game plan; my own fire-free zone.

The result was a noticeable increase in the morale of the gunners. Testing the guns settled their nerves early and had them mentally primed for opening fire when it was called upon. Who knows, maybe they were also pissed off with not being allowed to have a crack at the bad guys. Perhaps the added cleaning and maintenance of their weapons in the evenings gave them a sense of pride. 'I'm cleaning my guns today because I have used them.'

As it was, the situation couldn't go on forever. The Wing Commander certainly wouldn't wear it for too long. He had already vetoed suppressive fire a week or so beforehand. Nah! Bollocks to him, with a bit of luck we could provoke Gunga Din into some really positive action that would be seen as far away as Headquarters in Colombo and thereby justify having a bloody good go at him. My very own version of '*Casus belli*' (Cause of war.)

It didn't work straight away. The only hot action seen during those first two weeks came from three sacks of dried chillies that were loaded for the Naval Base at Karainagar.

The downdraught from the rotors swirled the chilli dust around the cockpit, into our mouths and eyes until we were all coughing and crying. Ariyaratna, our starboard sidegunner that day, started laughing between his tears at some point, and in no time at all we were all laughing, at ourselves and at the Navy who apparently needed so many chillies to get themselves fired up for action.

On the few occasions that we did go into Point Pedro we still came under fire. The gunners acquitted themselves well, but things did not come to a head until the beginning of September, by which time I had almost given up hope of prodding Gunga Din into a head-to-head open conflict.

Karainagar navy base where's north

My first trip to the East Coast came up during those waiting days. The venerable Wing Commander Perez, magnificent bushy moustache and all, probably wanted me out of the way to prevent any further conflict between him and his backsliding, pension-pushing buddies at the local Army Headquarters in KKS.

With Namal as my companion, we were sent away to China Bay in support of a Cordon and Search operation on one of the small coastal towns on the southern edge of Koddiyar Bay.

As ever, by time the Army had completed a blundering two-day approach march through the jungle to cordon the landward side of the town, the birds had flown the nest. That didn't stop the Army from giving the remaining population a good going over.

We were given the task of covering any roads out of the search area that the Army had missed. By the time we arrived the tracks and paths out of town were full of fleeing civilians.

Namal was flying right seat that day. With him as Pilot in Command I should have known that the trip would be a real bastard.

We had hardly arrived on station when we came upon a group of stragglers leaving the town. They just didn't want to stop when they were circled and waved back by the gunners. They simply fled, scattering and disappearing into the undergrowth. Why Namal couldn't control his frustration at arriving too late I don't know. He couldn't help it. It was the Army's cock-up. Initially Namal had flown low small orbits around the front of the fleeing villagers. The side-gunners waved their hands and shouted at them to go back, but it did no good.

The tremendous noise from the thudding rotor blades and the sheer size of the 212 at close quarters frightened them witless. They scattered and disappeared into the scrub and jungle.

The last of the group was a grey-haired and skinny old chap clothed in flapping rags who, in total and utter desperation, climbed a tree. Oh shit! Not a good place to hide from Namal with a monk on.

What sticks in my mind to this day is that when we left the area there was a tattered rag-covered body hanging out of that tree.

Totally sickened, I tried to reason with him. It didn't do any good, it just made him angrier, and more determined to make somebody pay for it. Turning back towards the town, we met another poor old bugger on an ancient pushbike who equally didn't want to stop when waved at. Namal swung the Trooper around the old man in a blade-slapping, racking turn, barking out orders to the gunners in Sinhalese as he did. The side guns hacked and rattled briefly. The old man fell from his ancient pushbike and died on the roadside. I was gutted, totally disgusted with the depraved little animal.

We left the old man there, a lifeless heap on the road, and turned away northbound for fuel at China Bay and our return to Jaffna.

Flying northwards along the western edge of the town, we passed about 400 metres from the houses there. To my mind we were too close in to the buildings for comfort, too low, too close for our own safety, and said so.

'Namal, don't you think we should fly a little further out?'

Namal sniffed and shook his head. He suffered from sinus trouble.

Suddenly there came the thumping clank of a hit that shuddered all the way through the airframe. The cockpit was filled with a stinging dust. The Trooper leaped as Namal jerked back against the straps in his seat with a choking gasp.

Grabbing control, I flung the aircraft away from the town, pulling pitch to get us up and away to safety. Throwing a quick glance back through the cabin for any signs of damage, I saw only the gunners staring goggled-eyed with shock towards Namal's seat.

Two minutes later, out over the jungle, Namal was still shaking his head and trying to clear his eyes of the fine ceramic chips and glass fibre dust that had filled the front of the cabin when the 7.62mm round had impacted the side armour of his seat. Me? Hell, no problem. My helmet visor was down at the time, a habit brought on by the amount of reporters and photographers around the place.

'Are you Ok now,' I asked, 'are you fit enough to go back and get the bastard?'

Namal shook his head again, this time though without the haughty sniff.

Realising that whoever had shot at us would be long gone, we carried on north-bound for China Bay. It certainly had to be admitted, they had some good shooters on the East Coast. One solitary shot, one good hit.

'Pity they hadn't hit the little bastard,' were my less than charitable thoughts.

As for Namal, he was one lucky fellow. It really wouldn't be long before he got himself and his crew into some real trouble by flying too low and too close in Bandit Country. I had no desire to be with him when it happened.

Later that afternoon, on our way back to Jaffna, we were ordered to make a diversion into Vavuniya for a few minutes to pick up some mail and passengers for KKS. We were taking a relaxed late morning coffee in the Mess when I was pleasantly surprised to meet the latest batch of 'Contract Pilots'. I hadn't even known there were any, but there they were. They had already been in the country for two weeks, and nobody had seen fit to tell me. They didn't even know that I was up at KKS. Still pale of skin and in clothes that reeked of 'I'm a new chap here, tourist, English on hols, don't cha know', John Winterbourne and Richard 'call me Rudi' Ramsden were full of the frustration of good ideas that had come to nothing because nobody would listen or 'It was too difficult', or 'There are peace talks on'. What was really meant was 'Why didn't I think of that' or 'Too difficult for me.' I'd met it all before and knew how John and Rudi must have felt.

For all the shit that was being stirred by me with the Army at KKS, the Sri Lankan Air Force knew that they had someone that they could use to good effect. Ranasinghe probably hadn't told me of the latest batch of pilots in case I demanded a rotation to another station that he'd promised. I had certainly done my time in KKS.

They probably also knew that the new guys wouldn't take kindly to Jaffna and Gunga Din and that they would, in all likelihood, throw in their hands and go home. I hadn't come across them before, but we talked of mutual friends and that broke the ice to some extent. What the hell, they were Whitefaces and I was in need of someone to talk to; and it was good to talk to them and to laugh quietly amongst ourselves at the gross ineptitude of the Sri Lankan Armed Forces and the most recent of their minor military tragedies.

According to John, a batman in the Officers Mess at Trincomalee had shot two Officers. When a Police Inspector later arrived to arrest him, the batman had shot him as well. The batman finally shot himself. He was probably pissed off with their holier-than-thou, haughty, look-down-the-nose attitudes.

I'd had a dose of those attitudes myself. It was all that was bad about the young British Officer magnified and multiplied. The thought crossed my mind as to how long Namal and Royce would have lasted if he had been their batman. I really felt sorry for the poor little bugger.

Later that afternoon we left Vavuniya for Jaffna, promising to send John and Rudi some books from the put-and-take library that I'd finished and also to keep them up to date on any Whiteface news by letter. It had been great to meet them, it made me feel a little more secure knowing that there were two more Whitefaces 'just down the road'.

Sadly, John and Rudi left just a few weeks later. I'd been away from Whiteface company for too long.

Back at KKS things had almost gotten out of hand. The Army had moved out from the airfield perimeter to take over a house near the quarry at the southern end of the strip. Nine hundred metres from the wire and 1200 from the Mess, the Army was really pushing the boat out.

Because of the military activity so close to the airfield, we spent the remainder of that day in enforced idleness awaiting the Army's call for support. It didn't come, although that evening the LTTE provided us with a bigger and better lights out display of mortar and machine gun fire. Their approach route to the Army Camp on the eastern side of the airfield was being threatened, and they didn't like it one bit.

The following day brought much of the same inactivity for us. Even the daily re-supply Avro turned up later than usual. When it did I was given the surprising task of going down to meet it and bring a Whiteface back to the Mess.

As ever, the area around the Avro was a seething mass of sweating soldiery heaving and pulling at a mountain of sacked food and supplies. The rush of conscripts trying to get on nearly overwhelmed those who were unhappily trying to get off. Amongst them all the fair-haired thickset bulk of my visitor was easy to spot.

Keeping a wary eye out for reporters, I waited until he was almost out of the crush before moving to intercept him. I helped him to grab his bags out of the pile, and with a jerk of my head indicated that he should follow me away from the crowd.

'Hi,' I said, once we were clear, 'Tim Smith, welcome to KKS.'

'Pleased to meet you, I'm Donald Skants,' he replied in what I took to be an educated South African accent.

At that moment the young Lieutenant who was normally in charge of the helicopter loading parties arrived, I knew him only by sight and his radio call-sign, One Two Sierra. Politely he explained that the Army's Officer Commanding in KKS, a Brigadier, would like to meet the new pilot. We looked at each other, shrugged, nodded in agreement, and followed him into the Headquarters building.

I thought it strange that another unknown Whiteface had tagged on to the procession. I hadn't been briefed on meeting two Whitefaces, but as the young Lieutenant seemed to know him I thought no more of it.

Inside the building we were asked to wait outside the Brigadier's office for a moment until he was free. We waited. Somehow I began to feel uneasy about the deal.

'Don, this is something new to me, I never had much to do with the Army here, and nobody ever invited me to meet the Brigadier. Maybe things have changed for the better.' Somehow I doubted that, but hoped for the best.

The unknown Whiteface eased over towards us and made himself known. My doubts rapidly became certainties.

'Hi, chaps. I'm Tom Ayling. Have you just arrived in KKS?'

One Two Sierra

With hardly a pause for breath, he went on to explain that he was a reporter for a UK newspaper, and started in with the standard set of questions.

'Could you tell me who you work for, what are you doing here?' he asked with his pencil poised over his notebook. I was bloody furious and immediately on my guard. 'How long have you chaps been here, oh! I don't suppose I could have your name . . .?'

'I don't care who you bloody are or which paper you work for. Who we are is none of your bloody business, so why don't you take your grubby little notebook and piss off out of here.' I turned my back on him. In retrospect we should have told him 'all about it'.

Just then the Brigadier's Aide de Camp reappeared and invited us into his office. The reporter came in with us, nodding 'Hullo' to the aide as he did, he was a persistent bugger. Me, well I was ready for a showdown with somebody. It turned out to be the Brigadier.

The Brigadier looked up from his desk as we went in.

'Good morning, take a seat,' it sounded more like a command

than an invitation. 'I like to meet all the new people that arrive in *my camp,*' he explained, leaning heavily on the words.

'*We* are members of the Air Force,' I replied sarcastically.

'I would like some information about you,' the Brig went on.

'Not with a bloody newspaper reporter present you don't.'

'He is a friend of mine, he can stay here. So, who are you?' he demanded.

'*We* are members of the Air Force and *we* are leaving now. If you want to know more about us then ask the Squadron Leader or the Wing Commander, but you don't ask us questions in front of the press, your friend or not,' I replied angrily.

Muttering savagely under my breath about a load of effing wankers in the Army and tosspot newspaper reporters, I got up and walked out. Looking behind me a few moments later, I was shocked to see that the new guy hadn't followed me out. Turning on my heel, I stomped back along the corridor to get him. 'Ahh, SHIT, where's he bloody got to?' He was leaving the office when I found him and just caught the tail end of a one-way conversation very much like my own. It seemed that the new guy certainly had the makings of a good lad in him.

The bad news of course was that where there's a reporter there's a cameraman. For the next few days we would have to keep our helmets on and visors down whenever we were around the helicopter pads.

The rest of the day was spent getting the new guy, Donald, settled in and introducing him to the crews: our new Squadron Leader, Sujith Jayasekara, Roshan and the rest of the crew, the haughty Namal and his snobby shadow, Royce.

At last there was someone to talk to, and the run-down on the situation that Don got helped me to see more clearly for myself how things really were on the Peninsula. By nine o'clock that evening we were just about finished and relaxing on 'the patio' with a warm beer and discussing the LTTE's love of playing their own version of the *1812 Overture* at lights out; when an enormous thump was heard from out towards the quarry.

'Well, I don't think much of this place,' Don drawled.

We finished our beers and went to our beds. The Army moved out of the house at the quarry under fire the next day.

Two days later we were tasked to go to Katunayaka with a Trooper for servicing and return with its replacement. Strangely

Squince at KKS on the sunporch

enough, Don was to go with me and he was to stay there. His posting to KKS had been a mistake.

The trip down country was a great pleasure. It was rare to have two Whitefaces in the same cockpit for anything more than very brief functional air tests. We were able to sit back and enjoy the view, secure in the knowledge that there wouldn't be any queries as to whether we were on track, no unexpected excursions to low level to investigate any green minibuses, followed by the standard destruction of them and their occupants.

Added to that, my brief stay waiting for the replacement Trooper 'coming on line' gave me the chance to top up my food supply at the Airport Garden Hotel and the local shops. My greatest problem that day turned out to be the fact that the local shops were unable to supply my ration of cornflakes.

Leaving Katunayaka the following day just after lunch got me back to KKS by mid-afternoon.

There was a pitched battle going on for the house by the quarry. The Artillery had sited their 105mm Pack Howitzers about 120 metres away in front of the Mess, and afternoon tea was taken to the thump and crump of the guns engaging targets less than a mile

105mm pack Howitzer KKS

away. Brilliant, one could see both ends of the engagement whilst sipping tea.

Namal was up in the Gunship between salvos, and all were able to watch as he broke every rule in the combat flying book. Too high, too slow, using the yaw-pedals when he shouldn't, sliding round turns with nothing but hope on the clock, and always pressing in too close with the attack. Rockets should still work well when used from 1000 metres out, so why did he always insist on putting himself and the machine at risk by pressing in to 500 metres. It was bloody foolish.

Break every rule

12.7mm I think

One day, yes, one day soon, he would get into severe trouble, it was only a matter of time. He did well enough that day, though, and survived it with only one bullet hole in a main rotor blade.

Peace was restored to the little house near the quarry by seven o'clock that evening. Sat on the patio with a warm beer, I realised that the mynah birds had started chattering again and the sound of the breeze through the palmyras had lulled my senses, like the sound of gently breaking surf.

Some weeks earlier it had occurred to me that the Tigers had changed their tactics and were leaving PPO and VVT out of their plans for the time being and were concentrating on easier pickings around the airfield and out on the islands, Karainagar, Mandaitivu and Kayts.

My chances of coming to grips with Gunga Din were fading fast, and my R&R in mid-October would come up without having completed my self-imposed task.

The truth of the matter was somewhat different. Reports coming in from Trincomalee and Batticaloa showed that the Tigers were now increasing the pressure on the East Coast as well. Maybe our day trip out there had something to do with it. Maybe Namal's slaughter of innocent civilians didn't go down too well with the Tigers. It certainly hadn't gone down too well with me.

Meanwhile on the Jaffna Peninsula there was the ongoing battle for the house near the quarry at KKS and also attacks on the tented camp at Mandaitivu and the Fort at Jaffna.

Several brief, but effective, hit-and-run attacks were carried out on the outstations and patrols on Karainagar and Kayts. The pressure was certainly building, the only questions that still remained to be answered were where and when the Tigers would make a really big effort.

In the meantime the Army and the Air Force were fully occupied with re-establishing control over their own doorstep at KKS. The Army were taking up residence in the little house by the quarry.

The next two days were spent lobbing High Explosive (HE) shells over our bungalow and into the quarry area, generally making a lot of noise and raising the dust around the Mess.

Breakfast on the first day was heralded by the arrival of four mortar bombs inside the perimeter fence at the southern end of the runway. Three more during breakfast had everyone running for their hard hats. Gunga Din obviously ate his breakfast early. The Artillery dropped their mugs of morning tea and replied in kind for the next two hours. At lunchtime Don turned up again with a replacement Trooper and was completely disenchanted with the prospect of staying until the show was over.

By lunchtime of the second day the action had petered out until it consisted of only an occasional crack of small arms fire from the quarry. We considered the fact that the Tigers might well have gone shopping in town with their wives and kids. Well, it was Saturday afternoon.

We thought that must be the case when suddenly the Artillery started dumping HE shells into the quarry at a furious pace. Walking round the side of the Mess, we stood and watched as the Army made their final assault on the house complete with armoured cars (Saladins, Saracens and Buffaloes) and close mortar support.

When they got there they found that the Tigers had left during the night, taking with them just about everything that was worth taking, tables, chairs, doors, window frames, walls and ceilings.

The Lads

The following day brought another trip to Katunayaka to replace yet another unserviceable Trooper. The replacement machine wasn't going to be ready in time to take straight back, and an overnight stay was on the cards.

That evening was spent with the whole of the Rotary Wing pack. It was one of those few rare occasions when we were all together. There was Greg from Katunayaka, Chris from Vavuniya, Don B from Trincomalee and Batticaloa, and Donald and me from KKS. We spent the evening having a good chinwag and getting right royally pissed in the Blue Oceanic at Negombo.

The Sri Lankans do such a fine job of distilling Arak from the coconut tree. We were happy to report that the stocks in the Blue Oceanic were up to standard, all of it.

We also did our bit for international relationships. The bar staff were keen to stand close at hand and listen to our conversation. We taught them that 'Piss off' meant 'Leave us in peace before your throat gets bitten out'. They were such obliging people. They left the bottle and retreated behind the bar.

Don B had spent a lot of time at Bati and Trinco, and declared to one and all that he had put down more lead and HE than anybody present. The others looked disinterested and I thought, 'What a gung ho arsehole, get yourself up to KKS where the bastards shoot back.'

It seemed that the others were on fairly cushy numbers at Katunayaka and Vavuniya. They didn't want to know about Don B and me, and couldn't care less.

The following morning I took the replacement Trooper back to KKS with a real blinder of a VSOA hangover and a decent cooked breakfast inside me. It was the last to be had for five weeks. I got back in time for the Air Officer Commanding's (AOC's) Inspection.

The bloody houseboys were everywhere, cleaning this and polishing that. Me? Well, to get me out of the way they sent me off for six hours of coconuts and cabbages.

By time I got back the AOC had departed, and the leftovers of the sumptuous lunch that had been laid on for him were being devoured by the Wing Commander.

We had curried something or other. Bloody charming, having already dined well on it at lunchtime, to the exclusion of all the others, the greedy bastard scoffed the remainder on his own at suppertime.

One day followed the next with boring regularity. The monsoon rains were still with us, and the smell of wet earth and rotting vegetation was pungent to the point of being almost unbearable. The cesspool out the back was almost overflowing from regular heavy bursts of rain, and the evenings were filled with the croaking of frogs that were as big as cats. Froggy Pond had come into being.

The mosquitoes that it produced were real beauties, and constant attention was paid to the state of the nets over my bed and on the windows. It struck me then that the reason for Whitefaces being in the back room wasn't just because it was furthest away from the remainder of the Mess.

The LTTE continued to play Last Post with a fastidious regularity and a certain amount of added fervour. Attacks on the little house at the quarry occurred on a daily basis, and much of the Last Post each evening was directed there. The occupants of the little house or the school at Vasavilan were not to be envied, not one little bit.

Donald was back with us on a permanent basis, 'learning the ropes' to take over from me in due course. He was grown-up and could look after himself, but I didn't want to leave him with the legacy of Gunga Din and his black pyjama gang running riot at Point Pedro and VVT.

Our evenings on the patio were spent in muttered conversation as he was carefully briefed on the firing points around PPO and VVT. We paused now and then to identify passing hardware as it sighed and riffled overhead. From the south-west there came a deep bup-bup-bup followed by the sound of the Tigers' 12.7mm rounds rustling through the darkness, and then from the south-east the dull thumping sound of the Army's outgoing mortars in reply. Over at the southern end of the runway, the more muted whump of the Tigers' response, an incoming mortar setting off, followed by a breathless pause while we waited, counting the time of flight, and hoping to hear it whispering by to land with a thump somewhere near the school or the house by the quarry.

There were only five weeks to go before R&R, and I seriously thought that there wouldn't be time enough get another good crack at Gunga Din before leaving. Time, as ever, tells a different story.

9 September 1986 was a real shitbag of a day. We visited every outstation at least twice, Point Pedro three times. On the first visit to PPO we had 2000lbs of HE and small arms ammo on board.

As we crossed the fourth breaker out we came under sustained fire from the east. Not just the standard three or four taps, but a good solid burst. Gunga Din and his boys really meant it this time. Rolling the heavily loaded Trooper left, we climbed and laid down a withering hail of fire from the side-gun. Continuing round in a left-hand orbit, we set up for another approach. The Tigers waited until we were committed to landing before they gave us another heavy burst of machine gun fire. The sea just beneath and beyond us was whipped into a storm of foam by the near-misses.

Seconds later I thumped the Trooper on to the PSP heli-pad in a cloud of dust. The place was buzzing with activity although no one was bothering to return the fire we had taken on the way in. Absolutely stunning, no one was returning fire.

Suddenly, 80 metres away to our left towards the main entrance, there came the concussive thump of a landing mortar bomb. The aircraft shuddered in the blast and the eastern part of the landing site was covered in a pall of dust and a hail of falling debris.

The young Lieutenant in charge of the outstation rushed up, and with much waggling of his head shouted through my open side window, 'We have secured the west side. You must come in from there, it is safe.'

'The bastards are on the east side, Lieutenant, secure that,' I shouted back.

'But they are a long way out,' he almost pleaded, agitatedly waggling his head.

'That, Lieutenant, is what guns are for. Shooting a long way.'

'You must approach from the west,' he shouted back, definitely pleading.

'Not fucking likely, get yourselves out there and secure the east side,' angrily now, I was beginning to lose my temper. An approach from the west meant flying straight down the gun barrels of the bastards sat out there in the Tigers' toilet bunker to the east.

'But they are in the east'.

'Ahhh, fuck off!' I bellowed, realising that we wouldn't get any cover on the way out either.

Pulling in a little pitch, I let him know that we were finished with

Point Pedro firing point (2)

Passing the buck at point Pedro

talking. He scurried back to his bunker on the west side. The thoughtless little bugger wasn't even concerned about the wounded that were even then being loaded into the cabin on sheets of corrugated iron and broken doors. Nor the fact that we were having to deny his own soldiers the pleasure of getting the hell out of there on the pretext of looking after the wounded in flight.

We departed in a hurry, not wanting to be trapped and helpless, strapped in the cockpit when the next mortar arrived. We left hastened by yet more fire from the east.

Back at KKS they didn't even know what was going on, or didn't care, for they loaded us up with another four bags of coconuts and three Police Constables for Point Pedro. Half an hour later we were back at PPO. Again we came under fire, heavy fire from the east, and decided that for today that was enough.

We went back to KKS and cajoled the Squadron Leader into coming along with the Gunship to see us into Point Pedro. Even Royce, my co-pilot for the day, was for once in agreement with me.

Sujith finally agreed, but with much waggling of his head he solemnly declared, 'With the peace talks on, we cannot go firing rockets into the village.'

'Sujith,' scorn dripping from every syllable, 'you don't have fire anything into any bloody village. The bastards have fortified the school toilets and changing rooms on the beach. That's where they are firing from.'

'I will get the Army to try and clear it,' he said, 'and then I'll come along to see what's going on.' He disappeared to find a telephone.

An hour later we were back again, this time with the Gunship on station at 2000 feet. This time for sure we would have Gunga Din on a slab.

On short finals to land we came under fire again, and to confirm that all was going as expected we called Sujith and Don on the radio. 'We are on short final approach and we're under fire from the east.'

There was no reply from the Gunship. Silence. Complete and absolute silence.

During the approach some Army guys had been spotted behind a beached log about 200 metres short of the changing rooms, with their heads down and their arses up as usual. I knew that Sujith wouldn't want to open fire with the Infantry so close. Disaster, Sujith should have been brassing them up with the .50in pod-gun; a nifty bit of gear that was really accurate when it worked.

Once on the ground I looked around to find our top-cover, but couldn't see them anywhere. The fact of the matter was that they were so close to the overhead that the only thing they could

Firing point at Point Pedro (small)

possibly have hit would have been way out of the target area. They were so close in that they were worse than useless.

Out with the coconuts and constables, quick time. Full power and off into the air, only to come under fire yet again; and that with the Gunship lurking around.

Rolling hard right, we put a whole belt of 7.62mm into the fortified toilets and then rolled left to use the other gun. We put another half a belt of ammo into the toilets before the gun jammed. (Pointless really; studying the photos much later, it was discovered that the firing point was in an atap-roofed lean-to 20 metres west of the toilets.)

Bitterly disgusted, we called the action off and buggered off out of it to KKS.

Back on the ground I stormed into the Mess and cornered Sujith. I was so bloody angry.

'How the hell did you expect to cover my approach when you were sat directly over the target, Sujith, you didn't even acknowledge my radio call that we were on short finals and taking fire from the east.'

He sheepishly rolled his head and casually shrugged it off as 'not realising that he had got too close in until it was too late'.

What he really meant was that he did not know how to provide top-cover; nobody had taught or shown any of them the basics of the job, and nobody had asked. Totally inept shower of bastards.

Realisation struck me only then that these people didn't even talk among themselves about tactics or local conditions. It was a point that would be brought home to me time and time again.

That was what Wing Commander Oliver wanted me here for, to teach them how to do it. The problem was that they were so full of their own sense of superiority that they wouldn't bloody listen.

The following day was spent within five yards of the toilet clutching a bog roll. A severe dose of the trots had made it impossible to fly. I couldn't even get to the Int Cell to find out the results of our action at Point Pedro the previous day. It would have to wait.

Life at KKS went on without me. The food was still half-raw, nearly cold and always curried. The LTTE still played the Last Post, and Sri Lankan Officers still said 'if' when they meant 'when', and 'maybe' when they meant 'impossible'.

Sujith wandered by my room that night. Quite unusual for a

Squadron Leader to seek someone out. They generally sent for them or passed a message by some Junior Officer. I was ready for the worst.

'Ah, Tim,' started Sujith, in his blandest manner, 'I have spoken with the Wing Commander about Point Pedro the other day. The CO has said that if you go to Point Pedro tomorrow you must ensure that the Army have secured the site or destroyed the changing rooms.'

'And what about the mortar team?' I asked equally blandly. 'We really should take the Gunship to cover the Tigers' mortar team.'

'I do not understand,' replied Sujith with much rolling of his head.

My stomach turned and I knew from the hollow feeling in my gut, it wasn't hunger, that I was about to get rubber-dicked into going into PPO without any cover, either from the Air Force or from the Army. I was beginning to lose my cool.

'Bloody hell, Sujith, don't you understand? Yesterday the Tigers set up a co-ordinated mortar and machine-gun attack at Point Pedro to coincide with the arrival of a helicopter on the landing site, and the Army did bugger-all to cover us.' The words were punched out at him.

It made no difference. Sujith merely rolled his nose in a figure of eight, smiled sheepishly and said nothing.

'Sujith, when the Tigers gave us this much trouble at VVT we had the Army, the Navy, the Artillery and a Gunship for top-cover.'

Anger boiled behind my teeth and spilled over my tongue. For certain tomorrow was going to be one shitty day.

'You must make sure it's secure,' said Sujith calmly and left the room.

They had said that it was secure three times the previous day. Sujith had been there, albeit in the wrong bloody place, but he'd been there and seen that they had done absolutely bugger-all to cover our arses.

Gunga Din and his boys were getting good, and his mortar team had only to build their confidence enough to stay around for that telling second and third shot. I wondered for a moment just what it would be like if they managed to get their own Western Mercenaries. 'Gunga Din bloody well deserves a Cocopalm and Bar,' I thought.

7

Countdown

Working out of their base in Tamil Nadu, the guerrilla groups have recruited young warriors from the ranks of the refugees. Some are devoted revolutionaries, but others are devoid of ideology, indulging in smuggling and piracy.

Newsweek 19 May 1986

One of the Liberation Tigers of Tamil Eelam's methods of re-supply for their Tigers on the Jaffna Peninsula was to run small fast-boats from Ramnad in the Tamil Nadu province of south-eastern India, some 20 some miles or so away across the Palk Straits, to the Jaffna Peninsula. There they were beached at pre-arranged remote spots and offloaded before stealing away again to Tamil Nadu.

The boats were generally between about 15 and 20 feet long. They were light and open, and when loaded showed little freeboard. As a fairly standard fit they had three powerful outboard motors on the back, two for getting across the Straits, one for loitering before they beached, and three for running like hell if they were spotted by the Navy's Coastal Fast Patrol Boats (FPBs) or the Air Force's Skymaster Offshore Patrol plane. Namal and me had already caught one some time before at Mulliyan and had burned it on the beach.

In mid-September Squadron Leader Sujith Jayasekara and Royce were called out in an effort to intercept a fast-boat that the Navy had been unable to stop.

Those boats were extremely quick with all three engines going. Sujith and Royce eventually came upon it just before it beached at a fishing village on the northern coast of Karaitivu, about 12 miles due west of KKS airfield.

They decided that as the boat had made it that far then good luck to them and had returned to KKS.

My own flying programme for that day was to take three loads of conscripts, constables, cabbages and coconuts to Mandaitivu. Having completed the C&C runs I was then to take a Sri Lankan TV crew on a filming run around Point Pedro, Kankesanturai and Jaffna Fort, with a quick jog out to the Naval Base at Karainagar for the finale. Happy snaps for the folks back at home.

Royce, who had by then finished with their abortive fast-boat intercept, went along with me as co-pilot. Somehow I always seemed to get the jobs where civilians were concerned, or jobs that, should they go wrong, would ruin any self-respecting officer's career.

Returning from the Naval Base at Karainagar, I decided to take a gentle swing past the fishing village on Karaitivu to have a look at the fast-boat. Sure enough, it was still there, pulled up on the beach by the village, with a group of people around it busy carrying stuff from the boat to some cars waiting nearby. At a reasonably safe height of 1500 feet I rolled the Trooper into a steady right-hand orbit around it. The people gathered down there by the boat immediately scattered to the nearby huts. For a moment it appeared as though they were trying to hide, but that thought was suddenly dispelled when they all re-appeared at a rush and grouped about the boat in kneeling positions.

'What the bloody hell is going on down there, Royce?' I muttered into the intercom.

'They seem to be pointing at us.' replied Royce smugly, with a tinge of young aviator's pride in his voice. The old aviator sat next to him was immediately on his guard.

Looking back into the cabin, I saw that one of the film crew had some binoculars hanging around his neck.

'Ariyaratna, take those binoculars from the cameraman. See what's going on down there,' I shouted across to the nearest gunner.

'Yes, Captain.' A huge smile spread across his face. He was doubtless pleased to be able to commandeer something from the film crew and at last get his own back, in some small way, for all the buggering around we had got from them in the past. A couple of seconds later I got the answer.

'They are all pointing guns at us, Captain.' shouted the gunner in reply.

Royce's smug look faded like a cheap T-shirt in a hot wash.

Pulling pitch fast, I hauled the nose up in a quick zoom climb. I just hoped that it was quick enough.

As we passed 1800 feet in the climb, there came a tremendous crackle of gunfire from directly beneath us. There must have been at least half a dozen automatic weapons down there, enough for me to keep the climb on whilst the camera crew blithely grabbed for their cameras and snapped wildly away.

We needed some help with this one, and fast if we were to make anything out of it. With blind faith, or was it empty hope, I called our own Ops Room in the Mess's lounge-cum-dining room at KKS on the Squadron's chat frequency. I prayed that they weren't deeply engrossed in a blue movie or playing space invaders.

As it was, we were lucky enough to catch the ear of Squadron Leader Sujith, who was having a well-deserved cup of tea after a stressful and harrowing morning avoiding action.

'We have a group of armed Tigers on the ground around that beached fast-boat on the north side of Karaitivu. Can you send the Gunship?' I asked.

'You mustn't open fire unless they fire at you,' came Sujith's infuriatingly mild reply.

'Bollocks,' I thought, 'mustn't interrupt his bloody tea and biscuits.'

'Send the Gunship, we are under heavy fire. Send for the Navy Patrol Boat, we need support,' I shouted angrily into the microphone.

Realising that we weren't going to get an instant response, I continued to orbit the fast-boat and used the sideguns in an attempt to hold the Tigers in the village. There was no way that we could risk the lives of the camera crew by going any lower to engage the Tigers in the village – or mine, come to that.

There was so much we could have done from low level at high speed to have given the Tigers a stand-up fight, but it would have to be a holding action at best. Enough to keep their heads down, enough to keep them occupied until the Gunship or the Navy FPB arrived on the scene.

Royce was already busy on the marine frequency, making contact with the Fast Patrol Boat, passing them the location of the village and giving them a description of the target for them to open up on when they arrived.

We had almost completed our second orbit and were levelling at

2000 feet, with the camera crew still snapping away madly in the back, when three black and grey mushroom clouds appeared about 200 feet below us.

Now this was something new. A 40mm grenade launcher with airburst shells, maybe. Whatever, they were firing something that airburst straight up at us. By now Royce was almost frantic on the radio, trying to get the Gunship launched in time to take those buggers out before they scarpered. It was the first time that he'd been in an open firefight where he could see both ends of the engagement.

Suddenly a man on a moped made a break from the village towards the coconut plantations about 600 metres inland. We swung out of the orbit and dived after it, with the side-guns chattering away at the village as we went.

Getting closer, Ariyaratna switched his fire onto the moped. The chap on the moped quickly decided that he didn't fancy his chances and scooted back into the village. Suddenly the radio burst into life.

'KKS Tower, this is Charlie Hotel Five-Three-Seven, lifting and departing westwards for Karaitivu, over.' At last, the comforting sound of Sujith's voice and the Gunship's lifting call came over the radio.

Out at sea, the Fast Patrol Boat was almost on station and was calling for a target to engage when one of the cars burst out of village towards the plantations. Again we dived after it with the side-guns rattling and streaming gunsmoke. This time, though, they were a lot faster than the moped and had some weapons along with them.

The car bounced and bumped along the track towards the plantations, swerving wildly from side to side. All of the windows in the car had Kalashnikovs poking out of them that rattled and left a trail of gunsmoke all the way behind until they made it into the coconut groves, where we lost sight of them.

The Gunship had arrived by then and, surprisingly, Sujith was calling for a target. Yet another car broke out of the village and the Gunship took off after it. In what should have been a set-piece attack dive, the Gunship opened fire from too far out and the rockets, as ever, went anywhere but straight and proved totally ineffectual. Both cars had made it to the plantation and disappeared amongst the trees.

Breaking off the action we swung hard right, back to the village and climbed again to 2000 feet, giving the Gunship all the space it needed whilst we continued to party with the Tigers that were left in the village. The Patrol Boat was just offshore from the village and the beached fast-boat, and was still calling for a target.

'Jesus H,' I muttered to Royce, 'we have just poured two thousand rounds and a slack handful of rockets into the area of that beached boat, and they are still asking for a sodding target.'

Royce was still chattering wildly on the radio, and at long last he managed to get the Navy to open up with their forward-mounted deck gun. Why the hell they bothered I don't really know. They had come in too close and were sat on the furthest and biggest breaker, pitching and heaving like a drunk on Saturday night.

Somehow they managed to fire from the top of every wave as it passed beneath them. They dumped 20 rounds of cannon fire somewhere between the beach and the middle of the island before they got fed up and buggered off out to sea.

Back on the beach the villagers were showing a strong belief in self-expression. Two small mushrooms of smoke appeared in the air close to the Gunship as two more 40mm grenades were fired at them from the village. Sujith really took exception to that, and broke off his attack and headed for home and another cup of tea.

At first I thought that the Gunship was repositioning for another go at the fast-boat but there was no excited chatter on the radio from the Gunship to set up another co-ordinated attack. Silence, dead bloody silence, as the Gunship slowly became a dot on the horizon. If it had been a proper village, I would have understood some reluctance to engage it with rockets and guns. Shit, it wasn't a village. It was just a huddle of five or six huts full of bad bastards, but Sujith just broke away and buggered off. What a bloody debacle. Utterly pissed off, I followed them back to KKS. The Tigers had won that one by default.

Ahh, but the day was not yet over, and on our return to KKS there were two casualties to pick up from PPO. I refused to go unless top-cover was provided by the Gunship. Sujith was the only other aircraft commander left on the station and wouldn't take a chance on having to fire at the Tigers twice in one day, so he decided to take Royce and go without the top cover. 'Not clever, bloody foolish.' I thought.

What he didn't say was that the Artillery at Tondamanna were shelling the shite out of the east side of PPO with their 105mm

Pack Howitzers. That should keep their heads down in Gunga Din's fortified toilets, and Sujith wouldn't have any need for top-cover.

Temporarily out of a job and with nothing better to do, I wandered down to the heli-pad to get ready for another couple of hours of conscripts and cabbages, and found the engineering staff gathered around the tail end of the Trooper.

With a broad grin on his face, the chief engineer turned round to face me. With his head rolling fit to fall off, he handed me the bullet that they had just dug out of the tail boom. 'A souwenir of Jaffna, Captain Ee . . . Smeeth,' he grinned.

My two side-gunners, standing behind him, smiled at me and rolled their noses in a magnificent figure of eight of agreement. Thanking them, I took it and pushed it into my flying suit pocket.

I was overwhelmed; it was the first act of kindness or recognition I'd had in four months. I still have that bullet to this day, as an ornament on my mantelpiece, set in clear plastic resin like a paper-weight.

That evening, when I had finished my day's flying, I dropped in at the IntCell to see if anything had been heard on the Tiger's radio frequencies regarding that morning's debacle with the fast-boat on the beach on Karaitivu.

'We have heard nothing yet about Karaitivu, but I have some wery good news for you, Captain,' said the young Second Lieutenant on duty. 'Two days ago at Point Pedro, when you came under a mortar attack, the second bomb exploded in the tube and killed many of the mortar team.'

'All of them?' I asked, trying hard to hide the excitement in my voice.

'Unfortunately no, one of them was only injured and escaped.'

Still trying to hide my pleasure and excitement at the good news I thanked him and left, hoping upon hope that Gunga Din was finished. Somehow, however, I knew that he would be back, but for the time being Gunga Din and his team were out of action. Wonderful, great news, I was on another cordite high.

What a day. In the aftermath of the utter cock-up at the fishing village and the astounding good news of the self-destruction of the mortar team at Point Pedro, I found myself in an emotional limbo. With Gunga Din out of the picture for the time being, quite possibly forever, I had nothing to keep me on edge. I relaxed to the point of almost falling apart. Laid-back? I was almost horizontal.

Cabbage trips into Mandaitivu and Navatkuli went off like pleasure flights, and by the time that I got around to taking some cigarettes into PPO and VVT the following afternoon, I was almost at the stage of being happy. Certainly I wasn't prepared for the landing sites to be secure with Army foot patrols out to 250 metres on either side of the heli-pads. I finished the day's flying in a state of near euphoria.

There was no time for an evening run. The next hour or so was spent putting together an evening meal to celebrate the day. I raided my stockpile of Whiteface grub: tinned soup and tinned hot-dogs, followed by tinned fruit. And to follow dinner, I allowed myself a beer.

I showered and shaved in slow time. I got dressed in my best gear, rumpled grey cotton slacks and a batik cotton shirt, courtesy of the Tamil traders in the Pettah District, and long cotton socks with leather sandals to finish.

Later that evening I sat and relaxed on the patio with my beer, listening to the gentle rustle of the breeze through the palmyras and let the peace seep into my mind. I went to bed early and lay quietly drifting off to sleep, waiting for the 'lights out' that didn't come. The last couple of days had seen a change. Thoughts of the taxman and holes in the roof had taken, well if not a back seat, a pouffe on the side.

The following days passed in total boredom and uninterrupted tension. Absolutely bugger-all happened. After two days of peace I was more twitched up than I had been the previous week. God, but my nerves were in an awful state.

Sat in the Mess at breakfast one morning, I asked the HouseBoy for some bread. There was no response. He stared at me and didn't move. Growling under my breath, well, I thought it was under my breath, I got up and fetched the bread for myself. Hesitantly he stepped forward, offering to cut the bread for me. Baring my teeth in a grimace, I waved the breadknife under his nose and glowered at him. With his eyes rolling fit to fall out of his head, he beat a hasty retreat to the kitchen and spent the rest of the meal watching me fearfully through the doorway. It seemed that I had somehow developed a reputation as a fighting, biting, tooth and nail bad bastard.

The state of temporary peace in Jaffna District didn't last. Donald had been doing the North Coast re-supply runs over the last couple of days. He had been getting quite confident when he took a good rattling of small arms fire from the west side at VVT, from the house set in high walled grounds about 400 metres from the LS.

Suddenly we were back to square one, just as it had been three and a half months earlier.

The following days passed in various states of nervous tension. One day uptight, the next really loose. Some mail had arrived from home for me, great day. I bobbed and weaved into VVT and still came under fire, bastards, awful day. My air ticket for home leave arrived from the downtown office, days-to-do euphoria.

We bobbed and weaved our way into Point Pedro one day and there was no response from the Tiger detachment at the Toilets, nothing happened, no hostile fire, nothing at all. Yee-haa, I'd beaten the bastards.

I gave it to Royce to fly out. He set himself up to take off into wind, overland that was. 'What in hell's name is he up to?' I thought, 'An overland take-off.' I was about to take the aircraft off him, but considering briefly that if it was a surprise to me I thought it would certainly be a surprise to the Tigers, so I sat there fat, dumb, and happy.

Yeah, I sat there until at about 200 feet, in a very student pilot climb out, there was a enormous explosion from below and behind us. The aircraft shuddered in the blast as I grabbed the controls and shouted, 'I have it.' Pulling all the torque available, I stuffed the nose down to gain some airspeed and rolled the Trooper seawards. 'Number one gunner, what can you see out there, what's going on back there?' I called on the intercom.

'Captain, there is a big cloud of smoke behind us on the ground,' he replied, as he hung from his safety harness and looked behind us. It was time to get us seawards for safety, away from the bastards in the coconut trees who had just connected a battery to a bloody great big landmine just 100 metres outside the perimeter of the camp.

There was a resistance to the controls, 'Shit,' I thought, 'we've taken some damage to the control runs. Gunners, look back at the tail of the helicopter to see if we have any damage,' I called, still pulling and pushing hard on the controls to get us out to sea, to

Landmine at Point Pedro

somewhere safer. They both lunged outwards on their safety harnesses, anxiously looking back down the tail of the Trooper for damage.

Looking quickly over at Royce to see if he was OK, I saw that he was fighting me on the controls. Hell no, it wasn't the controls runs that I was fighting against, it was bloody Royce.

'You're pulling too much torque,' he whinged indignantly.

'Bollocks, Royce, when you're under fire and in danger of losing it all, bollocks to the rules,' I shouted back, 'I have control.'

Still pushing the cyclic stick hard forwards for speed, I turned away from the hidden dangers of the coconut groves. Bloody incompetent, self-important, know-it-all junior pilots flying like they were still under training on the airfield.

They would be the death of some poor bastard, and it wouldn't be me. They could take their righteous indignation and stuff it. From total complacency to wildly angry in 30 seconds. Rock and roll.

Safe out at sea and heading homewards a few moments later, the radio crackled into life. Velvettiturai were calling for a Cas-evac. They had taken a few hits on the securing party during our last landing at VVT.

We were almost abeam them by then, homeward bound. Rolling left and diving for the wave tops, I set us up for a very fast landing at VVT.

We arrived so quickly that the Tigers in the Big House hadn't time to get a single shot off at us. Aye, it had proved to be the case in the past and had proven itself again. Don't tell them you're on the way, and the welcome mat doesn't get put out.

We quickly loaded the casualty, the 106mm recoilless rifle with a few cases of ammo for it, and poked off out to sea before anybody had a chance to think. Everybody except for Gunga Din, of course. He gave us his standard salute as we left.

Looking back into the cabin to check that all was well, I saw that the port gunner was staring steadfastly into the cockpit. He was a new guy on the Squadron and I reckon that he'd had enough for one day. Hell's bells, it had been his target, his responsibility to respond. He was new and no one was hurt. Shit, you can't expect to win them all.

Back at KKS the area was gently throbbing with explosions. Welcome home, chaps. Kapila, the instructor from Katunayaka, had arrived some time during the afternoon, and as soon as I could I got him on one side to find out what the bloody hell was going on with our new Squadron Leader and Royce.

'Hi, Kapila. How ya' doin'?' I started, softly, softly catchee monkey. 'Hey, do you know that Point Pedro and VVT are back to the same state they were in three months ago?'

Kapila nodded in greeting, he was one of the few that tried to get it right. 'Hi, Tim, what's going on then?' he asked.

'You know, today when Royce took off from Point Pedro we got a bloody great land-mine set off underneath us. They seemed to be ready for us. I thought at the time that taking off into wind and overland would surprise them, but they were ready for us,' I explained, as coolly as my ragged temper would allow.

Our new Squadron Leader had been standing very nearby and was obviously listening in to the conversation. He ambled the few steps casually over to us. 'I've been teaching Royce how to take off from Confined Areas,' he proclaimed grandly with the same stupid look on his face that I'd got from him before.

'You cannot possibly practice such techniques in an operational area, you must be sensible and employ other tactics to get out of there.' Thankfully Kapila had immediately backed up my thoughts on the subject.

'Aye, and if you make any change to the standard operational procedures, it would be nice for the rest of us to know what you're bloody doin',' I interjected. 'Today Royce nearly got us blown out of the sky by following your bloody stupid route out of Point Pedro.' I was bloody seething. Someone had risked my life without telling me. 'Just how many times have you been in and out of Point Pedro overland.' I finished angrily.

Royce

Give him his due, he realised how bloody stupid he'd been, it was written all over his face. 'Oh, maybe every time for the last week,' he admitted with the standard sheepish figure of eight roll of his head. Bloody wonderful, I'd allowed Royce to fly us over a landmine that had been laid for himself and Sujith.

Aye, I was sorely pissed off with myself for ever believing that anybody in the Sri Lankan Air Force had actually got it right. 'Never again,' I vowed, 'never again'.

The Squadron Leader wandered off to lick his wounds whilst I managed to get Kapila to agree with all my thoughts about LS security and the lack of top-cover. He promised that he would take the matter up with Wing Commander Perez and the Army that very evening, and until he had got it sorted out we were not to go to PPO or VVT. He wandered off towards the Wing Commander's rooms, leaving me wondering just how long that would last.

Kapila's first line of approach to the situation had to be through the Wing Commander. The Wing Commander doubtless didn't want to piss off his friends at KKS Army HQ, and they wouldn't want to do anything to upset the peace talks.

The short answer, they put me on anything but runs to PPO or VVT for a couple of days. Donald got them instead, and complained bitterly about the Army not securing the sites properly and coming under fire on every approach and departure.

It didn't count for much, though, they made him the same promises that they had made to me some four months earlier.

Cornering Kapila again a couple of days later, he was able to come up with an answer. 'I will come along in the Gunship with Squince, and I will see for myself what the Army say and do.'

So, off we went, carting corned beef and cigarettes into VVT, complete with the Gunship lurking at a discreet distance to the south.

Royce called for a secure site and, quite unexpectedly, the Army replied immediately, 'We're ready for you, the firing points are cleared.'

So in we went and immediately came under fire from the usual firing points at the Little House, about 250 metres from the LS. We were completely buggered. We couldn't see anyone on the ground, we couldn't be sure how far out the securing party were. We couldn't just open fire on the houses for fear of hitting the poor bloody infantry.

'Royce, ask them where the securing parties are, ask them in Sinhalese, so that they understand exactly,' I demanded insistently. There was an awful, pregnant pause.

'They were 200 metres out,' came the Army's reply.

God, how could they lie so blatantly about something so important?

Kapila, listening and watching from the Gunship, must suddenly have realised what we had been up against for the last four months.

'VVT, this is Gunship Charlie Hotel Five-Three-Seven, I am running in to fire on the firing point, tell your patrol to step onto the beach very quickly,' came Kapila's call from the Gunship. With that the patrol leader stepped out from behind a bush just eighty metres from the LS.

'Enough, enough,' said Kapila, 'we go back to KKS.'

Breaking away to left and to right, we departed. The point had been proven in a very direct way.

Ten minutes later back at KKS, Kapila stormed away from the Gunship and disappeared into the Wing Commander's office. How I would have loved to have been a chit-chat on the wall.

He didn't emerge for quite a long time. When he did he declared quite positively, 'It will definitely be clear tomorrow.' Kapila was due to return to Katunayaka the very next day. Life's a bitch and then you burn.

An early start the following day turned to worms within ten minutes of starting.

God, but I was a good lad. I had even got up extra early so that I could take things easy and still be on time to do top-cover for the Avro when it arrived.

Whoops, no bloody chance. As soon as the first engine was fired up we got a Chip Light on the warning panel and it had to be closed down. What the hell, being seven minutes early wouldn't have made any difference anyway. The Avro arrived ten minutes early. This was going to be a grand day out.

I'd finished my breakfast by time the engineers had the Trooper back on line, and was quite happy to get on with delivering conscripts and cartridges to Karainagar, Mandaitivu and Elephant Pass.

At ten-fifteen we landed back at the loading bay heli-pad at KKS for the next run, and I was more than a teensy bit surprised to have a manifest sheet for Point Pedro and Velvettiturai thrust through the window.

'Uh, One Two Sierra this is Five Four Six, we're not going to Point Pedro or VVT today,' I called on the radio, 'we're closing down.'

It seemed to me like a good time for a coffee break anyway.

Back in the Mess ten minutes later, all hell broke loose. Twenty minutes later I was escorted into the Brigadier's office in KKS Army Headquarters. Just to keep me company were Squadron Leader Sujith, Donald, Wing Commander Perez, some Major or other, probably from the QM's department, and the Colonel Commanding Operations for Jaffna.

The shit had finally hit the fan. Yep, it was the same Brigadier that I had given a mouthful to when Donald had first arrived at KKS.

The Brigadier was very unhappy with me. In the most imperious of tones I was commanded to explain myself for refusing to fly into Point Pedro and VVT.

'Bollocks to it,' I thought and waded in. For the next five minutes I held forth and told the Army their fortune with no holds barred. In reply I got the same shit that we had received time and again in the past about the distances that the soldiers were expected to go, and that the Tigers would shoot at us anyway. Donald backed me up all the way, but without Kapila there it was pointless.

'The Commander Air Force will have to be informed.' declared Perez, puffing importantly through his handlebar moustache. With the Brigadier glowering sternly at us, Perez led us out of the office and back to the Mess.

The Wing Commander obviously realised that we were not going to do as we were told on this one. He couldn't really put us under Mess Arrest, or charge us with disobeying a direct order. We weren't supposed to be there. So he did the next best thing and used us to provide top-cover for Sujith and Royce while they did the runs into PPO and VVT.

Sujith, being the complete pacifist prick that he was, didn't even say that they were under fire until we got back to KKS. If he had, we would have shown him a brassing-up of the Tiger that would have made his hair stand on end.

Squince had been in the left seat, I was in the right seat. Two Whitefaces on top cover; shades of Western mercenaries commanding Gunships.

Surprisingly, that evening after supper the Wingco eased up to us and very chummily agreed with our actions during the day and our reasons for it. He even said that he would cover us if it got to the ears of Ken Who? We'd long since given up calling him 'our local Team Leader' or 'Ken Whyte'. He didn't know what game we were playing, and we thought that he probably didn't know who he was himself.

Before he left us to our own devices, however, the Wingco did suggest that when the Chief of Staff arrived the following day that we should perhaps put our case a little less bluntly and not be too hard on the Army.

'Yes sir, of course, sir,' we agreed patronisingly. 'Why the hell,' we wondered, 'didn't he say anything in the Brigadier's office earlier today'? Naturally he had been covering his own back and, of course, he didn't want to lose either of his two faces.

Later that same evening we sat and listened to Mr G. Din's comment on our activities of late. 'Lights out' consisted of three hours of mortars and small arms fire, all directed at the Army. That evening we counted 22 inbound mortars and a similar number of the Army's 84mm mortars as they rustled through the night sky over our heads on the way outbound.

'Hell's name, what was I fighting for? Why should I get my guts in a knot?' I thought. All that I wanted was for the Army to do just a little bit towards stamping their mark of authority on the area.

I'd gone a long way down the line from being there to 'learn the ropes'. I was taking a much more personal interest in the outcome of the conflict. No longer was I just an observer, nor was I content to sit back and let them get on with it. I was beginning to make the running in a fight that was rapidly becoming my own.

Mercenary, well, I don't think so. Reluctant, well, maybe not as much as I had been.

8

Peace at Point Pedro

20 September 1986. The Chief of Staff (COS) was due to arrive before lunch to preside over an investigation into the antics of the two Whiteface contract pilots on the Jaffna Peninsula. To keep me out of trouble pending his arrival, Perez had me put on top-cover duty for the midday Avro, with Royce in the left seat.

The COS didn't turn up until the afternoon, however. He had decided to stop off at Vavuniya on the way and found the grub there to be so good that he stayed on for lunch. Eventually he arrived, and with all due pomp and ceremony we were ushered into the Hallowed Presence. We were suitably unimpressed.

Much the same teams were lined up as before. The Brigadier sat at the COS's left side behind a large table. Facing them on the other side of the table were just me and Squince at my right shoulder. The remaining teams were sat, suitably distanced, behind us.

The Army, to our left, included the Colonel of Ops and his second in command, a Major. There was also an infantry Captain from Headquarters. He was, quite possibly, the Adjutant. He didn't say a lot, maybe he was there to make up the numbers.

The Air Force, to our right and behind, were fielding a fairly impressive team. The two newly promoted Wing Commanders, Oliver from Katunayaka and Perez from KKS, and finally our own Squadron Leader Sujith. Complete farce though it was, I knew that we would do okay. *The Chief of Staff was an Air Vice Marshal.* Come on, the blues!

The COS started the ball rolling by solemnly asking me to explain the problems of flying into VVT and Point Pedro. 'Captain ee-Smith, why do you refuse to fly into VVT and Point Pedro last week?'

'Er . . . Sir, the situation at VVT and Point Pedro has deteriorated over the last few months to the point where it is impossible to fly into either LS without coming under sustained small arms fire. The Tigers have increased their anti-helicopter activity to the extent that they have used co-ordinated mortar and machine gun fire attacks on landing helicopters.'

A shuffling of chairs and feet from the Army team to the left.

'They have also used land-mines just outside the perimeter fence to try and catch us if we try to take-off over land.'

A shuffling of feet and chairs from the Air Force Team to the right.

'All of these attacks have been uncontested by the Army . . .'

More shuffling of feet and chairs from the Green team to the left, '. . . and as the Air Force do not permit suppressive fire, even on known terrorist firing points . . .'

A muted choking sound came from Perez, which was hastily covered by some tactical coughing in the Blue team.

'. . . we are now stuck with the unenviable situation of having to go into the Landing Sites without ground support from the Army. With no support from the Air Force there is a distinct chance of losing a helicopter and its crew for a bag of coconuts.'

I was using my posh 'talking to serious officers' voice.

Going on, I carefully explained the build-up of the situation. The location of the firing points at the school toilets and changing rooms on the beach to the east of Point Pedro. The Little and Big Houses to the west of VVT, and the results of the Army's pitiful efforts to remove them.

The Chief of Staff listened attentively to it all. 'Thank you, Captain.' he murmured at the end. 'Now, what have the Army to say about all this?'

He had turned inquiringly towards the Brigadier. The Brigadier turned inquiringly to the Colonel Ops. The CO Ops blustered and explained that 'the Tigers could see the Security Forces moving out and so moved into the firing point early', and 'they moved in overnight so that we can't see them.'

Squince, at my right shoulder, almost leapt from his chair. 'Rubbish, those firing points are constantly manned and are less than six hundred metres away from the landing sites in both cases,' he almost shouted at the CO Ops.

'We don't have enough troops to send out holding detachments,' replied the Colonel, 'it would take at least a hundred men to take the west bunker at VVT,' he finished, almost pleading.

'Great', I thought, gloating at his discomfort, 'at last he has finally admitted that there is at the very least a bunker in the Big House.' I was ready to go in for the kill in this discussion.

'Sir,' I put in, 'there is more than a bunker in the Big House. There are trenches, at least six sentry towers. There are sandbagged sangars against each and every wall of the grounds. The Little House that they often fire from is only four hundred metres away from the camp and less than three hundred metres from the LS. I have some photographs that prove it.'

The Colonel wasn't finished, though. The next bit was right out of World War One. 'We would need ropes and scaling ladders and grappling irons to get over the wall, we do not have any rope,' he calmly stated without even blinking, or thinking come to that.

Squince spluttered and nearly choked. I was astounded. Sujith sat looking at the floor, and amazingly they had all listened attentively to what the Colonel had to say. The LTTE were allowed to have their wicked way because the Sri Lankan Army did not have any rope. One thing was sure, they wouldn't hang us, for they didn't have enough rope.

The hearing broke up in a sudden outburst of squabbling as it suddenly came home to the Air Force that things were not as rosy as they were made out to be by their local commanders. The Army suddenly realised that their months of backsliding inactivity had been brought into full view. The Chief of Staff rumbled into activity like a small volcano. Everyone shut up, sat up and listened. 'We must communicate and we must co-operate,' he boomed, and he skilfully guided the argument between the Colonel Ops and me.

'We cannot allow the Tigers to get away with shooting at our helicopters,' a small dig at the Army, 'neither can we allow them to prewent our helicopters from flying to our outstations,' he went on, sniping at the Air Force with more accuracy than Gunga Din's black pyjama gang.

The COS went on with his diplomatic engineering, 'Captain ee-Smith, and you Captain Skince, must make every effort to assist the Army in overcoming the problems of flying to the outstations. You must help them to identify the firing points and put them out of commission.'

I wanted to say that they knew already where the firing points were and that they did bugger-all about it, but I knew it would be useless. We would have to accept that this was a new starting point, and from here on in we should be able to expect more co-operation from the Army in putting the Tiger back in his cage. I silently nodded my agreement.

The Brigadier had been quiet up until then. He turned slowly, almost imperiously to the Colonel Ops and his team. 'We must give the Tigers a bloody nose, we must whack those bloody buggers. You must co-operate with these pilots to sort them out,' he proclaimed in sonorous tones.

Aye, and there we had it. The Sri Lankan stand-off again. As far as I could see, the buck was well and truly passed. It was down to me and some, as yet unspecified, young officers at VVT and PPO to sort out Gunga Din. All with the total blessing of the Chief of Staff, the Brigadier, the Colonel Ops KKS, two Wing Commanders, and a Squadron Leader. What a way to fight a war.

We, at least, were exonerated; it was time that the Army had a kick at the ball. And kick it they did. They spent the next 30 minutes discussing the taking out of the Big House and its bunkers by various *Boys Own Annual* methods.

'Captain Smith, we would like to see your photographs so that we can brief the officers at VVT,' asked a respectful CO Ops.

Big House before the mini-war

'Totally bloody hopeless people,' I thought, as I carefully explained that their own Intelligence Cell had the cameras and equipment to produce bigger and better photos than mine. 'Bloody hopeless.' Anyway, I didn't want the Army to get hold of my photographs, for I knew that once they had their grubby fingers on them I would never get them back.

At four o'clock we broke off for lunch. We had won, but at a price. We had to make it work. Perez had also scored some Brownie points for eventually backing us.

The Colonel Ops had drawn the match, his situation was bad, but he had put forward a *Plan.*

Wing Commander Oliver had lost because he had been in the

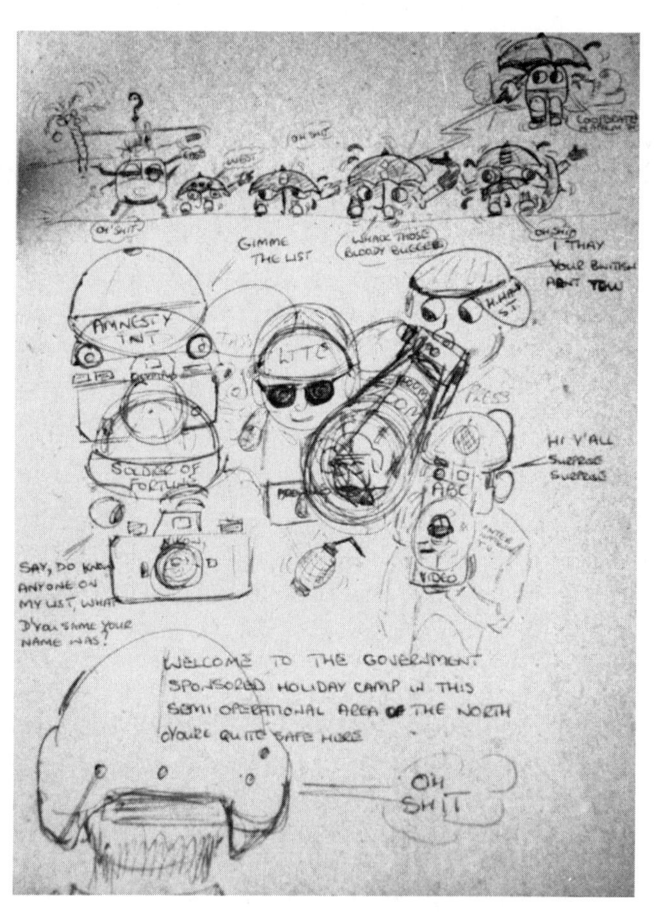

Toilet cartoons

dark regarding the situation in one of his own units. Sujith had lost for not keeping his Wing Commander in the picture.

Sujith got his own back, though. I was sent to do a ground run just as we were about to sit down to supper that evening. When I got down to the hangar the engineers were still working on the aircraft and knew nothing about it, so I trailed all the way back to the Mess and a cold supper. Some you win, some you lose.

The following day was Sunday and was usually a quiet day for the Whiteface crews, maybe they thought that we were Christians or something. As it was, we got down to some serious cartoon drawing.

I was scuffing about doing some sort of housework when Royce came trundling by. It wasn't like him to be so friendly, and my immediate thoughts were that he had heard that we had won the match against the Army the previous day.

'We have been to Point Pedro,' he said with a confident swagger and a truly magnificent figure of eight roll of his nose, 'it's quite safe now.'

'Well done, Royce,' I thought, 'gave 'em hell, did you?'

'How's that, then?' I asked with an innocently inquiring smile. For those that knew it, the smile was like a hand grenade with the pin out.

'The Army carried out a night raid on the toilets at Point Pedro,' he said, full of pride, 'they killed two and captured three Tigers with no injuries to the Army.' With his nose up in the air and his head rolling fit to fall off, he went on into the Mess. I put the pin back in the grenade.

So it wasn't just 'a little bunker,' it had been manned with five Tigers even at night. It was only 400 metres from the camp and not 'miles away' as they had constantly claimed. We'd been so bloody right to kick up a fuss.

Obviously the Chief of Staff had said a little more to the Army after we had left our private court-martial. The Army had finally got its finger out. In the Sri Lankan scheme of things, they had to recover some face. Yes, we had won yesterday, and so had the boys on the ground at Point Pedro. That should really poke it up Ken Who's arse if he ever got to hear about it.

Later that day, Sujith and Royce went to PPO to pick up the three captured and the Colonel Ops to bring them back to KKS. I

Firing point at Pedro manned

waited for their arrival with baited breath, wanting to know if, this time, Gunga Din was really in the bag.

The CO Ops arrived without any terrorists. How odd that, more often than not, captured Tigers never seemed to make it to formal interrogation. 'Where are you now, Gunga Din?' I thought.

Whether or not Mr G. Din was dead, captured or had escaped, the recent loss of a mortar team and the taking of the toilet at PPO with the loss of five Tigers should have made life on the peninsula positively peaceful.

Monday, 22 September 1986. Back to work. I was full of 'I told you so' confidence and more than ready to co-operate. First stop VVT, with the Gunship skulking about two klicks to the south. The crews were briefed, and we were ready to rock and roll.

We were at 200 feet and 400 metres out from the LS at VVT when the Gunship started the ball rolling with a run past from east to west, laying down some suppressive fire from the 7.62mm side-gun and the .50in cabin gun. Rolling right, we took up a parallel course offshore and put a belt of 7.62mm into the Big House.

They were ready for us and returned our fire as quick as they could screw themselves around in their dugouts, trenches and towers. 'Not for long,' I thought as we continued rolling right and climbed away from the beach and cleared the area for the Gunship. Rolling left and running in from the south, the Gunship crew dumped a string of rockets into a deserted Kovil some 200 metres short and onto somebody else's patio before they got the third one through the letter-box of the Big House. The Tigers were taking it from three sides now.

The Army had moved out from the LS into the coconut groves towards the Little House and were putting down their own covering fire from the earth walls and ditches of the coconut groves.

The Gunship had rolled away to the left and taken up an orbit around the area. We took up a right-hand orbit opposite them and we both poured in covering fire whilst the Army moved up on the two houses.

In no time at all the Little House was taken and the infantry had moved on through its grounds towards the Big House. The Sappers had moved into the Little House behind the infantry and were already preparing to blow it into dust.

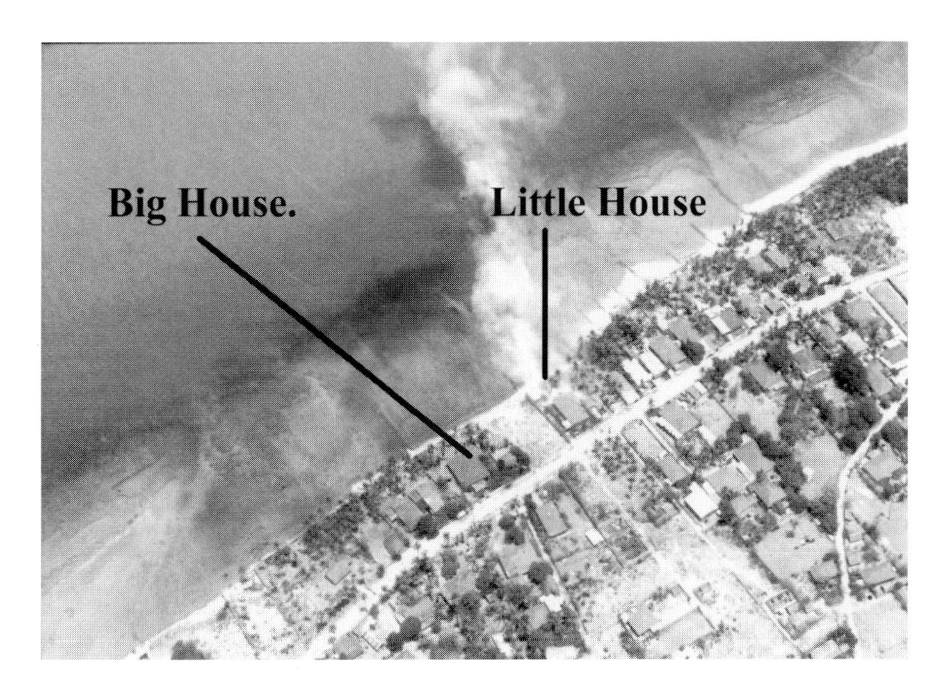

Big House and Little House

We maintained our orbit and laid down box after box of 7.62mm from our side-guns. Unfortunately the new gunner on the port side was not content to lay it on the Tigers in the Big House and the snipers in the factory just to the south of it. Seeing the infantry running through the groves, he lost his sense of direction and started having a go at them.

The Army screamed at us and I screamed at him to stop. The Gunship was going for fuel and ammo, so we continued with our right-hand orbit and transferred the port gunner's ammo across the cabin to Ariyaratna at the starboard sidegun. We could so easily have killed a stack of our own troops, and life for the Whitefaces would have been one big bucket of shit.

The infantry were now closing on the Big House, but the Tigers were not giving up. To the south, behind the Kovil somewhere, a Tiger mortar team had set up and was lobbing mortar bombs into the coconut groves. We sprayed the likely points within the area in an attempt to harass them, but to no avail. They added their own piece of chaos to the scene. We were getting short on fuel when the Gunship returned to take over from us. We stayed on and watched as another pod full of rockets went into the Big House and its grounds before heading back to KKS for replenishment. The infantry were stuck in the coconut groves short of the Big House. 'Were they waiting for someone to bring up the scaling ladders and ropes,' I wondered as we left for KKS.

The outstation at Tondamanna had been having their own little fracas at the same time, and on our way back to KKS we dropped in to pick up two of their casualties. How the LTTE could field so many players and teams at the same time amazed me. We had taken eight of them from PPO in the last fortnight, and still they were able operate where and when they pleased.

Back at VVT half an hour later, the picnic was still going on. We took up our orbit opposite the Gunship and fired on anything that moved. We rattled the corrugated tin roof on the factory until the snipers in there must have been deafened by the racket, but still they moved around and put down sporadic bursts of fire on the infantry as they moved towards their objective.

Looking down from our orbit, it was easy to see where the Tigers' bullets were going. They kicked up the dust around the feet and legs of the soldiers as they dashed from tree to tree and ditch to ditch on their way to the Big House. It wasn't so easy to see where they were being fired from and do something about it. Our port-side gunner was still having difficulty with his sense of direction, and Ariyaratna was doing most of the work with the starboard side-gun.

The situation was still hotting up as more and more terrorists were flooding into the area. We watched them as they dashed from bush to tree and from house to house on their way towards the fight. I don't know how many we killed that day. I do know that they kept on coming, on foot, on pushbikes and in cars. We knocked them down and they crawled on until we hit them again. It was surely one hell of a way to secure a landing site for a bag, full of coconuts.

Suddenly the infantry were ready. They had taken the Big House from the Tiger. I think we must have killed them all, for I had not seen anyone withdrawing from the area. The Sappers moved in and, having laid their charges, rapidly withdrew under our covering fire. Lickety spit, they ran through those groves faster going out than when they went in, and dived for the cover of the ditches around the Little House. Seconds later there was an enormous explosion and a huge cloud of dust and smoke which took several minutes to settle. When it did, the Big House and the walls surrounding it were still standing.

There was no time to hang around and admire the view, we were again short on fuel and ammo. We went into the LS to pick up four casualties, four walking wounded, the only casualties on our side, and took them to KKS for attention. The Gunship had departed some time before, and as we left the area all was quiet and, for the time being, it was secure.

An hour later we were back to re-supply VVT with ammunition and explosives. All was quiet. The Army had withdrawn to camp, having given all they had to destroy the Big House, but still they had failed. The Tiger, though, was a different animal altogether, and as we approached the area a few latecomers were still arriving on pushbikes. We took the easiest one and presented him to the new port-side gunner, who shot him off his bike. When we turned our attention to the others, they had wisely and very rapidly made themselves scarce.

The landing site at VVT was peaceful enough as we dropped off their supplies. Our next stop on the routing was to be Elephant Pass, so we rolled right on departure and flew east down the coast past Point Pedro. A foot patrol was out looking around the area of the toilet bunker that had been taken during the night less than two days before. They were experiencing some difficulty with the local hard nuts, so we laid a belt of 7.62mm rounds into a small group of houses they were trying to clear and continued on our way to Elephant Pass.

Returning to KKS an hour later, we thought that we would slide by PPO and take a look at Mr. G Din's toilet bunker.

Surprisingly Point Pedro came up on the tac-radio and told us that the foot patrol had a casualty to shift. The cabin was full of troops going on R&R, so we scooted back to KKS and picked up 700lbs of fuel and replenished our ammo for the return trip.

Back at Point Pedro a short time later, the patrol had already withdrawn to the camp and the LS was declared clear and secured out to the white house about 120 metres east of the landing site. We took another swing round the toilets on our way in just to have another gloating look at the scene of G. Din's defeat.

Rolling on to final approach, we got a tremendous burst of fire from the toilets.

'Dear God,' I thought, 'the fucking Army can't get anything fucking right. You are surely a better man than they are, Gunga Din.'

That evening we sat and waited for the Intelligence Reports to find out the final score. Our crew had put down 7000 rounds, 28 belts, of 7.62mm that day, and I wanted to see what we had done with it. The chance didn't come, for the casualty that we had lifted from PPO was in a bad way and had to be taken to Anuradhapura Hospital for treatment. As it was well after dark I was selected to go, taking Royce along for the experience. Already tired, I was in no mood for buggering around.

Left to the Sri Lankans it would be a case of IFR, I Follow Road, but it was down to me and I was more inclined towards SWAG, Scientific Wild-Arsed Guess. Back in the UK I'd been an acknowledged expert at such things and could navigate by various Rules of Thumb with extreme accuracy. I wanted to get this trip over and done with and go to bed.

I grabbed a 1:500,000 map and folded a crease along the line of the route. In less than a minute I had mentally dead-reckoned our heading and distance. A quick feel for the wind as we walked to the heli-pad gave me a wind velocity. A quick mental calculation of our heading, airspeed and the wind velocity produced the timing for the trip. The rest could be done in the air. Five minutes later we were airborne.

Royce bitched all the way, he couldn't see where we were going. Mind you, it was bloody dark down there and there was nothing to confirm whether we were on track or not. Reaching into my flying suit pocket I got out my whiz-wheel and a home-made compass rose to check my figures. They seemed OK, so I sat back and waited.

Anuradhapura turned up less than a mile to the right of the nose 50 minutes after take-off. We landed smack on time.

Royce still wasn't impressed, but said nothing on the return trip. We arrived back in KKS at one o'clock in the morning. They'd had me flying for nearly nine hours that day, and I fell into my bed totally exhausted.

The next ten days followed in what passed for peace on the Jaffna Peninsula. It seemed that we had dealt the Tigers a telling blow at VVT and Point Pedro.

Ten almost idyllic days of cabbages and coconuts. Letters from home and pleasant evenings playing cribbage with Squince. The Sri Lankans had still not mastered his surname and called him anything that they felt was close to the real thing.

There was an effort to cut down on the amount of flying to the outstations. Anything less than three passengers outbound from KKS and the trip was cancelled. Surprising how the manpower requirements went up to six when there were only three men going to PPO with the cigarette ration. Ration re-supply to Point Pedro and Velvetitturai was to be done by the Navy. In less than a week we were back to square one, with twice-daily trips everywhere.

There were still occasional bursts of machine gun fire over the airfield boundary, but nothing that really disturbed the peace.

We took the Army Band to Karainagar Naval Base for an Officers Mess dinner and cadged a few bottles of lemonade from the mess while we were there. We chased the occasional truck. One had knocked a cyclist off his bike and buggered off at high speed. We left the truck smouldering on the roadside whilst the driver made good his escape with a minor bullet wound to his backside.

Mr Mahindapala and Mr Siripala had worked miracles for the Whiteface food store by bringing a three-litre carton of Maçon

Rouge back from Colombo with them. Those two had the nous to go uptown to the bigger shops and ask for what we wanted. They doubtless pocketed a little more of our cash than was necessary for the job, but who were we to argue?

It was time to check out the Army cookhouse.

There was a trick to going in there. The first time that I went in I had opened my mouth to speak and promptly swallowed a couple of flies. After that I did a sort of Bogey takeoff and spoke through clenched teeth. It made no difference to the cooks. They didn't understand what I was after whichever way I spoke. They just let me have the run of the place and gave me whatever I pointed at.

Home-made mashed potatoes became a regular feature of our evening meals after that. Life really was quite pleasant for a while.

One evening Donald and me were sat discussing the inadequacies of the company and the devious means they used to get people to do the dirty work in Sri Lanka for themselves and the MOD. We were savouring a shandy of Army beer and Navy lemonade after an excellent evening meal of corned beef and mashed potatoes and some unidentified cookhouse curried vegetable.

'Haven't heard any good bangs for a while,' said Squince.

'I was just thinking that ... it wouldn't half stir things up a bit if a rocket came through,' I mused.

There was a pause of about two seconds before the mortar bomb landed 300 metres away just behind the Mess.

'Bloody hell,' I said, quickly grabbing my shandy to stop it from spilling.

'Shit,' said Squince with feeling, as another landed even closer than the first.

'Keep your bloody mouth shut, Squince, just look what you've done now,' I chided.

People were running everywhere. The lights went out as another mortar arrived even closer than the last and took out the power lines.

Little brown faces under steel helmets came running past us. They all clutched their AK 47s as though their lives depended on it. 'We should go to the bunker until it is safe,' said one as it ran by, teeth and eyes flashing white in the darkness.

'Bollocks,' said Squince without feeling.

'More shandy, Donald.' I asked, as we continued discussing the shortcomings of the company and Ken Who. That bunker was the

Officers' bunker at KKS

most unsafe safety device I had ever seen. It was full of snakeskin's and cat's piss.

The meringue that I'd planned for dessert later that evening turned to rat shit, and when the emergency generator cut in a hour or so later I found that some light-fingered bastard had lifted the washing bucket from the shower cubicle in the darkness. Maybe it was the Tigers on a morale-breaking mission.

The Brigadier had got his co-operation and we had our mini-war at VVT. The Army had done their thing at Point Pedro. We had got ten days of peace whilst the Tiger licked his wounds. It seemed to me that the Tiger was fit again and telling us just what he felt about us. We would have to think of something else.

9

Goodnight Captain

With the end of September there were only 15 days to go until my UK leave began. I hadn't left Jaffna for more than a few days during the last four months, and a rest was badly needed. Just 15 days and I would be out of KKS for good. Where the SLAF would send me when I got back I didn't know, and didn't really care, it had to be better than the Jaffna Peninsula and KKS. How much of an instructional role I would then play was in the lap of the Gods.

The idea of being an operational or tactical instructor wasn't totally out of order. There was a lot of experience locked up in my head that I could pass on to those that wished to listen. I still felt that teaching was my vocation, and could think of no finer thing to do with my life, even in Sri Lanka.

The Navy had in the meantime stopped re-supplying Point Pedro and VVT from the sea. The only positive thing that they had done was to take four Tigers off on one of their re-supply launches for interrogation. Quite where they took them I don't know, probably to Karainagar.

They turned up again at KKS the following day, but instead of being handled through the loading bay they were off loaded on one of the heli-pads near the Air Force Officers Mess and were kept there under guard for 20 minutes or so.

When I next went by they had gone. That intrigued me more than somewhat, for I had kept my eyes open in the chance of seeing them again and getting a photo of Gunga Din or some of his men in the flesh.

I waited for several more days in the hope of seeing them again. They would eventually have to be sent to Colombo for internment, either by helicopter or on the daily 748.

The days of waiting were filled with the standard drudgery of C&C from KKS.

The Army had set fire to something or other on the north-eastern, the 05, end of the runway, and for a couple of days I used it as a homing beacon whilst it burned. On the second day of waiting I finished flying in time to take a run around the airfield. Jogging along towards the 05 end of the strip, I noticed that a pack dogs were scavenging around the still-smouldering fire; fighting among themselves for whatever it was that they had found there.

They had spilled onto the perimeter track, and I wondered if it would be safe enough to pass them at the trot. Grabbing a handful of small stones I jogged past them, shying stones at any that came too close.

The following day the same thing happened again, so grabbing a handful of stones, I ran straight into them. They scattered and loped around me at a distance as I continued on towards the smouldering fire. The last dog to leave dropped whatever it had in its mouth and backed off a few yards, snarling it's defiance at me. Slowing to a walk, I stopped a few feet from the still-smouldering fire and turned over the dog's booty with the toe of my running shoe. It was a large bone with blackened and charred flesh still attached to it, not recognisable as any cut of meat that I had ever seen before, I wondered at the generosity of the Army Cookhouse in throwing away so much meat on the bone. I wondered too at their generosity in throwing away the bones.

Moving into the centre of the fire, I turned a few more charred lumps with my foot. There were more than enough to make up for a couple of the lightweight cows that they produced in Sri Lanka. The ribs were not long enough for a cow and didn't seem quite right for a pig's. Pork wasn't on the menu that often, anyway.

That evening I couldn't get the thought of those charred bones out of my head. If they had been burning all day, then there must have been a sight more meat on those bones at the beginning. If the dogs had been there for two days, then there must have been a lot of bones there in the beginning.

Over the last few years as a born-again bachelor, I had bought and cooked for myself. The bones were not recognisable as anything that I had seen before in my life. They were actually about the right size to be human. Right there I thought that I had it.

Was that where the captured Tigers had gone? They had not survived the interrogation. Had they died somewhere in the camp and been disposed of in the simplest, most effective way?

I felt it wise not to make any further enquiries about the fire or the captured Tigers' apparent disappearance. I knew that over the last few days I had used a funeral pyre as a homing beacon.

Small wonder then that the LTTE turned their attention to the Naval Base at Karainagar. Late in the afternoon of 30 September a foot patrol from Karainagar had got themselves caught in an ambush mortar attack. The Gunship was called out to cover their withdrawal to the Base. Ten minutes later they called for a Cas-evac. Royce and I fired up the Trooper and got ourselves under way as quick as we could. We went down to Karainagar at 3000 feet, admiring the glorious sunset as we went.

Closer in to the Base, I asked Royce to get on the radio and find out the situation on the ground at Karainagar. The patrol had, apparently, recovered to the camp, but they were still under fire. From the frantic messages that were being passed to us and the Gunship that was already on station, it seemed that they were well nigh bloody surrounded and in a state of near panic.

I had been in this situation with Namal several weeks before and had managed to get into the LS with an off-the-cuff spiral dive. I felt it was now time for me to put a bit of polish on the technique and show this haughty little shitbag of an Officer Cadet something new. We climbed to 4000 feet again and I set the Trooper in a slow orbit, waiting for the moment when it was clear for us to make our descent.

Kapila had been making strafing runs from the seaward side to the south-east in the Gunship and concentrating its fire on a group of buildings across the narrow stretch of water between the Base on Karaitivu and the island of Kayts.

It was nearly dark, and the Gunship was making one last run to keep the terrorists' heads down during our approach. I made one quick call to Kapila on the tactical radio to watch out for the high tension wires between the islands to the east of the camp, and dumped the collective pitch lever. Within seconds the vertical speed indicator was off the clock as we rocketed downwards in an autorotative spiral dive. My hands and feet and mind were full as I juggled with the airspeed, rate of descent, rate of turn and rotor revs. We were riding Smithy's A1 air-mobile express lift, and I had no time to think about anything other than getting it absolutely right. One slight misjudgement in the gloom would result in an expensive smoking hole.

Once, twice around; as we went round the third orbit I started easing the power in and gently increased airspeed. More and more power, quicker now to slow the rate of descent, collective lever coming up 'til it was almost under my armpit, ears listening to rotor revs, feeling the balance of the tail through my backside, eyes flicking from instruments to outside and back again.

Rolling off some bank, I lined us up with the lights of the camp through the lowest coconut trees as we came whistling out of the third orbit. Royce had his eyes shut as we pulled out at the bottom and flashed between the coconut trees to land in the middle of the cricket pitch. The side-gunners had been very quiet.

The Brigadier was visiting the base from KKS, and as soon as we were down the Naval Base Commander ordered up a mini-war to impress Him. 'Everyone is inside the wire, shoot anything that moves.'

As we left with four casualties they opened up with their 25mm cannon and blew away a house in completely the wrong direction. Still, the racket of it pounding away kept the Tigers' heads down while we staggered into the air, and it probably impressed the Brigadier no end.

Ordering up a mini-war was all well and good. Rather than wiping out anybody that just looked suspicious, the Tigers were near enough to be engaged directly, with the exception of the house. I could live with that. What was needed though was a more permanent means of engaging the enemy on a day-to-day basis.

The problem, however, was that we in the air were quite often unaware of our own dispositions on the ground, such as they were, and were unable to engage on many occasions purely because we didn't know where our own troops were.

Honestly, I think that most of the time the ground troops didn't know where they were themselves. There was obviously room for some thought and planning. What we needed was *communication.*

Towards the end of our private court-martial many weird and wonderful ideas had been brought out into the open, one of which covered that very problem. It was maybe time to see if it worked in practice.

Not only was there a shortage of rope and scaling ladders in the

Sri Lankan Army, there was also an extreme shortage of Tactical Radios and, of course, people trained to use them. A system of coloured flags had been suggested as a means of identifying the forward position of our troops on the ground whilst they were out securing the LS for our approaches and landings.

With that in mind Donald and me pitched up to Sujith and suggested that the Army probably had a 'very good idea' and 'why didn't we try it for them'. Well, if someone had to take the blame for it all turning to rat shit, let it be the people that had suggested it in the first place. Let it be the Army. They would probably get it wrong anyway.

For a couple of days everything went well with the flag system. We still got shot at, and on some occasions it was difficult to actually see the flag. Which complete prat ordered jungle green flags one day I don't know. The side-gunners were young and sharp of eye, though, and often enough we were able to reply in kind when we came under fire. The plan didn't solve the problem of the troops not going out far enough, and on many occasions they might well have stayed in camp.

The situation came to a head a few days later. Donald returned from a run to VVT and Point Pedro at lunchtime and stomped straight into our room with a face like thunder. Lying on my bunk, I was taking it easy. I'd had another dose of the trots and was feeling particularly rough.

Even Ken Who's letter from Colombo 7, exhorting us to take greater care with our hygiene hadn't helped. We had waved it at Froggy Pond, but it had made no difference. Ken had obviously not seen Froggy Pond in all it's glory when he had come to visit us. It was a breeding ground for dengue fever, malaria and dysentery.

'Smithy, you should have seen it, it was a fucking farce,' exploded Donald as soon as he got into the room. 'We were on short finals, taking the shit from the Little House as ever, when a blue flag appeared eighty metres out from the landing site, eighty fucking metres, I ask you!'

Don stood in the middle of the room, hands on hips, with a look of pure murder on his face. He was surely upset about it.

'Easy me old lad, easy, what else did you expect?' I tried to calm him down.

'I didn't expect Gunga Din to wave another blue flag from two hundred metres further down the beach.'

I rolled about on my bed, clutching my aching sides in a sudden burst of uncontrollable laughter.

'It's not fucking funny,' he almost shouted, 'when we got to Point Pedro there were two flags on that fucking bunker at the toilets.' I sat up on my bed, head thumping from the Plague of Froggy Pond, and eyes streaming with tears of laughter. Don sat on his bed and glowered across the room at me.

'You've just got to see the funny side of it, Don,' I tried to placate him.

'Funny, it's not so fucking hilarious when he's put security lights up as well. And they work. They're better equipped than the Army, they've probably got a whole trunk full of coloured flags in the Big House.' There followed a minute or so of thunderous silence. Finally he smiled. 'How are you today, any better?'

'Aah, my head aches something wicked, but the trots have finished, I'll be OK.'

We lapsed into silence again for a moment while Donald got over his rage at being thwarted by the Tiger, and I wiped my still-streaming eyes.

'Don,' I started quietly, 'we knew it wouldn't work, nothing ever does for long up here, but you've got to hand it to Gunga Din, he always comes back. We knock him down, he stands up. We come up with something new, he comes back with something better. He is one hell of an innovator, he deserves a medal, does Gunga Din.'

'Crossed Coconut Palms and Bar,' said Don grinning.

'You can just imagine it, Don,' I sniggered, 'Mrs Din slipping next door for a cup of sugar, "my boy Gunga, well, I mean, he just has to have some sugar on his cornflakes, he does." ' I rolled off my bed and we went for lunch.

Lunch was Curried Something-or-other with enough chillies in it to make our eyes water. We ate it anyway. We wandered back to our room for a proper coffee. Well, as proper as we could make it with what we had.

'Don, how do you fancy chips tonight?' I asked, 'I'm pissed off with eating this shit. What do you think?'

'Chips. Chips! You gotta be joking. These people can't do a curry without fucking it up. What are they going to do to chips?'

'Nah, no problem, I'll make 'em. Good old English chips, without the newspaper, but chips all the same.'

'Smithy, we'll need proper fat and some decent spuds.' He was a complete pessimist when it came down to getting things organised at KKS. Maybe he had good cause, but I was going to make some chips, one way or the other.

There was nothing for me to do that afternoon, so I wandered across to the Army kitchens. With my teeth firmly clenched against an intake of flies, I managed to talk my way into the butchery area. Ten minutes later I wandered out again, clutching a soggy brown paper parcel.

Back at our own 'kitchen' I cleaned off the worktable and opened my parcel. The Mess boys all gathered around to watch and help. I told them all to bugger off out of the way and got on with chopping the beef fat that I had scrounged into smaller pieces to put in to my own pot and render down to dripping. Yes, I was going to have chips that night, come hell or high water.

It didn't take long to fill the small saucepan with bits, and in no time at all I had the pan over the gas ring. The process was extremely slow. By teatime I had just enough to roast a few small potatoes, but I wasn't going to be beaten.

By the time that Donald got back at the end of the day's flying, I still had barely enough to fry off a small handful of chips.

'Shit,' he said, peering theatrically into my pot, 'there's hardly enough to fry an egg.'

'Piss off,' I countered, 'oh ye of little faith. We will be eating chips tonight.'

His face was enough to tell me that he still had little faith.

'Come on, there's just this pot to finish, and we can at least fry some or even roast a couple. It's got to be worth the effort,' I pleaded.

'Well, all right. Let's have a game of darts while we're waiting.'

The Mess boys were sat on their lemonade crates a couple of feet away at the back door, so I left the pot on the stove and followed him into the Mess. Roshan and Namal were lounging in front of the TV watching some Indian film.

'Five-oh-one, double in, double out, nearest the bull to start,' said Don, and off we went. I couldn't get started, and it took us what seemed like ages to get to the last hundred.

Now and then I peered round the corner of the lounge to see that my cooking pot was OK. There were no signs of activity from the Mess boys, so I presumed that everything in the kitchen was all right. I was still struggling with double 19 when Don asked if I could smell something burning.

'Less noise from the spectators, please,' I said, but still took a brief glance round the corner of the lounge. No, Roshan and Namal were still lounging in front of the TV, still watching their Indian film. There always seemed to be a predominance of blue in them. No, the Mess boys were still by the back door, I could hear them chattering away.

I had a go at double nineteen.

'Close one, Smithy. Are you sure your cooking pot's OK?' enquired Don humorously.

'Piss off Skince, I'm trying to win this one,' I countered, lining up on double 19 again.

Then I could smell it as well. Smell it, I could hear it. I rushed through the lounge, almost tripping over Roshan and Namal in the cloud of smoke that issued from the 'kitchen'. My pan of dripping was a smoking, burning mess on the gas ring stove. The Mess boys were almost gagging on the smoke as they sat at the back door, still chattering away.

Grabbing a filthy rag from the kitchen table, I lifted the burning pot from the stove and doused it under the cold tap at the sink. Holding the still-smouldering pot at arm's length, I tipped the contents into a rubbish bin near the door.

In the lounge Roshan had half sat up. At the back door the boys had finally stopped chattering. In the kitchen I looked at the blackened and twisted remains of my only cooking pot and totally lost my cool.

Why the hell any one of them had not seen or smelled the burning of that fat I don't know. How the hell Roshan and Namal could sit in front of their beloved TV and not say anything when the screen was almost blotted out by smoke from the kitchen less than five yards away, I couldn't figure. What I did know was that we weren't going to get any chips that night.

'Bolllllocks!' I howled, and hurled my pot out through the back door into the darkness. The Mess boys dived for cover as I stormed out behind it, muttering black oaths and dire threats beneath my breath.

'Goodnight Captain,' came a quiet voice from the darkness.

The whole day had been a complete cock-up anyway. Gunga Din was back in residence and would doubtless be back in business before the week was out. The Lieutenant down at the loading bay, One-Two Sierra, had promised to get us some lemonade to go with our sundowners and had failed miserably.

The Army had spent the day clearing a fire-free zone to the south of the Mess and had subsequently been frightening the shit out of me by blowing things up without warning. To cap it all, my chips had turned to rat shit and my only cooking pot was a twisted and blackened lump lying somewhere out there in the darkness.

Sat on the side of my bed that evening, silently grieving for my cooking pot and the promised chips, I had little time for small talk. Squince sat quietly busy with his writing pad for a while before he came over and dropped his finished work on my lap.

It was a cartoon of a Mess boy with a blackened and twisted saucepan fitted firmly on his head. The caption beneath it said 'Goodnight Captain'. I smiled wryly for a moment. Then we both laughed like hell and turned in for the night.

After that the Whiteface pilots knew me as Captain Goodnight; particularly when my back wasn't quite turned.

There were only ten days to go before getting out of KKS on R&R. I had hoped to spend it peacefully trotting about the outstations delivering groceries without the attentions of Mr G. Din and his black pyjama gang. My nerves were at full stretch. Just about everything that I had thought to be organised or dealt with was coming rapidly unravelled.

Down at the loading bay I had spent some time explaining the intricacies of helicopter loading and centre of gravity to One-Two Sierra and his loading gang. There was no way that we could actually get seriously overweight with the sacks of supplies. Weighing the sacks was well-nigh impossible. There were no scales available, and if there had been they would have been inaccurate, or the Jinglies would have misread them or got their sums wrong, but a guess at 100lb a sack wasn't that far out. Looked at from that point of view, life should have been easy. With a disposable load of about 2000lbs, that made a maximum of 20 bags a load, 20 bags of coconuts and chillies and cabbages. Loading, well that was the easy bit. Centre of gravity was just a little bit trickier.

The loading bay crew really loved to chuck those bags in and stack them up to the ceiling just behind the pilots. I had convinced them some while ago to start at the back of the cabin and lay the sacks just over the outside edge of the cabin floor. The sacks on top would hold them in place. My, but they didn't like that, more of the Wing Commander's fallout theory I had no doubt, but they did it.

That morning I had been particularly terse with One-Two Sierra. It was no bloody wonder that we didn't get any lemonade out of him. We had loaded up at the bay and gone lumbering off to VVT in the normal way. Over the fourth wave out I'd flared the Trooper hard, decelerating for the landing, pretty much as usual. As we passed over the beach, still going at a fair old lick, it became clear that we were not going to stop in time for the heli-pad.

I tried increasing the flare, but nothing happened. With the collective lever fully down and the cyclic stick hard back in my stomach, we just kept on going. 'Bollllocks,' I thought, 'out of C of G.' There was nothing else for it. Go round. Overshoot. Shit, no, this was Bandit country. 'Bolllockss, bollocks and double bollocks.' I thought again as I pushed the cyclic stick hard forward and pulled in full power. Rocketing over the landing pad at about 20 feet, I rolled the Trooper hard right and kept the power on as we swept around the clearing in a blade-slapping and thumping steep turn. Scraping past the coconut trees surrounding the heli-pad, I headed back out to sea.

We had got no hostile fire on the first approach and didn't expect any on the second. VVT and PPO had been quiet for many days since the mini-wars, and I hoped that it would stay that way for just a little bit longer as I was going in to give it a second try, but this time much slower.

Three minutes later we were on the pad at VVT and I was carefully counting the bags as they were off-loaded. They carried away 17. Seventeen bags, 1700lbs and four passengers with their baggage. Overweight, maybe. Out of C of G, definitely. 'Bollocks and double bollocks.' I'd trusted the Sri Lankan system again. 'Ah, to hell with it,' I thought, 'this is my last run for today.'

Back at the loading bay I shut the aircraft down and left the engineers to get on with a turn-round servicing. I ambled across to the young officer in charge of loading, a new guy, One-Two Sierra's leave relief, and explained the problems of the morning.

The new guy had obviously not been fully briefed on his job when he took over. Either that or he hadn't listened, probably both. I think that his idea of weight and centre of gravity was a fat man stood on one leg

'Lieutenant, on that last run to VVT we had too many sacks on board.'

'They asked for seventeen bags of supplies today,' he replied, rolling and shaking his head at the same time.

'Lieutenant, we were supposed to have twelve hundred pounds and three passengers on board for that last trip.' I was being very patient with him, exasperated, but patient.

The plan had always been to increase the load in the cabin with each successive run. As the fuel load burned off the cabin load was increased, it generally worked, and up until then I had experienced no real problems, particularly if the bags were stacked towards the rear of the cabin, close to the helicopter's centre of gravity.

'They had requested seventeen bags of supplies, Captain, and there were four soldiers ready to go to VVT,' he replied equally patiently. I was losing my temper rapidly, and it was time to back out before I hit him. It would have to wait until the real One-Two Sierra returned from his R&R and hope that no one crashed in the meantime.

Namal and Royce were sauntering across the heli-pad towards us, ready to take over for the remainder of the day's flying. Namal had obviously heard some of the conversation. He swaggered up between the Lieutenant and me. 'Captain ee-Smeeth, it is no problem. Go for lunch, I will take over now,' he declared with a casual wave of his hand.

He was playing the Big Man for his shadow, Royce, and I was being dismissed from the conversation.

I gritted my teeth and took a deep breath. Clenching my fists to my side and trying hard not to snort like a bull through my nose, I thanked him and walked calmly away. I could almost feel the static charge coming off me. God, but I was livid; absolutely seething with pent-up anger.

On the edge of the strip I stopped for a cigarette to calm my nerves before going on to lunch. Sitting cross-legged in the dust with my T56 slung across my shoulders, I watched as Namal clambered into the cockpit and the aircraft was loaded. I smiled to myself as I watched and worked it out in my head. Royce was in the right seat, doing pre-start checks and firing it up. Namal was sitting casually in the left seat, waving more and more sacks on board. Standard fuel load, full crew and the cabin almost bulked out with sacks. They had to be overweight, and with that many sacks loaded forward in the cabin it was probably out of C of G limits. 'This could be interesting.' I mused, smirking to myself.

The loading was finished and the beat from the blades increased as Royce pulled the Trooper towards the hover. The blades coned upwards as the skids became light on the ground. Miniature tornadoes from the downwash played in the dust around the heli-pad. The heels of the skids came off the ground first. In my mind's eye I could see the cyclic stick being fed further and further backwards.

The thump of the blades deepened as the front of the skids came off the ground. Immediately the Trooper started to slide forwards, the cyclic stick was fully aft trying to hold against the forward movement. Before Namal and Royce were six inches off the ground, the nose of the aircraft was down and the front of the skids were bouncing off the tarmac. They were well out of limits. The only real answer was to bang it back on the ground and reload the cabin, but not Namal. I almost laughed with near-manic glee as he frantically took control from Royce.

Pulling all the collective pitch that he had left they bounced off down the strip, struggling to get airborne. After 50 metres they had managed to stop bouncing the skids on the ground. Lumbering unsteadily into the air, the Trooper accelerated rapidly down the strip.

It took them another 200 metres to get enough height to clear the coconut trees at the end of the runway. The landing, wherever it was, would be interesting. I only hoped that it was far enough away for them to burn off enough fuel to get the C of G back into limits. Giggling like an idiot to myself, I stubbed my cigarette out and sauntered off to lunch. I was one happy teddy.

One boring day followed by another boring day, followed by yet another. Strange how the crew at the loading bay had suddenly got it right. Namal probably had a word with One-Two Sierra when he got back from his out of limits trip.

No matter how much I had dug my heels in about all or any of the operational problems around the Jaffna Peninsula, the only time something positive got done was when it was too bloody late.

Odd that the Air Force should clear a fire-free zone behind the Mess the day after they had been subjected to a mortar attack. The

Army spent three days blowing up houses and bulldozing away the trees and scrub to clear it.

Kapila crashed a 212 Trooper in the dark. He was trying to make an approach into Elephant Pass using an open fire as his reference point. Oh, he managed to get in to the site, then he got disorientated and stuck it on its tail and rolled it while trying to hover away.

He never was much good at night flying; he used some rough old techniques, but then you can't teach them that don't want to learn. Maybe in future they would practice using some of the simple but effective night landing aids that Greg had told them about. On the other hand they probably wouldn't, for at the root of it all the Sri Lankans were bone bloody idle and would never plan ahead if they could do it off the cuff. Whatever the problem, they always responded with too little too late.

One week to R&R, and it's still the same old system. Early get-up and fly 'til breakfast, pause. Fly 'til lunch, change crew, and fly. Still the same old lack of planned movements. The Army wanted this and that done because it didn't need planning if the Air Force could do it. Just chuck it at Air Force and let the Whitefaces sort it out.

The Air Force had no policy to accommodate the Army's ad-hoc requests, and it boiled down to doing it as best you could, planning as you went. The only decisions taken on the ground were purely personal. Would it affect their social standing, promotion or personal gratification?

Squadron Leader Sujith had gone to Colombo, to a court-martial. The Wing Commander went the following today. Apparently a Junior Cadet had a go at a Senior Cadet with his T56, twice, and emptied the magazine. He had missed his intended target but plugged a bystander in the arse with a ricochet.

The same Wing Commander that would help to decide the fate of the Junior Cadet had briefed the Sri Lankan pilots in his 'Command' that we must not use angles of bank of more than 10 degrees now in case the passengers fell out. There were to be no quick-stop approaches into the Landing Sites. There was to be no firing unless we came under fire first, and no warming bursts. To cap it all, we were expected to do the evening engine washing runs in our flying suits.

There were only seven days to do, and I was counting. We flew four and a half hours that day, during which we stopped two cyclists out on the sand at Elephant Pass, nothing. Two fast boats offshore to the north of Elephant Pass had looked highly suspicious, but we had to leave them alone due to a lack of fuel. A real bummer of a day.

The bloody idiots next door were still buggering around with the toilet doors. It was a shared toilet with two doors for access. When you entered the toilet from your own room, you locked the door to the other room. When you finished, you simply unlocked the door to the other room before you left.

The pair in the next bunk continually left the door to our room locked, which wasn't a problem until you had a dose of the trots and suddenly had to make a run round the block to get in to the john from your neighbour's room. On top of that the new washing bucket had been full for the last four days with the same rotting clothes, and the place stank more than usual.

I'd had beans on toast for breakfast that morning, such a breakfast as should be repeated at lunchtime. Except that the Mess labourer, who wouldn't normally clean the appalling filth from the kitchen table, floor, walls and utensils, had decided in one dark moment of near-insanity to clear away the beans. My bloody beans.

The selfsame labourer who had saved tidbits of curried God-knows-what to reheat umpty-ump times had suffered a complete mental aberration and, overcome with an almost puritanical urge for cleanliness, had chucked away my fucking beans. Why me, dear Lord, why me?

There were just five days left for me in that shithole, and I seriously wondered if I would make it without breaking down in tears. It was easy to see that Wing Commander Perez and the Squadron Leader Sujith were not on station. They certainly had their uses, no matter how limited.

Weejita, a Flight Lieutenant had been sent up to replace Squadron Leader Sujith while he was away at the court-martial. Weejita quite obviously didn't like Jaffna, and planned to do as little flying as possible. He also planned to enjoy himself as much as he could, and he celebrated his birthday in fine style.

We finished partying at one in the morning. I had spent the

evening on local gin, and Don had drunk Very Special Old Arak. It wasn't so funny at five the next morning, when I had to get up to do top-cover on the incoming Avro. It wasn't at all funny several hours later, when I finished the morning's grocery flights with a visit to VVT and PPO. Our landings at Point Pedro that morning had been no problem, and I had hoped to finish the morning's flying without any hassle and get my head down for an hour or so.

VVT put an end to that. The starboard doorgunner spotted some movement on the ground to the west as we approached VVT from the sea. I was in no mood for any buggering around and aborted the approach even as we came under fire. Ariyaratna was quick off the mark and was already laying down a stream of 7.62mm as we climbed away.

The Tigers continued to fire at us as I rolled the Trooper right and turned overhead. They were as determined as ever, and it was hard to believe that we had not had any trouble from VVT for the last 18 days. The starboard gunner stopped firing and reloaded as the first belt came to an end. Rolling left, the port doorgunner continued the engagement until the Tigers' guns were silenced.

We broke off and turned back towards the landing site. In all that time the Army had done absolutely bugger-all except watch the action from the safety of their Sangars. On final approach for the second time, the Tigers opened up again. My thoughts right then were sanguine to say the least, and I had no real consideration for the Army at VVT other than 'to hell with you and your fresh rations'.

Rolling right again, I called upon Ariyaratna to give them a good working over. As soon as the next belt was empty I told Royce to get on the radio to VVT and tell them that they were getting no rations from me that day, and we buggered off back to KKS. With only three and a half days left in Jaffna, I didn't intend to get involved in any more mini-wars delivering a few bags of rations to an outstation that didn't give a toss if you got shot down doing it. Anyway, the noise was doing my hangover no good at all.

In four days I would be back in the UK. And then a whole month of doing what I pleased, when I pleased. There would be 30 days of walking down the street every day. Just four days to do.

The Company was sending a team up to visit PPO and VVT. 'Ha,' I thought, 'that should open their eyes a bit.' The boys on the ground were coming out of their sheltered little house in downtown Colombo to visit the 'cowards' in Jaffna. I was ecstatic; I could go on R&R knowing that Ken Bloody Who had found out the true depth of the shit that he had consigned us to without a second thought. Lack of moral fibre was what he had called it. Lack of company back-up was more like it.

Once he'd been into a few outstations under fire, I felt that my attitude towards the situation here would be vindicated. As it was they didn't turn up, perhaps they didn't have the time or maybe they didn't like the idea. Bastards.

There was a Trooper scheduled to go back to Katunayaka for servicing at 1500 hours that afternoon, and I had packed my bags and got everything ready to go back to Colombo with it, and them, after our local Team Leader's non-existent 'visit'.

Still, I was going home, and that was the main thing. Whether or not I had done a good job in Jaffna was for me to know and for the company to guess at. In five months I had been personally involved in the death of 152 Tigers. Well, to be totally accurate, at 152 I had given up counting. Perhaps the company in their comfortable offices in Colombo and Kensington would never know what it was like in Jaffna. I had come to Sri Lanka to teach in Katunayaka, and would leave Jaffna having at least shown them how it was done.

10

An Interlude in UK

Low flyers, and rum and black.

I had a mountain of gear to shift. The accumulation of five months of Whiteface goodies. Paperback books to be delivered to Vavuniya for Don Burton. Cooking pots and brew kit. T56 and ammunition, flak jacket and flying gear. It was just as well that Ken Bloody Who and the team had not turned up for their visit.

The trip to Vavuniya was absolutely brilliant. No Tigers to look out for. If we had seen some, I wouldn't have bothered my arse, I was on my way home. We went down via Kilinochchi to drop off a couple of base-wallah passengers.

At Vavuniya we met yet another of the unheralded 'contract pilots'. Tony Willings, aged and venerable, with a magnificent handle-bar moustache, web belt, and a Crocodile Dundee knife. Topped off with a red sweatband tied around his balding pate, he looked the very picture of a modern major head-case. He later became known as Captain Fantastic. Every other sentence started with 'When I was in Nigeria'. Tony was a life member of the Firm Handshake Club.

As we left Vavuniya a massive thunderstorm was brewing to the south and west of us. Right on cue Tony said, 'When I was in Nigeria they covered the sky,' and Don Burton said, 'When you get south of here it will be all right.' We spent an hour with Colombo Radar and our onboard Weather Radar dodging those storms. So much for DB's local knowledge and 'great experience of Sri Lankan weather'.

Katunayaka was the same as ever. People came and went with no apparent aim and under no obvious control. Except for the engineers, nobody seemed interested in our arrival, so I signed the aircraft down in the Technical Log and left it there.

I dumped my ammo and T56 in the armoury and my flak jacket

in the Squadron Stores. Ten minutes were wasted on a flying visit to the instructors 'shack', but there was no one at home. I chucked my local gear, the stuff that I would need on my return, into a steel locker. After a quick shower I changed into some fresh clothes and left hotfoot for Negombo. The next stop was the Blue Oceanic for a beer and the start of one really fine piss-up.

Two days to go. The worst bit was having to give up a couple of hours somewhere along the line to check in with Wing Commander Oliver Ranasinghe and find out where I was going when I got back from R&R.

There was also a trip down-town to be made to see Ken Who at the office and give him a piece of my mind and let him know that I was coming back. It would just have to be the following day, I had a hangover to find.

The following morning I left Squince at the Airport Garden Hotel. How the hell we got there I don't know. I had one hell of a head on me, and Don had a replacement Trooper to fly back up to Jaffna. I said my goodbyes and scooted off to Colombo in a taxi. I planned to stay in town that night, so I dropped by at the Taj to book a room for the night and have a liquid breakfast before I went on to the company office in Kollupitiya.

It was during that late liquid breakfast at the bar that I bumped into Andy Vine and John Winterbourne and discovered to my utter disgust that Ken Bloody Who had spoken to everyone about the 'deplorable lack of moral fibre in their staff in Jaffna'. I felt that it was a bloody shame that he couldn't have spoken to the people concerned before he called them down in front of the rest of the world. It was a crying shame that he couldn't have made his visit to KKS and come under fire a few times.

Dave Warton had finished his time and gone home, but the shit would follow his name everywhere when people met and talked of Sri Lanka. For myself, I felt that I had acquitted myself more than adequately in Jaffna. It was well past time to go and get things straightened out with the company's local Team Leader.

Fired up with indignation and a head full of alcohol was perhaps not the right way to go about it, but that was how I was and the time was right. The great pity was that Ken was not in to hear it all. The secretary explained that he would be away for a couple of days at the Training Camp, so I just left a note that I would be back at the end of my R&R to finish my year and buggered off back to Katunayaka. Someone would have to hear what I had to say, and it looked like it would be Wing Commander Oliver Ranasinghe.

The news back up at the Squadron wasn't good. An operation in the Mannar District had gone seriously wrong. The Army had screwed up, and DB had got caught in some serious action. As I heard it, he was trying to get in to recover a foot patrol that had been ambushed and had a large chunk taken out of his seat's side armour; his starboard side gunner was dead in his seat.

He had pressed in too close during one hell of a firefight. The Tigers had then carried out a bayonet charge on the patrol and slain 15 Sri Lankan soldiers. Another section of 12 men and their officer in charge were missing. One really bad day.

On one hand we had gung ho aviators that pressed in too close with a weapons system that operated quite adequately from 1000 metres out, and on the other we had Commanders who insisted that we shouldn't operate the same equipment to its fullest capacity. The whole damned shooting match was without direction and order.

Unfortunately for him, Wing Commander Oliver was in to hear my views on the matter. Fortunately, for the future, he listened to what I had to say. I poured the lot out. Ten minutes later Oliver Ranasinghe proved that there was more to him than at first met the eye. The Wing Commander paused for a few moment to collect his thoughts.

'Captain Smith, I have had nothing but admiration for your work in KKS. I have left you to get on with it in your own way. I have never told you how to fly the aircraft and I never intend to, but I will have to handle the matter of Wing Commander Perez and his briefings with some diplomacy. You see, in the past he has only flown tourists on pleasure flights, he has never flown operationally.' he explained carefully,' but you may rest assured that I will speak to him at the earliest opportunity.'

Listening intently, I nodded my understanding. It didn't exonerate Perez for the poor decisions he'd made as a Commander, but it did explain a lot.

'As for your feelings about the lack of ground support at Point Pedro and VVT, well, I agree with you entirely. If I had been in same situation myself I would have done exactly the same,' he went on.

'Yes Sir, that may well be so, but there is still the matter of me refusing to fly the Gunship, and the company's attitude towards me and the others at KKS because of that.'

'Captain Smith, I personally feel that you were right in refusing, you didn't come here to fly Gunships. If I had taken up the matter on your behalf no one would have listened to me, but because you spoke out for yourself on that point as well as the matter of site security, something was done. Of course it will not take long for them to forget about all that was decided or achieved, and we will sadly be back at the start again. Having read the reports on your flying and your actions under fire, I cannot imagine where anyone could get the idea that you or your fellow pilots lack moral fibre. I am extremely happy with your performance,' he smiled as he finished and started to rise from his seat behind his desk, but I wasn't finished, though.

'Thank you Sir, it is a comfort to know that at least you are aware of, and appreciate, what has been going on at KKS. There is one last thing I'd like to clarify before I go on R&R, Sir. I would like to know where I shall be stationed when I get back.'

'Now that I cannot say, Captain Smith, but what I will say is that it will not be KKS. I would hope to send you somewhere where your experience and ability may be used to the full. Now, off you go and have a good rest and recuperation,' he stepped around his desk, smiling, and warmly shook my hand, 'I don't suppose you could bring me back a dozen of those wine glasses that you get from the petrol stations in the UK when you come back.'

'No problem Sir, no problem. Thanks for listening. See you in a month.'

Ah, well, I had said what I came to say and had got a half-decent answer, there was no more to be said or done. I had a plane to catch and a hangover to nurture. There was just enough time to collect my gear from the Taj and to get a few beers down my neck before then.

Six hours later I was sat in the departure lounge, waiting for the flight to the UK to be called forward. The boys had already warned me that the bar didn't serve any alcohol at all, and I was suitably armed with a bottle of whisky. Unfortunately there was a shortage of glasses and I had to make do with a plastic film container. I sat in a corner, furtively sipping neat whisky and chuckling to myself. I was people watching.

An absolute cracker of a dolly girl, in hotpants and a loose-sleeved T-shirt, was strutting about the place, jiggling her tits and flashing an occasional brief glimpse of her nipples through the armholes of her T-shirt. The Jinglies were walking around backwards with their eyes on stalks to watch her, and I was waiting for the moment when one of them tripped arse over head.

'Would passengers for flight number HMU 7 to London Heathrow via Dubai please now board the aircraft through gate number two.'

Stepping down from the train in Carlisle some 16 hours later, I was completely knackered. A great flood of relief washed over me. It was great to be home, home to the bosom of my family, even if it was only a 32B cup.

My wife was there at the station to meet me. Her blue eyes were flashing all sorts of signals that were all too easy to read. I put my arms around her and kissed her warmly, passionately, and knew immediately that I'd missed female company for too long.

She was on her own, having left my son Chris at home looking after the latest addition to the family. 'Well done, lad,' I thought, thinking that all at home was beauty and light. The car journey home went without thought other than it was just great to be away from all of the hassle, and that night would be spent in a far different bed than those that I'd slept in over that past five months.

The bosom of my family turned out to be more like a viper's nest. An hour after arriving in Carlisle, I was sitting in my own front room once again in front of a roaring fire. The only difference was there was no sound of running water, the roof had been fixed, and I could feel the tension. I'd lived with five months of tension and quite frankly could have done without it at home.

There was obviously something wrong. Chris had given me a warm welcome and disappeared upstairs to his room. Some homework on his computer, I presumed innocently, glowing with inner pride, and thought no more of it.

No sooner was he out of sight than my wife started. Christopher had done this and that, he hadn't listened to her, he was going round with some older lads, he spent all his time with role-playing games, he had spent all his savings during the school holidays rather than go to work for a bit of extra cash. It was a litany of despair, a catalogue of disasters, and right then I didn't want any part of it.

What a shame that I couldn't do the Sri Lankan thing and just let it lie in the hope that someone else would fix it. To give myself some time to think I mumbled some excuse. Yes, yes, I would speak to him about it at the next best opportunity, and hid myself quietly in the Grouse bottle for a while.

The days fled by. Days of walking about the streets of the town without beggars or pimps to bother me. The bright and cool November mornings were spent out on the fells, helping out with Robert and Anna's sheep and cattle. During the afternoon's we stole away and left the farm to Anna whilst we skived off shooting pigeons.

Saturdays were spent out on the shoot with my old friends Robert and Algie, Davy, Thomas Gilbert and the rest of the lads. It was great to get away from the hassle of family life for a while. With my favourite 12-bore under my arm and some dogs around my feet, I hadn't a care in the world.

That first Saturday I spent the morning as a walking gun, a flanker, beating the edges of the woods and only taking a bird if it flew back away from the line of standing guns. Looking back on it, I should have known that things wouldn't happen as they should have. Somehow I had a mental itch that I couldn't scratch. There was something on the edge of my mental view that I couldn't quite see.

I was very much switched on, and no matter how many times I shouted 'Forward' or 'Over' my opposite number could only drive the birds back towards me, where I despatched them with remarkable speed and accuracy. Yes, I was very switched on to killing.

Lunch was taken sat on bales in the barn at Greenside. It was a good-natured affair, full of jovial banter and more than a little leg-pulling for the poor performance of the standing guns during the morning's shooting.

'Ay, Jonesy, what was wrong wi' ye, man? Auld Smithy nearly ran out of ca'tridges back in the Quarry Wood,' declared Robert to all in earshot. 'Aye, it's the fost time I've known a beater to shoot more than the standing guns.' The barn nearly fell together in a gale of laughter.

The second part of the day was to be spent on a tremendous hike over the moors and bogs out to Haining House, a disused farmhouse about six miles away. As ever, the less active members of the group declined the offer to join us, so the six of us set off for a good afternoon's walk and the prospect of some really wild birds.

There was everything on that moor. Grouse and blackgame on the tops, partridge and pheasant in the gullies along the sides. Snipe and woodcock in the rushes and rides, mallard and teal in the watery bottoms. And hares like donkeys, for the unwise to carry home.

I should have enjoyed myself no end. But I didn't, for the mere act of carrying a loaded gun brought its own problems. I had lived for five months with a loaded gun at hand both day and night, and had seen no reason to unload it when I climbed in and out of an aircraft.

Out on the shoot the same apparently nonchalant attitude raised a few eyebrows as I leapt ditches and climbed fences without unloading. I was very fortunate to be with friends, friends that were man enough to remind me of my apparent disregard for safety without being embarrassed at saying it. But it did put an edge on the pleasure.

Slowly my lifestyle of the last five months was making inroads into my family and social life.

Christopher was the next to find out about it in no uncertain manner.

'Dad, can you come up for a minute?' he called one evening from the top of the stairs.

Two minutes later life had suddenly taken a three-month step backwards.

'What can I do for you'? I'd asked as I entered his room.

He'd been preparing some role-play game or other, and for reasons best known to himself he wanted to know the effective range of an RPG7 and the destructive power of it on impact. I was taken completely unawares by his line of questioning and responded without thinking.

'Destructive power,' I screeched, suddenly incensed with a nameless rage, 'you want to know about destructive power. If you want to know about destructive power, then bloody well watch this.' Without thinking, I reached out and picked up a large loudspeaker that stood in the upstairs hallway outside his room and tossed it the full length of the hall, where it rattled off my old

Singer treadle sewing machine, taking lumps of woodwork with it. Ah, shit. I liked that old machine.

'That is all the destructive power that you need to know about, now bloody leave it out, and give up this role-playing shit right now.'

I stormed off downstairs, where Eileen was very, very quietly getting the evening meal ready. Calm to cyclonic in 20 seconds, aye, it was still rock and bloody roll.

That was the first time that they had seen me lose my cool since I had been back, and they've seen it many times more since then. I was angrier with myself for responding that way than at the stupid bloody question, but it was too late, I was already mentally back in Sri Lanka.

The level in the whisky bottle was already well down, and the rest of the evening was spent in morbid reflection. That was the first of many times that the episode with the lady in the blue-green sari came back to me, the first time that I relived a mental action replay of the nasties that I had been involved in on the Jaffna Peninsula. Once I'd started, it just seemed to go on and on. RPG7s and 40mm grenades, burning boats and broken bodies, chattering guns and the beat of the blades.

Home leave in the UK, R & R. A month of Rest and Recuperation. Not bloody likely, it was more like Rage and Recrimination. I shook myself hard after that, mentally, and really struggled with myself to let sleeping dogs lie. I almost succeeded, but I hadn't counted on my brother-in-law's mind being even tackier than my son's.

For some reason my wife's family had decided to hold an enormous thrash at the Rugby Club in town. I can't remember now just what it was for, a wedding anniversary perhaps, or maybe a birthday party of some sort.

Most of their enormous family turned up, and it wasn't unlike a re-run of our own wedding reception. My father-in-law's family was quite large, ten brothers I seem to remember. They were all built on generous lines and looked so alike that you couldn't have recognised one from the other from back of a galloping horse. They'd all been cut from the same large piece of cloth.

What the hell, I knew them for a jolly bunch, and I felt that an evening spent with them would be a grand way to get away from it all and enjoy ourselves. Eileen assured me that the whole bloody family, and her brother in particular, had been well warned to keep off the now tricky subject of Sri Lanka. Yes, it would be a great evening amongst all those roly-poly friendly people.

Shortly after our arrival I installed myself at the bar and quietly enjoyed myself watching them all enjoy themselves. Eileen mingled socially and disappeared into the crowd. Happy that I wouldn't be imposed upon to recount any of the gory details of the last six months, I took a chance on rum and black for my evening's tipple. Tricky decision that. I love rum and black, but it tends to make a animal out of me, and like all rum drinkers I should be left quietly in a corner to drink on my own.

'Hullo Tim, how are you doin', do you want another?' Gordon, my brother-in-law, had arrived a little late and was standing at my shoulder.

'Hiyah, me old lad, I'm fine.' He fumbled for his wallet.

'No, no, I'll buy these, I'm on shorts,' I burbled happily, smiling and shaking his hand. We squabbled for moment or two about who was buying what, and finally settled for me getting the first round in. We spent the next few minutes in pleasantries. Kiss the wife's cheek and ruffle the son's hair, where was my lovely wife and how did I find the latest addition to the family? You know the stuff, it generally comes a couple of hours before setting the world to rights. His wife moved on to look for mine, and his son went to find somebody that wouldn't ruffle his hair. We got on with the serious business of having a good drink and a chinwag, knowing full well that we both had our wives to drive us home at the end of the evening.

He bought more than his share there at the bar that evening. Knowing him for a generally tight git, I wondered at his sudden generosity. It didn't take him long to get round to what was on his mind. What he really wanted to know was how did I like killing all those people for a living? How did it feel to have so much power?

In an instant I could feel the memories crowding in on me, the thump of the blades and the rattle of machine guns, bodies writhing as they died in the dust and the sand. I was angry with myself for allowing the past to intrude on the present, but I was determined not to submit to it. I was determined to use it. I was angry with him for bringing the subject up, so I poked it straight back in his face. He got the whole bloody lot, firsthand and more than a little embellished to suit his tacky little mind.

Ah, well. It didn't make me feel any better, but it did make him take a mental step or two backwards. I should care, I'd been taking mental steps backwards for the last five months. However, I was in no mood to let him off lightly, and with a devilish delight that was a fine cheesewire's width away from ghoulish glee, I told him 'all about it'. The more his eyes widened the more I poured it on. I revelled in it, like a pig in shit.

When he'd had enough he left me alone at the bar, which was just as well, for I'd got to the stage where I wanted to wash the overpowering feelings of self-disgust and recrimination out of my head, particularly with rum and black. Eileen had noticed us together at the bar from across the room and was making tracks towards us even as he left me. She collared him before he'd got out of earshot and the last I heard was Eileen giving him a good rollocking for his stupidity.

The rest of the evening was spent in morbid introspection and a vast amount of rum and black until my wife dragged me away from the bar and took me home.

Home, such a strange place. Full of tension and people mentally tiptoeing around. The only place that I felt really at ease was up on the farm with Robert and Anna, among their sheep and cattle or up on some lonely, windswept hill, rebuilding one of their dry-stone dykes. At least up there I didn't have to paw over the past or think about the present or future. It was one day at a time up there, and right then one day at a time was all that I could handle.

Home, where my role-playing son scowled around thinking God knew what about his bad-tempered, explosive and destructive father. Home where my wife tiptoed about like I was some sort of mental bloody invalid. Aye, it was great up there on the hill, where the only things I had to keep me company were the sheep and the curlew. The only thing I had to think about was the next length of wall to be put back up.

In the meantime the company had sent my air ticket for the trip back to Colombo. I can't say that I felt anything but relief at the thought of going back. At least it put a positive end to the length of time that I would spend being treated like some sort of unwanted relative that had overstayed their welcome.

On the other hand, it gave me a little over a fortnight to make my R&R worth coming home for. On 14 November I would be on my way back to Sri Lanka.

Over the next couple of weeks we worked hard at being normal. Somehow it just didn't seem to gel. At home Christopher still managed to scowl his way around the house. Even though he kept a low profile by escaping to his room whenever he could, there was no doubt that Chris was unable to handle my mood swings.

Obviously there wasn't a lot of love lost between him and my wife. His insolence towards her one afternoon got him a dig in the ribs from me that took his breath away, and distanced us still further. From her point of view I was to be treated as though I was convalescing from some sort of illness. As far as I was concerned, that only made the situation more difficult, it made the gulf between us just that little bit deeper and wider.

Shit, I'd gone through all the crap that Jaffna could produce in order to put a watertight roof over our heads. Aye, it was dry enough beneath it, but somehow I seemed to be drowning in an atmosphere of antagonism and mild tension.

We spent what time we could out of doors. When I wasn't up on the hill mending walls we went for walks or went out on shopping trips into Carlisle. Anything and anywhere to minimise the amount of time cooped up together.

There was, however, no avoiding the evenings and the sense of enforced tranquillity that they brought, and most of them were spent partway down a bottle. I'd spent happier evenings on the patio in KKS listening to the passage of hardware as it whispered overhead.

Okay, so I couldn't have been that good to put up with. I was withdrawn maybe, but in no way was I that morose or moody that folks couldn't talk to me. Not until someone pressed on the wrong button. Somehow, at home, that translated into 'keep out of the old bugger's way'. My family left me pretty much to my own devices, and it was down to me to open out and make the running in the sociability stakes.

Try as I might, nothing seemed to go as planned. One evening during the latter half of my leave, I made a positive effort to explain why I was somewhat remote. The thoughts came out in a jumble. I tried to explain my sudden bouts of anger in terms of Jaffna and the frustrations that it had produced. The bouts of morbid introspection were put down to the ease with which I'd snuffed out so many lives. When it came down to it, I'd really had enough of the family bickering and I was filled with an unrecognised self-disgust. I wanted a home life full of the tranquillity that I had denied to so many Tamils. I was suffering from PTSD, Post Trauma Stress Disorder, and didn't even know that it existed.

That evening I withdrew into the whisky bottle and hid myself in a book of German poetry. Reading German poetry took me away from everything, my mind was fully occupied in a foreign language, my spirit driven by the power of the words. Not for the first time, I read the poem of King Etzel's Sword.

The young knight knelt at his lord's feet. His shattered sword hung from his hand in the dust. In recognition of his valour on the battlefield, he was offered the freedom of the King's armoury to replace his broken sword. Prowling through the vast array of armour and weapons, he came across a truly unremarkable sword that somehow had a feel about it. The grizzled and ancient armourer in attendance advised him to look elsewhere for something better.

Perhaps I too should have looked elsewhere, for something better. I felt that I knew the story too well.

The honourable young knight wanted nothing more than a replacement for his own broken sword and, against the old armourer's advice, took the unremarkable sword and returned to the battlefield. All day his arm swung. Left and right the enemy fell to his sword, the ground about him covered with the bodies of his foes.

Evening came upon them, and still the sword swung as if it had a life of its own. The more blood the sword drank, the thirstier it became. At last there were none left to contest the strength and skill of his sword arm, but still the sword twitched and quivered in his hand. Staggering with weariness the valiant knight fell, the sword flying from his hand, impaling him even as he struck the ground.

Aye, there were more similarities to the story than I cared to think of. There are more ways of dying by the sword than just falling on it. I drank some more and forgot for a brief while.

After several weeks of enforced family unity, I'd had enough. It was time for me to get the hell out of it and back amongst people that didn't have to make an effort to keep off the wrong subjects. Four weeks before I had been overjoyed at the prospect of leaving Sri Lanka, but right then I was only too glad to be going back.

Packing my bags was a lot easier that second time. On the one hand I had no qualms about going, on the other I didn't have to think about what to take, the minimum. When the time came to put my bags in the taxi for the trip to the station, I was more than ready to go. This time that uncertain sense of freedom to be felt in railway stations became a feeling of long-awaited relief.

Tuesday 15 November 1986. Dressed rather more appropriately this time, I stepped down from the plane in Colombo with a good stock of cigarettes and whisky in my bags. I had half-expected to find Ken Who lurking in the background, but was disappointed. The last hour of the flight had been spent in psyching myself up for showdown with our local Team Hero over his loose tongue.

Out in the Arrivals Hall a few minutes later, I was greeted by Ken's driver, who quickly took me round the airfield to the military side and dropped me off at the bungalow to a welcome surprise. Don and Tony Willings were in temporary residence.

Nothing had changed, I don't think that I had expected it to. The place was still a tip, the lockers were still full or busted, and there weren't enough serviceable beds to go around. Still dodging the cockroaches, I took a tepid shower and changed my clothes for something that didn't smell of 18 hours of travel. Strange how good it felt to be back. Sitting beside the phone some time later and giving the downtown office an earholing for not sending my expenses up with the driver felt almost like being normal.

Wandering into the hangars just after lunch to see Oliver Ranasinghe seemed quite a normal thing to do. I wanted to know what was going on, I wanted to get back to work. I should have known better. As ever, there was nobody around that had the slightest idea what the hell was going on.

With nothing better to do, I dropped by at the armoury and drew up my trusty T56 and the standard load of 120 rounds just to fill in the time. I loaded the magazines right there and then, cadging some tape to bind them back to back. It all seemed so natural, so normal. Doesn't everybody do that before they start work?

Eventually I decided that if anyone knew what the hell was on the cards it might be the Engineering Section, so I continued my wanderings back to the other side of the hangar to see what they knew. As ever, they were more than a little sparing with their information but were willing to admit when pressed that something might be happening 'tomorrow morning'. Aye, I was back at work.

11

Operation Phantom Strike

After five months of being shafted in Jaffna my mind was finely attuned to the inverse workings of the Sri Lankan if, but and maybe. Thinking that it would be wise to prepare myself for the worst, I spent the afternoon scouring the local shops for the goodies that I would need in whatever shithole that I would be consigned too soon.

Cigarettes, tins of frankfurters and fruit, cornflakes, anything that would relieve the painful monotony of curried God knew what. Mosquito coils and soap powder, everything possible to raise the standard of life from the gutter to the pavement. I returned to the bungalow later that afternoon, clutching the bundle of the creature comforts that I'd gleaned from the rickety tin-shack shops of Negombo.

An anonymous brown envelope addressed to me had appeared under the door of the shack. My expenses had finally arrived.

It looked like I was staying. The next task in hand was to find somewhere to dump my personal gear. A firm shoulder applied to a previously locked door along the porch suddenly gained the instructors' bungalow an extra bedroom.

In no time at all my gear was stowed in the new annex. I was home, with money in my pocket, and it was time to celebrate. Calling up the local taxi yet again we legged it, lickety spit, to the Blue Oceanic in Negombo and toasted the indeterminate future in VSOA, lots of it.

We hoorawed and boozed all evening with a grim determination that kept the worried waiters a little fearful but extremely attentive from a respectable distance, more often than not with the bar between them and us.

Sometime later that night we climbed out of a rickety Morris Minor taxi at the security gate, and with some small difficulty staggered happily through the coconut groves to the bungalow.

The gentle evening breeze had settled to a soft, scented zephyr, like a woman's hand stroking your skin. Somehow I felt that it was good to be home again. It must have been about then that I finally accepted what I was doing there as more than a means to an end. Reluctance had fallen to its knees by the rocky wayside of life.

'bout a night-cap?' muttered Squince as we climbed the steps to the veranda.

'bout we don't answer tha' bloody phone?' I slurred as we stumbled our way into the darkened sitting room. Donald fumbled with the light switch as I knocked over the phone.

'Instructors Residence, Cap'n Smith speaking,' I intoned plummily.

'Captain EE... Smeeth, this is the Squadron's Duty Clerk. We need you and Captain Skuance to go to Vavuniya with a Trooper tomorrow morning at six o'clock, please, thank you.' Captain Skuance yet, would they ever get it right?

'Yeah, okay, no problem. We'll be at the Squadron at five-thirty, see ya. Goo'night.' Drunkenly I clattered the phone back onto its cradle and took the whisky and beer chaser that Squince had drummed up from somewhere. In all probability it was Greg's beer and Tony's whisky, but who gives a shit when you are supposed to be tough and mean and going back to work on a mini-war. Surprisingly we were ready to go on time, but due to one thing or another we actually didn't get airborne until nearer seven o'clock. Just as well really, for it gave us an extra hour to scratch around for a cup of coffee and a bite to eat. The engineers' sandwich shack took it as an honour to provide us with breakfast for a few rupees.

Suitably fed and watered, we set off. It then took us three attempts to get past seven miles out. We came under fire twice from the same place. On the first occasion we had levelled off over the jungle at 1500 feet and had just cleared with Colombo Radar. We had been idly chattering away about the smart new waitress in the Blue Oceanic and the God-awful state of the whores in Negombo when a sharp crack from behind silenced us.

'Bloody hell Squince, what was that?' I asked, ever quick to couch things in the most complicated terms.

'Dunno Smithy, sounded like something snapping down the back end,' replied Squince, equally at home with technical terminology.

Developing a sudden interest in not crashing in flames in the jungle, and with every fibre of our abused bodies, overhung brains attuned to unusual vibrations, we made a quick scan of the engine instruments. Nope, they all seemed to be pointing the right way, they showed that nothing was apparently wrong. Rolling the aircraft left and right, we tried to see if there was any smoke trailing behind us. There was nothing but a large question mark hanging in the cockpit above our Arak-soaked heads.

Prudence is a fine airhostess. She travels with all the old aviators. We turned back and had the airframe checked out for mechanical damage. After an hour of diligent searching the aircraft technicians gave it up for a bad job and declared us fit to fly. Well, the aircraft was fit to fly, so we tried it all over again.

On the second try it sank into our slightly befuddled senses that it was actually gunfire that we had heard. Gunfire sounds so different with the cabin doors fitted. At that time in the morning after a heavy night, nobody needs shit like that, particularly when you haven't got any side guns fitted. Orbiting the area a few times, we strained our bleary, bloodshot eyes in an effort to identify the point from which we'd been fired upon.

No muzzle flashes in the shadows, no gunsmoke in the morning sunlight, no black pyjamas legging it through the trees. Nothing. It was bloody hopeless. Turning back to the airfield once again, we called the Squadron office on the tactical frequency and explained the situation.

The Wing Commander joined us on our third departure in an armed Trooper. As we passed the same spot for the third time, we again came under fire. We left him there with the almost impossible task of finding the concealed marksman in the middle of a bloody jungle. Continuing northbound we took our hangovers for a caffeine stop at Vavuniya.

Vavuniya was in a state of near-chaos, it almost vibrated with activity. We had hoped for another coffee break to ease our aching heads, but no sooner had we arrived than we were set to work. Instead of being allowed to ease our thick heads we were tasked with ferrying hundreds of troops to the outstations to the north and east. They were preparing for an operation that was due to take place in three days time. Operation Phantom Strike.

The operation was doomed from the start. Phantom, hardly. Such a massive, lumbering wind-up could only warn the Tigers that something big was in the wind.

With only two Troopships to carry out the task, it took ages to

Marchettis at Vavuniya

get the ferrying done. The only thing that could be said for it was that I got a good idea of the layout and operations of the outstations in Northern Province. The camp at Vavuniya, a couple of kilometres to the south east of the town itself, was, at the time, the last outstation going north to have its own permanent airstrip. Resupply to it was generally by road convoy from Colombo. Standing squarely across the main road from Colombo and Anuradhapura in the south to the Jaffna Peninsula, the camp at Vavuniya also controlled the most northerly road across the country from Trincomalee on the east coast to Mannar Island in the west.

The task of controlling the huge surrounding area was for the Sri Lankan conscript Army almost insurmountable. The main road northbound through the jungle to Kilinochchi was a nightmare to patrol, as was the railway line that ran alongside it. The 60 kilometres of road to Kilinochchi were just a series of culvert-mine and bomb craters that took two full days at walking pace to traverse in a convoy. The railway had been out of commission for several months and would remain so for the better part of a year.

Leaving Vavuniya at first light, a convoy would hope to make it to the Armoured Squadron's base at Mankulam before dark on day one. Patrols from the outstations en route would clear their section of the road in turn.

The first stretch of 20 kilometres from Omantai to Puliyankulam was the easy section, although it wasn't unknown to find culvert mines under the road even there. From Puliyankulam to Mankulam the thicker jungle gave the Tigers greater cover to approach from and fade into. Hit-and-run attacks on the convoys were rather more commonplace, and all concerned were relieved to make it into Mankulam before dark.

Day two took them from Mankulam to Kilinochchi almost unaided, for there were no outstations along that 40-kilometre section, nothing except the guard on the TV and radio transmitter at Kokavil.

Any helicopters that happened to be going that way would keep a watchful eye on the convoy as it crept northwards. Out on a limb to the north-east, the outstation on the coast at Mullaittivu was virtually unsupported. Their nearest neighbours were an Engineer Squadron in their ramshackle, do-it-yourself camp near Odduchu-dan, nearly 30 kilometres away along Route 34. The same could be said for the troops stationed on the Mannar Island peninsula to the north-west, in Mannar District, where part of Operation Phantom Strike was due to take place.

Re-supply convoys had a 100 kilometres or so of Route 14 to cover in much the same way as the northbound convoys on Route 9, except that there were no bases in between for them to fall back on for help. The railway line that paralleled the road had been cut in many places, and the road around Giants Tank was pitted with craters.

For the Army to mount any form of successful operation with the forces at their disposal was well-nigh impossible over the distances that they were forced to travel. Purely for that reason alone Operation Phantom Strike, like many others before and some after it, was doomed to failure before it started. There was no element of surprise.

The basic idea behind Operation Phantom Strike was to carry out cordon and search operations on as many villages and small towns as possible in a specified area at the same time, denying the Tigers the chance to slip away into the jungle at the first sign of trouble. It should have also denied them the opportunity to group, train and re-supply for their guerrilla activities elsewhere. However, by time the Army had got itself into position the Tigers had long since faded into the jungle.

Vavuniya, then, was a somewhat more relaxed, better supplied and supported station than KKS. Unlike on the Jaffna Peninsula, the Army and Air Force had a different role to play. Coconuts and cabbages were of secondary importance; the movement of troops and weaponry came first. In an effort to deny the Tigers places to group, train and re-equip, foot patrols were more common than in Jaffna. Immediately I was reminded that my first Dust-off sortie out of KKS was for a foot patrol out of Mullaittivu so many months before.

During those first few days I once again set up a routine of housework and personal administration during the day, with a run in the evening whenever possible. There was also a re-supply system to be organised among the Mess servants.

The rooms that we moved into were smaller than those at KKS but still sported shared toilet facilities. They were at least clean. Unfortunately, the toilet seats were so small and set so close to the ground that a daily constitutional was taken with your knees somewhere up around your ears. Open drains were still the norm. One area of the camp was almost constantly under water during the wet season and a swampy bog of dirty water in the dry season.

As in KKS mosquitoes were an ever-present menace, and a practice constitutional on day one of my stay at Vavuniya resulted in several mosquito bites on my arse. An overwhelming feeling that I would make medical history assailed me. I feared that I would suffer from malarial bum, that I would contract sleeping sickness of the arse. On the bonus side, we weren't just two Whitefaces among half a dozen SLAF pilots.

At Vavuniya we were bunking alongside a larger group of Army officers. We had the opportunity to talk to people of an older age group and a similar military upbringing, which was a distinct improvement on Kankesanturai's segregated camp. When it was discovered that a large part of my own military life was spent in a Tank Regiment, I almost became one of them. We regularly spent an hour or two in the evening talking tanks and armoured cars to the Armoured Squadron's Commander, Major Karunatilake. A man of stern character, he.

The story going the rounds was that one of his troopers had run amok on parade one day with a hand weapon of some sort, killing or wounding one of his comrades. The Major, man of iron discipline that he was, stepped forward and ordered the man to lay down his weapon. When the soldier refused to obey and continued to threaten all and sundry, the Major drew his service revolver and shot him dead where he stood.

Coffee in the Mess after meals gave us the chance to meet many of the Army officers in their own environment and talk freely about the problems they faced in their efforts to defeat the Tiger.

My friendship with the armoured chaps led to a grudging acceptance by the Infantry Officers. They were frankly surprised that someone who flew helicopters could still be soldier enough to run three miles a day around the perimeter fence with only his personal weapon for company. They had been subjected to the whims and fancies of the slothful prima donnas in the Air Force for far too many years.

Yes, certainly, run for your life was still my philosophy. As much as it was good to meet and talk to real soldiers, the Air Force chaps at Vavuniya were still bound up in their smug feelings of superiority. The Army would have a long wait before the Air Force were capable of thinking about the Tigers as anything more than 'the Army's problem, let them sort it out we're only here to support you, what do you expect us to do?'

On top of it all there was Greg's latest batch of fresh out of the bag pilots to sort out. They felt that they knew it all when in fact they only knew the basics, and without careful bringing along they were just so many accidents looking for a place to happen. Even the two senior pilots, Gagan and Roger, were hidebound with the same lumbering thinking and clinging rules that had applied in Jaffna.

Without help they would think no further than coconuts & cabbages for the rest of their days. It was a crying shame. The Army in Vavuniya was hampered by a lack of speed in response. The Air Force was hampered by a lack of imagination. It took several months of talking to change it around and to eventually do something really positive.

Day two of the build-up to Operation Phantom Strike took me out to Mullaittivu several times. We shifted mountains of food and ammunition in preparation for the start of the Operation, just two days away. Towards the end of the day we were called on to lift some casualties from Talladi to the hospital at Anuradhapura. This was my first trip out to the Mannar Island area. The main base for

Mannar Island was at Talladi on the mainland, at the eastern end of the causeway.

On the island were two more outstations, Pesalai, on the northern edge of the island, which covered a radio transmitter station, and Talaimannar at the western end, which covered the ferry to mainland India. The scrub jungle on the mainland concealed much of the Tigers' movements and gave them ample opportunity to mine the road to Mannar Island whenever they chose.

Whilst we were away in the north-east re-supplying Mullaittivu for the impending operation, the Liberation Tigers of Tamil Eelam were busy blowing the shite out of a convoy on Route 14 to Mannar. Heading due west from Vavuniya, we picked up Route 14 at the road junction to the east of Giants Tank and followed it north-westwards towards Talladi. In no time at all we came upon the scattered wreckage of what was once part of the convoy. One truck lay in the irrigation canal to the south of the road. On the road itself a large crater showed where the Tigers had struck. A short distance away another damaged truck was still parked haphazardly against the trees at the roadside.

Convoy route 14 at Uyilankulam

Culvert mine route 14

We swung around the area left-handed. Pryantha, one of the new Officer Cadets, was flying from the left seat. I was taking in the sights and familiarising myself with the layout of the area. Looking down on the carnage, it was too easy to be reminded of similar scenes in Northern Ireland some fourteen years before. Preconception, as does ignorance, numbs the mind. Like the glare of a car's headlights to a rabbit on a darkened road, it blinds you.

The convoy leader had set up a protective cordon on the area and had sited his control post on a track to the south of the main road. Very professional and switched on. I thought, 'These guys are pretty good.'

Swinging into wind for a very standard flying school approach, Pryantha set us up to land inside the perimeter. Only in the last hundred feet of our approach did I realise that we were about to take out a set of power cables that stretched across our path. Shit, but I was angry with myself. Fresh out of the bag, Officer Cadet Pryantha Weeraman was a smoking hole in the ground looking for a place to happen. The army guys had waved us in through a set of wires and I had sat there, fat, dumb, and happy.

With a hastily muttered 'I have control', I quickly pulled some collective pitch to clear the wires and land a few metres further on. It was obvious to me that I would have to sharpen up my act even here, in a much more professionally policed area than Jaffna ever was. The casualties were quickly loaded and we shuffled them off to the hospital at Anuradhapura. I had just got my first taste of the future in Vavuniya. Less Tiger-induced terror, more like a case of pilot terror.

Tuesday 18 November 1986. The next two days involved us in dragging mountains of supplies to Mullaittivu and the Engineer Camp at Odduchudan. How anyone could imagine that the Tigers didn't know that something was in the wind I don't know, but the Army at Vavuniya seemed to be driven by an enthusiasm for the job that wasn't apparent in Jaffna. I couldn't make head nor tail of it but would discover the reason for it the very next day.

Rostered to fly with yet another new Officer Cadet on the day, I had walked down to the aircraft that morning in somewhat of a gloom. Kotakodeniya met me at the aircraft.

'Good morning Captain Ee... Smith, I am Officer Cadet Kotakodeniya, I shall be flying with you for the next few days'.

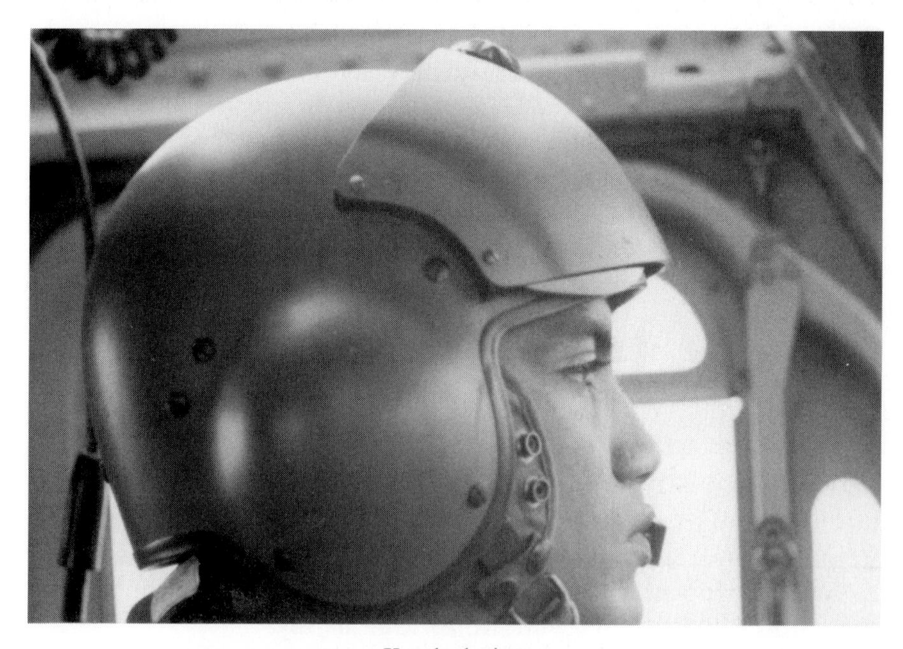

Kotakadeniya

Now that stunned me. Good manners, respect, if only for my greying hair. He'd almost stood to attention. Not the sort of British Raj-induced arrogance I'd come to expect.

'Good morning.' I reached out and shook his proffered hand. 'I'm pleased to meet you. Well, what have we got for today?'

'Captain, we have to take some supplies first to Mullaittivu and then to Mannar, where we shall remain on standby at Talladi until this afternoon.'

We turned and walked on together towards the Trooper that the engineers were preparing for the day's flying.

'Young man, my name is Tim, and I'd prefer it if you called me that when we're flying. If that's too difficult you can call me Smithy,' I let it hang for a moment before going on, 'let's enjoy our day's flying.'

Kotakodeniya looked at me strangely and uneasily nodded his assent.

'You check out your side, I'll check mine,' I called cheerfully, referring to the pre-flight inspection, and ambled away down the starboard side of the Trooper, leaving him to assess as to whether or not he should be bold enough to use my first name in future. The doorgunners were already mounting their machine guns in the back of the cabin and checking over the action of feed trays and working parts.

'Morning, chaps.'

'Good morning, Captain,' came the chorus of replies.

Aye, it was good to be back. Even better with such a different, friendly crew.

Talladi. We'd left Vavuniya after our runs out to Mullaittivu and headed due west, paralleling Route 30 en route to Mannar just before lunchtime. Swinging around the north edge of Giants Tank this time, we picked up the main road again at Uyilankulam and followed it to the roadblock set just short of the causeway to Mannar Island. Clouds of flamingos lifted from the lagoon and filled the air with a floating, swirling mass of pink and white. Idyllic, absolutely bloody idyllic. Kotakodeniya eased the Trooper around the birds whilst I pulled out my trusty old Nikon and took a few very quick photos.

Kotakodeniya was doing very well for a beginner. Widening our orbit, he swung us around the camp and into wind for a landing on the lawn in the centre of the main buildings. Five minutes later we were sitting with our side armour slid back and the doors open, waiting in the rapidly building heat for the main rotor blades to slow down enough to use the rotor brake to stop them.

The camp itself was set on the only firm ground in the middle of the salt water marshes at the base of the small peninsula that was Mannar Island. The wooden buildings set around a large central grassed area gave the outstation the air of a holiday camp. Mature trees dotted about the camp provided shade and created a gentle breeze. Only a scattering of armoured cars around the edges of the lawn, and the odd artillery piece or two laid out on a couple of display plinths belied the fact that this wasn't a holiday camp.

As the main rotor blades finally came to a stop a young lieutenant, braving the heat of the day in his crisply starched fatigues, walked smartly across the grass and actually welcomed us into the Officers Mess for refreshments.

Slightly run-down in appearance from the outside, the Mess was a haven of sanity. Ceiling fans chugged softly in the gloom, stirring the humid air to a sticky coolness. Cold drinks were brought to us as we lounged in comfortable rattan armchairs. The place beat the hell out of KKS, and even Vavuniya to some extent. There was no doubting that both the camp and the Mess belonged to an Armoured Squadron. This was one of Major Karunatilake's outstations, and it showed. Without being obsequious the young officers were well-mannered, respectful and polite. It was a pleasure to sit amongst them and listen to them whilst they chattered away to each other in Sinhalese, talking about God knew what. Inconsequential chatter it may have been, but somehow they seemed to show an air of confidence in their manners and bearing that had been missing in Jaffna.

The Major himself was not in station. That was another pleasure I was to experience many times in the future. In the meantime we were made welcome, and it was pleasant just to sit on my arse and do nothing for a few hours.

Leaving Talladi later that afternoon, we took a straight line back to Vavuniya. We climbed to 2000 feet and left the flamingos to settle back in the salt marshes. Passing north of Giants Tank again, we crossed the Madu Road and the Elephant Sanctuary around it.

The vast area of rice paddies surrounding Giants Tank gave way to the open bushland of the Elephant Sanctuary. It was hard to believe that this was the area where DB and his crew had taken such a lethal pasting only a month before. Aye, and it was somewhere down there that the Tigers had carried out their infamous bayonet charge and wiped out a complete section of infantry.

Not unlike the Spanish uplands really, the only things missing were windmills and *fincas*. This was the area where so much more was to happen in the not-too-distant future. For the time being I was happy to sit there in my ignorance and take in the surroundings, to store away a mental map for future reference.

Beyond the Madu Sanctuary the bushland gave way to denser forest with a scattering of lumber yards and sawmills interlaced with logging tracks, tracks that provided the Tigers with a complete network of unmapped roads to use.

Eventually we picked up the main north south road a couple of kilometres south of Vavuniya. Swinging left towards the airfield, we called the tower for landing clearance and parking instructions. We were cleared to land and, as the day's flying was complete, to park inside the wire.

The helicopters were kept inside the wire overnight for added security during the hours of darkness. The compound had very little in the way of paved surfaces and for the best part was covered

Heli-pad at Vavuniya

in packed earth. As we approached our landing point the downwash from the blades created a storm of eye-stinging dust. Volleyball players on a makeshift court nearby ran for cover.

Pushing down through the miniature dust storm as quickly as possible, we landed on a rough concrete heli-pad next to the small, corrugated tin hangar that served as a workshop. I signed the Trooper down in the technical log and left the engineers and armourers to get on with their end of day inspections and servicing.

With my T56 slung across my shoulder I made my dusty way over the hard-packed earth to the Mess. During the dry season that ground was packed hard enough to take a squadron of tanks. Later, in the rainy season, it would turn into a red morass, as slippery as a greased pig.

It was nearly sunset by time I got back to my room. Too late to go out for a run before the fast tropical sunset rushed upon us, but time enough to take a lukewarm shower and get changed for supper. Time to sit in the cool of the evening watching the fiery sunset behind the tail rotor of the Gunship. Time to think a bit about the future in Vavuniya before the mosquitoes made a meal of me.

Over the last couple of days I'd seen most of what there was to

Sunset at Vavuniya

see of the Northern Province. From Mannar in the west to Mullaittivu on the east coast, from 2000-year-old Anuradhapura in the south to Kilinochchi in the north. The outstations were much farther apart, not cut off but too far apart to provide much in the way of mutual support. Large enough to stand alone, too small to operate effectively within their own areas.

In both cases the rail link had been cut in many places and trains had not been run on them for several months, forcing re-supply onto the two main routes, Routes 9 and 14. For the greater part of their length jungle and thick scrub bordered both roads. Both were also pockmarked with craters that made them equally difficult to negotiate.

So there we were then, in Northern Province. Enough troops on the ground to maintain a reasonably strong presence in the area, but lacking the ability to respond quickly to any trouble that the Tigers chose to inflict upon them. What was needed was some sort of Quick Reaction Force that the Army did not have and the Air Force were unable to move.

I had the feeling that Oliver Ranasinghe wanted me in Vavuniya as more than an addition to his aircrew. The idea lurking in the back of my skull was that he wanted no more repeats of the fiasco in the Madu Sanctuary area. He didn't want any more aircraft damaged for nothing by gung-ho pilots. He didn't want any more side-gunners dead in their straps.

Out in the bush Operation Phantom lumbered on.

The following day I was blessed with Kotakodeniya's company again. Inexperienced he may have been, but there was no doubting his pleasant-natured friendliness. In the end it didn't matter too much, for like in Jaffna the Whiteface was not allowed any more insight into the short-term reckoning than finding out what the daily plan was as it happened.

That day was no different, except that for the first time I was to meet the man who would listen to what the Whitefaces had to say. A man who would do more than push our suggestions aside as too difficult, not suitable, or some such.

Brigadier Denzil Kopekeduwa had no delusions of grandeur, and no hang-ups when it came to asking for advice. He listened to what his subordinates had to say and thought about more than just his pension. Today the Brigadier was to visit the outstations.

We had started work a little later that day and hadn't even fired the engines up when a gaggle of sari-clad females appeared at the edge of the pad. They were escorted by a slim-built and slightly hunched officer with the look of an asthmatic academic rather than a soldier. With his hands clasped lightly behind his back, they looked for all the world like they were out for a stroll before tea on some lawn somewhere.

'What the hell is this?' I muttered into my microphone with an air of almost quiet exasperation.

'Those are lady doctors,' said my man for the day, with more than a touch of pride in his voice. 'They are going with us to visit the villages in the District with the Brigadier. He will talk to the village soldiers, and the doctors will open the surgery for the first time in many months.'

It was a pleasant surprise, for I hadn't been told that the Sri Lankans even had a Home Guard, let alone visiting doctors. 'Who's the chap with them? Where's the Brigadier?' I demanded.

Brig. Denzil and sari-clad doctors

My exasperation was rapidly overtaking my impatience with the standard 'keep the Whitefaces in the dark' attitude. The young-looking officer with them looked for all the world like an Army Medical Officer, or perhaps a schoolteacher in uniform.

'That is Brigadier Denzil, he is a good man. We must wait until they are on board before we start the engines,' explained my man with the sort of patient air of a father talking to his child. 'Now they bloody tell me,' I thought.

The party approached the Trooper in deep conversation until they were about to get into the cabin. The Brigadier stopped, looked up at me and smiled. 'Good morning, Captain Smith. Thank you for not starting the engines until we are on board.'

'Good morning, Sir. My pleasure,' I lied glibly, and smiled pleasantly back. I'd flown my share of VIPs in the British Army not to be caught off my guard in such a pisspotical way. Mentally I thanked Kotakodeniya.

The man was obviously very sharp and had done his homework. Well, at least he had got his Aide de Camp to find out who was flying him that day and had gone out of his way to speak to me. Clever man. I'd have to watch him.

Operation Phantom was well under way, and Brigadier Denzil wanted to follow it a little closer than sitting at his desk reading Intelligence Reports. The white saris climbed gracefully into the cabin without showing more than a trace of ankle. The Brigadier settled himself on the front seat. He opened out his map of the local area and busied himself with identifying the route we were about to take. No, no fool he, the clever little man who directed operations against the Tigers in Northern Province.

An hour later I was lounging in the cabin behind a door gun with my feet up on a seat back. Brigadier Denzil was addressing the Home Guard. Although he was speaking in Sinhalese and I could hardly understand a word that he was saying, his air of calm assurance and the tone of total conviction of his voice was quite striking. Somehow I knew that working in Vavuniya with this man in charge would be a totally different kettle of fish.

21 November 1986. The camp at Mullaittivu sits on the arid coastal plain that is northern Sri Lanka. Constructed from locally made airbricks with corrugated asbestos sheets for roofing, it was the absolute pits as a camp. Surrounded by two barbed wire fences, it

looked more like a prison camp. We were to spend that day there on standby with a Trooper and a Gunship. The local Infantry Company had taken some shit from the Tigers during the run-up to Operation Phantom; they wanted some close support.

Approaching parallel to Route 34, we swung round the Nanthi Kadal lagoon and descended to land on the grass and dirt airstrip on the western side of the camp. There were signs of recent work on the strip and, much to my surprise, I discovered that they intended to land a re-supply plane there sometime over the next few days. I wondered how and what the hell for.

The day dragged on and the heat built up under the asbestos roof until it was almost unbearable. Wandering into the Control Room to find out how long we were expected to stay there, I found the Radio Operators frantically busy. They didn't seem to mind that the ceiling fans just stirred the air into soggy wet lumps that stuck to your skin. The place was filled with an air of excitement.

The Duty Operations Officer came purposefully across the room to meet us. 'We are bringing in many Tigers,' he said, looking at us both, but speaking English for my benefit, 'if you go outside you will see them coming in.'

Brig. Denzil at Ittikulam

Truly surprised at the apparent success of the operation, I congratulated them; perhaps I shouldn't have bothered. 'Excellent, well done for the troops on the ground,' I smiled at him. He returned to his maps and radios with a positive glow about him, and I wandered outside to see the action.

Sure enough, some distance away across the scrubby, barren landscape, a stream of people filled the approach road to the camp. They all seemed to be carrying things, and initially it was difficult to make it out, but as they drew closer it was apparent that they were carrying oil paintings of some sort. 'Oil paintings? Bloody oil paintings?' I thought. Yes, sure enough, it was oil paintings.

The Sinhalese Army had swept hundreds of ordinary people from their homes. Hundreds of people, pissed off with the Sinhalese Government, had been dragged from their shacks and shanties, bringing with them pictures of their local heroes as evidence of their being bad-arsed Tigers. Tigers, they were bloody pussycats.

Yes, they may well have been supporters of the LTTE, but would you arrest everybody in Wales that had a picture of Rhodri Mawr, or Owain Glendower, or even Prince Charles on their front room wall? No, of course not.

Villagers of Chilvatai

Killed in action Mullaittivu

So on they came, those people. Young and old, all male, all in sarongs. Nothing to say, 'I am a Tiger.' No uniforms, no weapons, no literature. Just oil paintings. And I was there with a Gunship to protect the Army against them. With a Gunship to blow them away if they put up any fight. The Tigers had slipped away into the jungle days before, taking all their gear with them. The last few had inflicted whatever damage they could.

The following day the 748 re-supply plane landed at Mullaittivu. With all due pomp and ceremony they lifted out the Army's dead. The number of prisoners brought in may well have made it look like a successful operation, but for the poor bloody conscripts that had died for a handful of oil paintings it was a complete failure. A body bag is worth absolutely zip.

12

Sitting Ducks ...

The days came and went with monotonous boredom. More often than not they were spent going up and down the north-south road, Route 9. Changing out the guard platoon on the television and radio transmitter at Kokavil. Occasional R&R trips for the troops from Kilinochchi who hadn't been involved on the latest convoy. Days spent on standby at Mankulam.

The still warm evenings took on a similar routine to that in KKS, with one major difference. The route for my daily run went round the outside of the perimeter fence. Jogging out past the main gate, I would wave a cheery hello. It was really important for them to take note of the fact that I was going for a run. Not to impress them with my fitness, but because I wanted them to recognise me on the

Vavuniya and running track

second lap. I wanted them to know, to remember that I was out there.

Leaving the main gate behind me, I turned right and followed the perimeter fence as it dropped gently away downhill towards the airstrip. The track was rutted and rough, but it was good running, even though the humid air was cloying to the lungs. A gentle breeze moved against the skin as I ran, legs moving smoothly, arms swinging freely, lovely. It was great to feel the muscles moving under the skin. The open scrubland to the left got thicker, restricting the view. Totally unsighted to the camp guards, I suddenly felt very alone.

An avenue opened out through the scrub to the left, several hundred yards long. The hair on the back of my neck started to rise. The avenue was a beautiful shooting gallery for anyone who chose to use it, and me at the end of it jogging gently along. Like a duck in a fairground side-show. Lengthening my stride, I crossed it as quickly as possible, as fast as the rutted and uneven surface would allow me. Moments later I was clear and coasting downhill towards the runway and the front gate to the camp. That avenue through the scrub always put the wind up me, and no matter how knackered I was my pace always went up a notch to get past it.

Saturday, 29 November 1986. Weekends generally brought a slowing in the operational pace. Op Phantom had faded from my memory like a ghost in the light of day. Sacked out on my bed, I was reading some old letters from home. The peace and quiet were shattered by the sudden rush of feet along the veranda.

One of our side gunners appeared at the door. 'Captain, can you come? We must go to China Bay.' He blurted his message out without waiting. His sweating face showed only the slightest signs of panic, but I knew that something shitty had just blown in.

'Yes, young man. No problem, I'll be along in a moment,' I answered casually, 'I will get my gear and see you at the helicopter in a minute.' The gunner disappeared in a rush.

Rolling off my bed, I pulled on my jungle boots. Slinging my T56 over my shoulder, I grabbed my flying helmet from the chair. Sauntering out as casually as I could, I did a quick mental equipment check. Cigs, wallet and money. Who the hell knew where we'd end up? Cigarette lighter and pocket-knife, first aid pack in my leg pocket, ID locket round my neck. Oh yeah, and safety catch still on. Well, one should never let them see you panic, it could spoil the image.

Down at the heli-pad a few minutes later, Gagan was already strapping in. Opening the co-pilot's door, I slung my T56 over the seat armour by its strap and clambered in beside it. 'Hi, Gagan. What's going on then?' I asked nonchalantly.

'There has been an explosion on the road south of China Bay, I think some soldiers have been killed' he answered. There was no doubting the concern in his voice, but I felt there was more to it than just that.

We went through the checklist in quick time and fired the engines up. Checking in with gunners on the intercom, I called the tower for an immediate takeoff from the compound. On a cloud of red dust we climbed away and departed eastbound for China Bay. From 2000 feet a short time later it seemed that the scrubby jungle beneath us stretched away beyond the horizon. Nothing to do but wait until the sea appeared.

'Well, Gagan, what's going on then, what's happened that we are in so much of a rush?' I never did find out why the Sri Lankans were so sparing with the facts.

'Ahh, Tim, I think a patrol has been caught in a bomb on the road. There are many dead.'

Many dead. My thoughts turned to Northern Ireland for a moment, NI and the Parachute Regiment at Warren Point. 'Bloody hell,' I thought, 'it must have been a huge bomb.'

Thinking ahead, I gently scratched my brain for the right things to do. First a recce for command wires, firing points and come-ons, secondary devices set to catch the unwary in a killing zone. Then a safe landing site covered by arcs of fire from the side guns. Lots to think on.

'How come there are so many dead, how many are involved?' I asked gently.

Gagan seemed distinctly perturbed, and I didn't fancy him doing anything rash when we got there.

'Twenty-two. The Army says there are twenty-two dead.'

'That must have been one hell of a fight, Gagan.' I'd had visions of another punch-up similar to the one that DB had been involved in out in Mannar District.

'Ah, Tim, they were riding in the back of a Buffalo armoured truck when the bomb went off.' Gagan seemed vaguely indifferent to the whole thing. He seemed to be almost uncaring, not a bad thing really. It meant that he probably wouldn't do anything silly when we got there.

Half an hour later we crossed the semicircle of hills that surrounded China Bay. The oil tanks that had been of so much interest to the Japanese during World War Two were still there, nestling into the seaward slopes. On the headland out across the bay sat Trincomalee. The old Dutch fort on the seaward edge of the town sparkled almost magically in the sunlight. The harbour, which should have been full of freighters and such like, was almost empty. Why the hell anybody had to fight in a country as beautiful as Sri Lanka I don't know.

Slipping down the hillside we descended to land for a quick refuel at the military airstrip. Fifteen minutes later we were airborne again, heading south over the bay for Muttur and the site of the explosion that had blotted out so many young lives so quickly. Approaching the site from the north a short time later, I found it almost impossible not to equate it with scenes I'd mentally mapped in NI so many years before.

The road on which it had happened wound through gently rolling open countryside. My eyes saw and my brain registered. The stream that wriggled its way towards the road and passed under it through a narrow culvert, the bomb site. To the west a gently rising hillside dotted with trees and scrub that had probably provided the observation and firing point. The treeline beyond that would have been the escape route.

Had it been radio-controlled or was it a command-line job? Shit, in my mind's eye I could almost see the command line as it snaked back along the stream bank and up the hill to the firing position. Why, in God's name, had they not had two lines of flankers out? One on each side of the road. The big 'V' of protection that would have found the command wire somewhere upstream, well before the Buffalo had even got near the culvert. What a disgusting waste. It was almost obscene. What the hell was Ken Who's boys teaching them in their nice little training camp down south? Half a mile away to the left were possible spots for a sniper to be tucked away behind the bushes with a bloody great rifle, patiently waiting for us to arrive.

There was one really sensible landing site for any helicopter responding to the incident. It was beautifully lined up with the possible sniper position. We would have to be a little circumspect about this one. The possibilities made my balls crawl and my teeth itch.

'Gagan, I think we should land over there,' I suggested quietly, nodding and pointing to another site some distance up the road, away from the huge crater. 'When the area's been cleared we can land closer in.'

There was no way that I was going to be sitting in any helicopter that had landed on the secondary device. On the one hand I really didn't want an argument, but on the other hand I didn't want a foot in one county and my itching teeth in the next.

'There is a good landing site next to the Buffalo. We should use that one.'

'Maybe they could have another bomb there.' I was trying hard not to make an issue of it, or in any way bring his sense of pride and heroism into it. His face showed a little doubt in my logic. This was what Ranasinghe wanted me here for, to show them what made my short hairs curl.

'This has happened in Northern Ireland so many times,' I explained, playing my trump card.

A strange sense of anger was welling up in me. I wanted to tell him of the tragic waste of life. The senseless destruction and loss of equipment, the hopelessness of defeating the Tigers if we didn't do everything possible to deny them the chance of even remotely getting the upper hand. I didn't want to die for nothing.

In the distance, some three-quarters of a mile beyond the gaping hole in the ground, an Army truck appeared, crawling along the road at a snail's pace. In front of it soldiers on foot. At last the Army was taking the situation seriously.

'Tim, you have control, I will speak to the army on the radio.'

'I have control.' Taking the controls of the Trooper, I swung us away from the crater and flew an enormous orbit around the area. Gagan was nothing if not an opportunist. He saw the chance of handing over any cock-ups or loss of face to a Whiteface. He was also something of a diplomat. He would go far in the Sri Lankan Air Force.

Checking out the surrounding high ground, I returned to the landing site that I had previously selected. From a high hover I checked out the surface for any signs of recent digging, signs of command wires, anything to show that the Tiger had outguessed us. Finally satisfied that all was as it should be, I landed the Trooper and wound the engines down to ground idle. There was no way that I wanted to close them down completely in that situation.

Gagan climbed out and wandered off to speak to the Lieutenant who had just arrived at the crater and was already directing his troops to gather up the bodies of the poor bastards that hadn't made it back from their last patrol.

Walking casually around the crater a few minutes later, I checked out the banks of the road, looking for signs of that lethal secondary device. A few yards away on the other side of the road the pile of bodies grew higher. I wandered back to the Trooper, leaving Gagan to talk logistics with the young Lieutenant.

Knowing well what was to come next, I called on the side gunners to strap the cabin seats up and wound the engines up to flying speed. Lifting into the hover I taxied down the road to land alongside the pile of corpses by the roadside. Gagan climbed in, fastened his seat straps, and plugged in his helmet pigtail.

'We have to take them to a temporary mortuary that the police have set up in the next town,' Gagan explained as soon as he was settled in.

The Army lads had already started to load the bodies into the back of the cabin. At first they laid them carefully on the cabin floor, but then there was no more space left, so they stacked them like so many logs or sacks on top of each other. Gagan busied himself with something in his flight bag on the cockpit floor.

Looking over my seat back my eyes momentarily caught the sight of a thighbone sticking through the torn flesh of a leg. My gaze was dragged unwillingly further up the body. Over the ripped clothes, the bloody shirt, over limbs that hung loosely, lifelessly. The light brown skin at the throat of a neck that had until recently pulsed with blood and drawn air. The eyes of the young soldier gazed back at me with a blank, uncomprehending stare.

Who, in hell's name, could take a patrol of young men like these into Bandit Country without putting out scouts to the front and to the sides? My thoughts right then were sanguine, to say the least.
'Shit, so young,' I sighed sadly to myself.

Looking back into the cockpit I saw that Gagan had finally got his camera out of his flight bag and was lining it up on the young soldier's blank, staring face.

'Shit, Gagan, you'll be asking him to fucking smile next. You've gotta be joking, taking happy snaps of the dead. Are you fucking sick, or what?' Anger got the better of me and flooded my voice with contempt. Gagan grinned at me sheepishly and put his camera away.

It took two runs to lift them all to the temporary mortuary, a large shed in an industrial site, that had been taken over for the task. Closing the engines down after the second run, we had climbed out to stretch our legs. The local Police Commander ambled over and cordially invited us to have a look inside.

'Good afternoon Captain, we have taken over this shed,' explained the policeman grandly. 'It has air conditioning,' he went on without a thought. 'We have laid out the bodies for the doctor and his team to inspect.'

'Sick bastards,' I muttered as I trudged across the dusty compound behind them.

Gagan gave no sign of having heard me. What was it that made them think that a Whiteface would be interested in a pile of bodies in a shed?

The local doctor had been called in to help with the operation. He met me at the door and welcomed me inside like some visiting dignitary. The shed floor was covered with body bags, some already full, others in the process of being filled by a gaggle of female nurses from the local hospital.

Dressed in his best set of fatigues, the Police Commander strutted along behind us like it was some sort of parade. I wanted to get out of there. Not because of the mutilated bodies but because of the mutilated minds that were treating the whole thing like it was something to be proud of. The senior nurse bustled up to the doctor like senior nurses all over the world.

'We have found one that is still alive,' she said matter-of-factly. She turned and bustled away. The doctor paled a little and rushed off behind her. The policeman disappeared like a fart in a strong wind. Someone had cocked up by not noticing that one was still alive, and the Police Commander didn't want to be around to answer any questions.

With nothing better to do, I made my way back to the Trooper. Nearby Gagan was talking to the same young Lieutenant who had been out on the road earlier. Gagan turned as I appeared, his face lighting up.

'Tim, one of the soldiers was still alive when we got here,' called Gagan; there was no doubt that he was really pleased with himself.

'Great, Gagan. Is it time for us to leave yet?' I didn't feel much like a rescuing hero. All I wanted to do was get away from these sick people that took one minor bloody miracle and turned it into their finest hour.

'Shitty death,' I thought, 'they've taken a complete disaster, and by finding one poor bugger still alive it's been turned into a resounding victory.'

My feelings of disgust stayed with me, are still with me. With an almost perfect example to learn from, the military powers had chosen not to do a damn thing about training their troops in the simplest techniques that had been learned and practised in NI for years. The disaster at Warren Point could have saved so many lives if only these people had learned something from it.

So, okay, the jungle, and scrubland of Sri Lanka might not be the moors and bogs of Ireland, but they were both equally remote and inaccessible. The Tigers were carrying out their operations on the roads and in the towns; now that was the same. They were striking at the military on the roads and in their camps, just the bloody same. All I wanted them to do was to learn from someone else's mistakes.

Aye, I knew it then and I still know it now. When did anybody's kids ever listen to their parents? What the hell, they weren't kids and I wasn't even their bloody uncle, but I did want them to learn so quickly, so badly.

Just think about it. If they had put out their flankers on either side of the road they would have found the command wires to the culvert mine. But then the Tigers, in time, would have resorted to radio-controlled explosions. So what the hell. The Sri Lankans would have resorted to frequency sweeping radio transmissions to detonate the bombs and mines prior to a patrol's arrival, and so it would have gone on. But it would have saved lives, on both sides, it would have reduced the awful waste of young lives.

I must have been in cloud-cuckoo land. The daily grind went on with the almost daily loss of lives. There was maiming death and injury on every route.

Talladi, four days later, produced a similar scene of death and destruction to that on the road south of Muttur, four days before and only 150 miles away. Anger and frustration boiled in my guts, it seethed in my brain, like some huge maggot.

Who the hell could I talk to about it? No bugger, not even Squince and Tony. They had both been moved on. Don had been sent back to KKS, and Tony had gone to China Bay, or was it Batticaloa? Once a Whiteface got sent somewhere, they might well have disappeared from the face of the earth. There was no contact, no organisation to pool our knowledge, our skill and experience. Nobody wanted to know.

Poling out to Tallidi with Roger that Wednesday afternoon, I had somehow hoped that a trip with the Squadron's Chief Instructor would give me the chance to voice some of my ideas.

No bloody chance. I think now, looking back on it all, that Roger somehow thought that pure flying skill was what kept pilots alive. Wrong, he was so wrong. Some skill, yes. The skill to utilise the techniques that the tactics demanded. The mental agility to adapt techniques to suit the tactics demanded on the day. The imagination to improvise.

Roger flew beautifully, with a confidence that showed. In no way did it help the soldiery who were so badly injured that we had to take them straight to the Military Hospital in Colombo. What would have helped them would have been helicopter support for the patrol in the first place. No need for Gunships, not even Troopers full of weaponry, just a bog-standard reconnaissance helicopter with an observer and a pair of stabilised binoculars would have done the trick. They would have spotted the signs of activity around the culvert or roadside and saved the unnecessary deaths and destruction that followed.

We stayed in Katunayaka that night. Roger buggered off home to his wife. For me the night was spent in the Mess. There was no way that I fancied a trip to Negombo for a drink, and staying in the bungalow on my own for the night didn't really appeal to me. There was too much on my mind to spend the night alone.

I'd been back in Sri Lanka less than three weeks. Already I was beginning to champ at the bit with the frustration of seeing so much go wrong that hadn't needed to. I needed an outlet for my thoughts on the destruction of the Tigers.

We flew back to Vavuniya the following morning. It was an easy enough trip, but I was moody to the point of being morose. Roger probably thought that I was hungover, and said little or nothing for the whole trip.

Kicking about in my room that afternoon, I could think of

nothing better to do with my time than to get my running gear on and go for a canter around the camp perimeter. What had been a means of clearing my brain in the past proved to be precisely the opposite that day. I ran with a tightness, with a feeling of despair that I couldn't shake off. So I ran some more, it didn't help.

The camp guards must have thought me to be completely insane. Mad dogs, maybe they were right, and Englishmen go out for a midday run. It didn't make any difference.

The black cloud was still hanging over me the following day when we went out to Talladi again, this time to pick up the dead from the culvert mine of two days before and take them to Anuradhapura.

Once more they loaded the bodies into the back like so many lumps of wood, stacked two deep in places, particularly behind my seat. I couldn't help but to look back into the cabin at them. Into staring eyes that looked at me in dull wonderment. Eyes full of dull pleading. The purple-edged exit hole in his neck said, 'I died because I wasn't properly trained or led, why?' The soldier would never hear, and I couldn't find anyone to explain it for him.

We did a couple more runs out to Talaimannar that afternoon with replacements for the dead and wounded, re-stocking the base with its working complement of potential bodybag cases.

My evening run was as full of anger as the previous day's had been. When I got to the shooting gallery through the trees I actually slowed down in the hope of being shot at by some dull bugger who really wanted to die. Nothing happened.

Some new guys had moved into the rooms across the veranda from mine. I'd just got in from my evening run. I was still pissed off, morose and moody to the point of feeling murderous.

Cooling off with a towel wrapped around me, I walked onto the veranda for a quiet cigarette. Sat on the chair five yards away was one of the new guys, cleaning a weapon. Odd that. It was something that was normally done down at the armoury, where the cleaning kit was readily available. Odder still was the weapon. Very new-looking, modern, fitted with sniper sight mounts and a silencer. Intriguing, very interesting. Ambling across the five yards, I stopped in front of him.

'Nice weapon, not standard issue, eh?'

'Captain Smith, good evening. It's a Heckler and Koch MP3.'

Bugger, how the bloody hell did he know who I was?

Taken aback by his cheerful recognition, I did a quick study of the man. He looked fit enough, and not quite as young as he might be for his Captain's pips. His voice had the ring of self-confidence that was not usual in young officers. Other than his rank, he wore no insignia.

'How was your run? It's good to see someone that keeps fit.'

He certainly kept me bouncing, I'd hardly time to think, let alone reply. 'Ah, it was OK. It would have been better if there had been more of it.' I'd finally got myself together. 'I've not seen you around before. Are you with the Infantry here?'

'I'm the leader of the Trackers, we are a new unit based in Vavuniya.' Again there was that confidence in his voice that had me thinking, now this was interesting

'Why are you here in Vavuniya, is there something happening?' I tried hard to put my question in a roundabout way and got nowhere.

'We will work in the jungle. We will stay out for many days at a time.'

The Sri Lankan idea of jungle was very different from mine. For me jungle is rainforest; jungle is where you have to cut a heli-pad out of the trees. In Sri Lanka you just had to look around a bit to find somewhere to land.

'Will you need any helicopter support in your job?'

'In the beginning we will be out on unit training and will not need you very much, but later we hope to work with you more often,' he quite happily explained.

My first thoughts were that 'these boys might just turn the job around.' Keeping my excitement at the prospect well hidden, I turned away to go for a shower and get changed. 'Speak to you later then. See yuh.' I ambled off to my room across the way.

Several days later we were tasked with the job of dropping the Trackers off in a stretch of jungle to the north-west of Vavuniya. They had asked for a covert insertion near a fork in a small river.

Dropping to tree top height several kilometres from the LS, we skimmed along the river following the bends. As the river fork came up under the nose of the Trooper, I flared off our speed and slipped into a nearby clearing in the scrub. Already I could hear orders being shouted in the cabin. Obviously someone was doing a good job of the map reading, someone was decidedly on the ball.

Without wasting any time I slid onto the ground between some bushes and turned to look back into the cabin. It was already empty. The buggers must have left the cabin even as the skids touched the ground. 'These lads will do, ' I thought and lifted into an immediate take-off.

We left them out there for a week. Meanwhile the mundane daily grind went on. Up and down Route 9 to every outstation. A day on standby here, a load of ammunition there. One day a crewchange to the Kokavil Transmitter Station, and on another a call out with the Gunship. A patrol out of Talaimannar got themselves pinned down by the Tigers. Somehow they managed to get the Tigers pinned down in a schoolhouse. Yeah, a fairly standard SL stand-off. We pitched in with the Gunship. Yes, I was flying the Gunship. Somehow the dividing line between morality and necessity had grown dim. It should have been so simple.

The Patrol Commander had briefed us on the target while we were still en route. From some distance out we identified the target and set up for an immediate pod gun attack. Sliding the sights down in front of me, I called for the weapons system to be armed and the pod-gun selected. Rolling into the attack dive I switched the weapon sight on. The red aiming circle framed the school buildings. I hoped there were no kids in there. The red aiming dot centred on the main building, around it a red ring of imminent mayhem. I pressed the trigger. The pod-gun thundered into life. Tracer rounds curved their way across the intervening distance and flickered out as they disappeared into the building. Bloody good shooting!

And then the bloody thing jammed. Shit, I'd been through all this before at the Karainagar Naval Base. This time it was no different. One after another the systems went down. No pod-gun, no bloody rockets, and a cabin mounted 0.50in HMG that jammed. We were left with only the side guns. The Tac radio squawked into life. 'The gunmen are running along the ditch behind the school.' The poor bloody Patrol Commander was almost beside himself. 'They are in the ditch behind the school.'

There was bugger-all that we could do as we repositioned to use the side guns. I flew a huge figure of eight based on the road with the school buildings to the front and centre. We pushed forward, driving the Tigers further down the ditch and giving the patrol enough cover to get their sorry arses out of there.

As soon as they had put some distance between themselves and the Tiger we disengaged and buggered off, back to base, in disgust. Right then I thought about the Trackers out there in the bush and hoped that when the time came we could put up a better performance for them.

13

... and High Birds

Brown paper packages tied up with string,
these are a few
of my favourite things.

Trips up and down the line to Kilinochchi became more frequent. It was obvious from the amount of trips to the hospital at Anuradhapura that the convoys and foot patrols were beginning to lose more men than they could sensibly afford. More and more we were being used to change out the troops from the bases. The Tigers were obviously biting hard.

There was a plan afoot. The increasing amount of time that we spent on standby at Mankulam was to cover the Engineers as they beavered away, carving a short landing strip out of the jungle. As ever, we Whitefaces were told nothing of what was going on. It was a long time before I found out how they planned to land the Avro 748s on the short length of strip that they were carving out of raw jungle. Bless 'em, they had ordered up a slack handful of Chinese STOL aircraft for the job. Brilliant!

What the hell, it gave me something to take my mind off the diet of curried anything that I was trying to survive on.

Work on the airstrip stopped at lunchtime. One day whilst I was waiting in the lounge for lunch to be served, the redoubtable Major Karunatilake invited me to take some time out and enjoy myself.

'Tim, you like shooting?' he enquired. The Major always seemed to have a twinkle in his eyes. I couldn't work out if he was taking the piss or not.

'Aye, yes, at home I go out every week. Mostly shooting pigeons' I offered.

'Come with me, Tim.' It wasn't a request, nor an order, maybe a dare. Five minutes later he was thrusting a .22 rifle into one hand and a box of cartridges into the other.

'Across the road from the main gate is a large grain store with lots of pigeons in it,' he explained. 'They are a pest, see what you can do for a while, until lunch is served.'

Ten minutes later I was prowling around the grain store, followed by every boy in the village who was big enough to climb a tree. Every time a pigeon fell out of the roof one small boy or another would dash in to recover the body. They were so pleased to be there, like kids all the world over involved in something they shouldn't be doing, something that their Mums and Dads didn't know about. They laughed and giggled uproariously.

When I left the grain store some 20 minutes later, the kids went skipping home, still laughing, and clutching a brace of pigeons apiece.

'Ah, Tim, come with me.' The Major had been watching from the main gate and escorted me to the Officers Mess. 'Here, sit opposite me.' We'd arrived in the dining room where all the young Officers were already seated, waiting for us to arrive. Huh, I felt like some sort of visiting dignitary, a VIP. I felt a little embarrassed.

We, the Whiteface pilots, had never been part of the team before, or a part of their society; even Ken Who and KMS disowned us. Now they, the Sri Lankan Army, were inviting me to join them for lunch. It was an uncomfortable feeling.

'How would you like your steak?' The question shook me. I hadn't eaten a decent steak since I'd arrived in Sri Lanka. Something to do with religion and draining the blood from the meat before it was used.

'Uh, rare, please. Yes, uh, rare. Thank you.' The chatter around the table stopped. Vaguely I heard the Major rattling off a string of orders in Sinhalese.

Had I committed some sort of faux pas, stepped in some lump of social dog shit? 'I should give a fuck,' I thought, 'I've drained more meat for their bloody politics than I'd care to think about'.

'Today we have wild boar on the menu.' The Major's voice brought me back to reality. 'Do you like wild boar?' Somewhere in the distance I heard myself answer, 'Yes, very much, thank you.' The chatter around the table went on.

Lunch went by in an absolute barrage of questions about my earlier life in the Armoured Corps and mouth-watering lumps of wild boar cooked beautifully rare. Which mark of Centurion Tank had I been in, what main armament had it carried? Had I worked with armoured cars? What had been my role?

The young Armoured Squadron Officers listened intently to my answers; answers that had rolled so easily off my tongue. It had been a part of my life that I wouldn't easily forget. Centurion Mark Fives, Eight and Nines. Main Armament, Twenty Pounders, refitted later with 105mm. And yes, I had worked with Ranging Guns in their infancy; I personally knew the people that had done the trials and development on it, Bertie Starr and Ali Gater. Armoured cars? Yes, of course. Ferrets, Saladins and Saracens in my day. I'd been on the gunnery side of things, a Gunnery Instructor. Something I would never forget, ever.

The food was marvellous. There were bottles and jars of sauces and chutneys that I'd almost forgotten existed, scattered the full length of the table. I only hoped that I would get more Standby Duties at Mankulam.

'Yes, of course you will,' promised my magical Major. 'I will also get more meat for you, different things. I notice that you are a hunting man with a taste for good meat.'

Nodding and smiling, I could hardly believe my good fortune.

As we left later that afternoon to return to Vavuniya, Karunatilake took me by the elbow and stopped me for a moment. 'Thank you for giving those pigeons to the children of the village. That was a good thing.'

'Hey, I enjoyed the shooting and the company of the children. It was great fun, and it took me away from our job here for a while. Thanks, it was you that made it possible.'

'No problem, Tim, no problem. See you again, Tim. See you soon.'

The days rolled on. There was still no news as to how they intended to land planes on that ridiculously short strip at Mankulam, or Mullaittivu come to that. The time spent at Mankulam was limited, probably because of the high standard of the food to be had there. Everybody wanted a crack of the good food whip.

My source of information dried up. More and more flights were used for changing out the troops on R&R. The Tigers were getting bolder. Omantai, the next station north from Vavuniya, took a hammering, with the loss of one dead and several wounded during a daylight attack. Convoys out of Talladi and Talaimannar were getting hit regularly. Gunship support and Cas-evac trips were an almost daily occurrence. Surface movement was slowly grinding to a halt. The Tigers needed to be hunted in the jungle, but our hunters, the Trackers, were still on training in the bush somewhere to the north-west of Vavuniya.

Strangely among all this, I was tasked to go up to Kilinochchi to pick up a compassionate case. The soldier's father was on his deathbed and the Private, for that was all he was, was to be sent home on leave. I was pleasantly surprised that compassion should rear its timorous head amongst such an atmosphere of murder and mayhem. I put it down to Brigadier Denzil, such was my respect for him.

Several days later, following yet another attack on Omantai, a task came over on the Tac radio to return to Omantai and pick up yet another compassionate case and bring him back to Vavuniya.

That time it was a young second Lieutenant. I thought no more of it until later that afternoon. We had finished the day's flying and were about to put the Trooper away for the night when the same young second Lieutenant strutted up to me by the helicopter. Standing directly in front, he blocked my path.

'You will take me to Omantai, now,' says he, without as much as please, thank you or by your leave. Stroppy little sod.

'Sorry, me old lad. I take my orders from the Air Force,' I chucked back at him and made to step round him.

He took his AK47 from his shoulder and waved it under my nose. Quite the wrong thing to do. I smiled my 'hand grenade with the pin out' smile and gave him that flat look that says, 'I've picked my spot.'

'You will take me back to Omantai now.' This time he was shouting as well as waving his Kalashnikov.

Sighing an 'oh bollocks' sigh, I made to step the other way around him.

'I must get back to my section at Omantai, I must go now. They need me.'

Yeah, like a hole in the head they needed an arsehole like that running around the place. He got the idea that pleading wouldn't wash either. 'Look, I've already told you. I go when the Air Force tells me, and not before. Now go away and ask the Squadron Leader or the Brigadier.'

The young man was by no means in control of his emotions and was being really persistent. Actually, he'd totally fucking lost it.

What I didn't know was that the letter he had produced claiming his father to be on his deathbed was written on Army notepaper. He was deeply in the shit and trying hard to dig himself out.

'You take me to Omantai now,' he pleaded. 'I order you to take me to Omantai, now,' he ordered. His voice went up and down like a whore's drawers as he cajoled and demanded. 'My soldiers need me,' he squeaked in desperation. I wished that he hadn't waved his gun under my nose again. If he hadn't, I might have asked someone to authorise the trip. His last chance of avoiding a court-martial had just gone down the river.

'Young man, just do as you are told. Go and get someone else to authorise the trip to Omantai. Now fuck off and leave me in peace.' That was my Sergeant Major's voice. The one that's used to tell some lower-ranking erk to do as he is told voice. It cracked out, lashing along the camp fence like a snapping tow wire. It stopped soldiers in their tracks at a hundred paces. Sentries at the camp gate leaned out of their sangars to see what was going on.

'You do not swear "fuck off" to me,' he screamed, 'I will get you for this, I will shoot you for this.' He waved his Kalashnikov under my nose again for good measure.

Turds that wave weapons around are not inclined to use them, I hoped. With my jaw set and a stony look on my face, I stepped towards him. He half-stepped aside. Brushing past him, I walked straight on. Without looking back I walked away and left him there. My anal sphincter puckered and the hair on the back of my neck crawled as I walked away.

My evening run had not been any fun. My trusty T56 had not left 'the ready' all the way round. At that moment it lay on my bed, loaded with the safety catch on. Out on the veranda the Tracker Captain was relaxing in a chair. We'd picked him and his boys out of the jungle the day before. They had appeared out of the scrub around their makeshift landing site like true professionals. I'd been well pleased with their performance.

'Captain Smith, good evening. You have had some trouble today?'

'Hi there. Aahh, just a little.'

He held my non-committal look with an inquiring gaze. He didn't seem convinced. When I had finished explaining it to him he gently shook his head. 'He is young and foolish. He should not be trusted.'

I followed his gaze across the veranda through my open door into the room where my loaded gun lay in full view on my bed.

'I will speak to the Brigadier, he will listen to me. We will put him in jail until he is sent to Colombo for his court-martial. Do not worry about it.'

'They've had a hard time of it in Omantai lately. He was afraid. People do silly things when they are afraid.' That's me, Devil's Advocate.

'He is an Officer. He should not have done or said such things. I will speak to Brigadier Denzil about it.'

The Tracker Captain had no such gentle feelings. The rest of the evening was spent talking Trackers and Jungle Operations. He was keen to know how their performance could be improved or enhanced with the use of Air Support. We talked on into the night about hot and cold insertions, cordon and search operations, covert drops and hot Cas-evacs.

We discussed the ways and means of making more helicopters available from the limited resources of the Sri Lankan Air Force (SLAF). We talked makeshift heli-pads and photo-reconnaissance. Anything and everything that concerned helicopters and Special Forces. Some time later that night we bid each other goodnight and went to our beds hoping that things would change for the better, and soon.

My next-door neighbour was a Major. We shared the washroom and toilet. For my part I kept it immaculate. My razor was always clean. Something to do with cleanliness and order, and self-imposed military discipline covering suppressed anxieties.

For his part he was the Brigade Major; Brigadier Denzil's right-hand man. He had a batman to look after his gear. We spoke rarely, and then only pleasantries in passing.

One evening there was a quiet knock on my door. The young Lieutenant from Omantai was still in the camp and my T56 lay loaded by my bed. Checking that it was right to hand, I finished the line I was writing in my letter home and opened the door carefully. My neighbour, the Major, stood at the door, smiling at me.

'Good evening, Sir, do come in, please. I was writing a letter home,' I explained, trying to cover the pause between his knock on the door and my answer.

'Thank you, Captain Smith.' Still smiling and nodding, he stepped into my room, carefully looking at my T56, which still lay loaded at my bedside. 'Tomorrow we are having a barbecue to celebrate a religious festival. We would like you to attend.' It was a gently placed order, almost an invitation, nonetheless an order. I felt it best to accept the invitation.

'Why, thank you. That's excellent. I'd be very pleased to join you,' I replied as graciously as I could. 'Tell me, Sir, what form of dress is expected?' Not that it really mattered, for I had very little in the way of uniform and even less in the way of tidy evening wear.

'You may wear something casual, civilian clothes. Long trousers would be expected. It will start about eight o'clock. The Brigadier will arrive at eight-thirty.'

I'd been given my orders. 'Yes, understood. That will be no problem. Thank you again.'

The Brigade Major took one more look at my running companion lying loaded on the floor and left. Moves were being made to ensure that I was socially accepted. A warning to other young bloods that they couldn't bugger about with the Whiteface pilot.

The next day was take it easy day. A day off; a day to get on with some housework. Women's stuff. Clean and oil my trusty running companion. Borrow an iron from somewhere and press my best, hell, my only pair of long trousers, and the only decent casual shirt that I had with me.

Around midday a young soldier from the resident company, unknown to me, knocked cautiously on my open door. I looked up inquiringly from my ironing.

'Captain,' he began nervously, 'I have a parcel for you.' His hands shook as he held out a brown paper parcel in front of him. About the size of a small loaf, it was tied with brown twine and leaking blood. No wonder he was nervous. Moving towards the door, I took it from him.

'Hmmm, thank you. Where did you get it from?' I asked him quietly, calmly, all the time thinking about the little shit Lieutenant from Omantai. I should have hit the little bugger at the time and taken his weapon off him right there and then. Ah, well, in hindsight we all have 20-20 vision.

'Captain, I do not know where it came from. I work in the mailroom,' stammered my little brown postman.

'Yes, okay, you can go now. Thank you.'

He left, trying hard not to hurry. Dumping the parcel on my writing table, I poked at it with my pocket-knife. Turning it over I found that it was addressed to me by name, Captain T. A. Smith, SLAF, Vavuniya. Sharpening my blade with a few strokes on the doorstep, I carefully cut the twine and eased away the paper. There was no doubt about it. It was a damned great lump of bloody flesh. Double-wrapped, there was a piece of bloodstained white writing paper between the layers of brown. 'Christ,' I thought, 'what's going on here?'

Easing the notepaper out between finger and thumb, I spread it on the table and read the scrawled writing. 'Tim, here is some fresh Spotted Deer meat that my butcher has prepared for you. You must ask the Mess Staff to cook it for you. Karunatilake.'

Relief washed over me. Thoughts of the threats and dire warnings dropped from me with a wry chuckle, which was soon replaced by a near manic-giggle. Moments later I was creased up in bouts of laughter until the tears rolled down my cheeks.

Brown paper packages tied up with string were delivered many times over the next few weeks. Each time it was something different. Peahen, guinea fowl, wild boar, spotted deer. Anything and everything that could be found and shot in the Sri Lankan jungle. Except tigers, of course.

The barbecue was a pleasant affair. What else would you expect of an Officers Mess on a tropical evening? Swaying palm trees whispering in a soft warm breeze, the quiet chatter of parakeets, and in the background some very restful Indian music. The only thing missing was some female company. A crying shame.

The Brigadier, when he arrived, was extremely polite and quiet-spoken, genteel; an altogether charming gentleman. In stopping to talk to me for a few minutes, he indicated to all and sundry that I was an accepted member of the Team in Vavuniya. The Brigade Major made a point of explaining that tonight was not the time to discuss military things, but would drop by the following evening to talk things over with me. Before they moved on he introduced me to a couple of chaps who appeared to be civilians. Certainly by their dress and bearing they were anything but soldiers. Puzzled by their presence at a vaguely formal Officers Mess function, I initially put them down as local civic dignitaries or even local newspaper reporters, and promptly forgot about them.

Billy and Arnold turned out to be the jokers in the pack. I bumped into them again the next evening on my way to supper.

Sat out on the veranda in front of their bunk with a cup of coffee, they were caught up in some discussion or other that involved frequent shouts of laughter. Aye, laughter, something that was rarely heard in any SL camp. They both went silent and looked up as I approached.

'Hello, Tim isn't it? Would you like to join us for a cup of coffee?'

That was the thinner one of the two. 'Generous,' I thought, 'why not?'

'Aye, thanks very much. I'll fetch a chair over.' Generous in thought maybe. I had for one giddy moment of madness imagined that one of them would put a kettle on or something like that.

'Waiter,' hollered the big one in imperious tones that would have had a Victorian maiden feeling for the buttons on her bodice. Like magic a Mess Waiter appeared at the end of the veranda. 'More coffee, and another cup,' he commanded, completely offhand.

Personally I had never got results by being polite to the Mess Waiters and had long since given up trying. These two had it down to a fine art. The waiter disappeared to fetch more coffee. Placing my chair, I sat down beside them. Billy and Arnold introduced themselves again.

'I am Alwis Feroze and this is Billy. We work on the tea plantations near Kegalla.'

They were both keenly interested in what I was doing there. Where did I live, did I have a family, what did I do at home? When it came to the bit about living on the north edge of the Pennines where I often went out shooting, their interest increased. In no time at all we were chattering away about shooting and fishing.

From being nosy buggers they suddenly became old friends. When it got round to me asking the questions, though, they weren't so forthcoming. As much as I could gather, they seemed to spend their time driving around the villages and towns of Anuradhapura District, drinking tea and eating. I thought it to be a particularly strange way of doing their annual patriotic bit as Army Reserve Officers.

They were a little tight-lipped and preferred to talk of other things. Before I left them to go to my bed that evening Billy and Arnold, as he preferred to be called, promised me an evening's entertainment the following day. Something to replace my daily run and equally as vigorous. All I could get out of them was that I was to meet them on the veranda at six-thirty. I was to wear something that would protect me from mosquitoes and provide some camouflage in the dark. It took me a long time to fall asleep. I lay awake for ages trying to work out what the hell Billy and Arnold got up to during the day.

After five months of mild mayhem in Jaffna and a month at home I really had felt out of it. Feelings of self-disgust had made me distance myself from society. In Vavuniya I began to feel accepted by those around me and had begun to allow myself to open out again, to rejoin whatever society there was there.

Whatever the Tigers got up to that following day, I was going to be back in Vavuniya for the planned entertainment. Tigers, they could go to hell.

Dumping the Trooper on the heli-pad inside the compound the following evening, I quickly signed down in the Technical Log and rushed back to my room. There was still some daylight left, time enough to get changed, have a fag and brew a coffee before things started. Stepping on to the veranda with my cup of coffee 20 minutes later, there was no sign of Billy and Arnold.

'Bugger,' I muttered to myself. I thought they'd left without me.

'Hello Tim, you are looking a little unhappy this evening.' The Tracker Captain had appeared from his room.

'Hiya, me old lad. I'm all right. I'm waiting for Billy to arrive.'

'He's been out today, he's been busy in Vavuniya.' That could have covered a multitude of sins. The question mark in my mind must have shown on my face. 'Billy and Feroze visit all the Tamil-speaking shops and cafés. They gather information for us.'

So that was it, Muppets. They just hung around doing nothing special. Sneaky-beakies.

'You see,' he went on, 'as Plantation Managers they are absolutely fluent in Tamil. All their tea-pluckers are Tamil, they have been for hundreds of years, since the British brought them over from Tamil Nadu.'

'Well, bugger me.' I'd wondered what they could be doing with the Army in Vavuniya. I couldn't think of much else to say so I settled back in my chair to finish my coffee and digest the latest bit of news. 'Uh, thanks, I'll sit and wait for them.'

Pulling out my fags, I lit one up and switched off the conversation. Brought over, sent over, forced over. What difference did it make? Whether it was Ireland, India or Ceylon, the old British Raj had done it again. The poor bloody, tea-plucking Tamils, like the Irish, were a displaced group fighting for survival.

I'd been having some nagging doubts about the entertainment, but this latest bit of information made them dissolve. Made them fade like farts in the wind. Anyone involved in work like that had to have some common sense. The evening might turn out all right after all.

The tropical night had started to squeeze its way between the buildings of the camp when Billy and Feroze appeared at the end of the veranda. Laden with weapons, they were followed by three Mess labourers carrying torches.

'We're sorry to be so late. We went straight to the Armoury to get the things we need. It will save some time. Are you ready?' Billy came shambling along the veranda with that confusing, mile-eating stride that some big people have. He thrust a single-barrelled shotgun into my hands. 'Not as good as your own perhaps, but it'll do.'

Another huge paw appeared out of his jacket. His big soft fist opened over my outstretched hand. 'We cannot get many cartridges in Sri Lanka. These are for you.' A good half-dozen Number Three cartridges dropped into my hand. Number Threes would knock big holes in a man at close quarters.

'You will not need your personal weapon. Leave it in your room.' Feroze had finally found time to say something. Stuffing the cartridges into my shirt pocket, I opened the shotgun and checked that the chamber was empty. The 30-inch barrel looked like it was fully choked and would throw a tight pattern at 50 yards. Murderous, especially with Number Threes. Closing it again, I slung it over my shoulder and followed them off the veranda and out into the camp.

'We must check out at the front gate,' Billy called back over his shoulder. 'The servants will help us later.' Billy hadn't stopped moving, or talking come to that, since they'd arrived.

Feroze strode along beside me. 'It will be a good evening for it.' He grinned in the gloom.

The three labourers clutched their torches and trotted along several paces behind us. What they were there for, I couldn't imagine.

Once clear of the main gate we turned right towards the town and followed the security fence along what had once been the airstrip's taxiway. It was now pitted and out of general use. Bushes and weeds grew out of the tarmac surface. Clearing the end of the runway, we set out across open grassland towards the lights of Vavuniya.

Very soon we came across the rear edge of a water reservoir; the tank that provided irrigation for the local rice paddies. The dark line of the dam at the front edge seemed to rise out of the ground to block out the lights of the town. We stopped there in the gloom to discuss the plan of action. At last I would find out what we were out there after.

'Tim, you go to the right and move into the water until you are close to the dam wall over there.' Billy pointed out over the water to a clump of bushes on the tank wall. 'There is a path along the top of it. No one should be on it. I will go down the middle, and Feroze will go left towards the town.'

I nodded my understanding.

'They should come from the West, just as it gets dark. Good luck.'

Billy turned away and moved into the dusk. Feroze and his man had already disappeared into the lengthening shadows. The soft, sort of hollow, metallic clunk of guns being loaded came to me through the closing darkness. It reminded me that all too soon things would start to happen. It was time for me to load up as well. I waded out towards the almost solid darkness of the dam wall. Close behind me came the soft, watery swish of my following servant.

The water lilies grew thicker and thicker around my ankles, slowing our progress until I thought that we wouldn't get into position in time. A furtive shadow moved along the dam wall in front of us. A darker shape against the deepening blue of the sky. I stopped, gun at the ready, rock still, I didn't want to get shot out there in the water. The shadows on the path faded. A villager on his way home, maybe. Maybe a figment of my imagination. Eventually, with the water just below my knees, we arrived at our position. With the dark bulk of the dam blotting out everything except the sunset I turned and squatted, waist-deep in the blood-warm water of the tank.

The sky seemed to be on fire. Pinks and oranges had turned to flame red and gold. The trees on our immediate horizon stood out stark and black, like the blackened grate of some celestial fireplace. Within minutes the fire died out and suddenly the tropical night was upon us. There was no sign of Billy or Feroze. Silence lay upon the water like a shroud.

My little brown man squatted on his haunches in the water beside me, his spaniel eyes ringed white in a brown face. A tingling expectancy ran down my spine. A shadow flickered on the extreme right of my vision, somewhere over towards Billy, and was gone as suddenly as it had appeared. A brief flurry of sound came on the soft warm breath of the light westerly wind.

Without thought my gun came up to my shoulder, the safety catch came off with a barely audible click that sounded to me like a door slamming in the darkness.

Out to the right Billy opened up, a bright flash and a bang. Another shadow flickered on the edge of my vision. Swinging to follow it, I squeezed the trigger. A dark shape was etched on my eyes in the muzzle flash; an inert darker patch against the dark sky. Lifeless, it dropped to fall with a splash in the water. My pulse thumped in my ears, blood boiled in my veins. Breaking the gun open, I fumbled another cartridge into the breach and swung the chamber shut. Another shadow flitted across the sky in front of me. Without thought the shotgun came up into my shoulder.

Over to my right Feroze and Billy were going through the same frantic sequence. Muzzle flashes ripped the darkness. Picking up another shadow I swung quickly, tracking smoothly, firing instinctively. Again, a shadow etched briefly on my eyes. Momentarily blinded, I listened. The silence rang in my ears, it was over.

Sat there, waiting elbow-deep in the water, I took time to look around me. The brass ends of four empty cartridge cases twinkled dully as they bobbed amongst the lily pads. Somewhere in the mad rush I had fired and reloaded four times. My man sat still beside, me clutching his torch to his chest like a shield. He grinned at me proudly, I smiled and nodded to him. Quickly he stood and sloshed his way into the darkness, his torch flickering briefly from time to time. Stuffing the empty cases into my shirt pocket, I rose and turned to follow him. Pointless really, for I hadn't a clue as to where our quarry had fallen.

For what seemed like several minutes I waited. The sound of splashing came from all around me. Still temporarily disoriented, I waited. A nagging doubt lurked in some dark and suspicious recess of my mind.

Shadows, darker shapes against the dark horizon, seemed to waver like reflections on moving water some distance in front of me. I tried to think it out. So, the dark bulk of the dam lay behind me. Okay, where were the lights of Vavuniya beyond it, to the north? Where was the dim glow of the camp security lights in front of us, to the south? The whole world was in darkness.

My man reappeared from the shadows, his teeth and eyes barely showing in the gloom. He'd obviously found what he'd gone out for.

We gathered in a huddle in the shallow water at the edge of the tank our three labourers in front of us. Arnold had called for a head count, and the labourers had held out our trophies. My man proudly produced two large plump duck-like birds.

'What are they then Billy? ... Arnold?' They were a totally unknown bird to me.

'Coots. Blue coots. They are Blue coots' said Billy.

'Well done, good shooting,' murmured Arnold.

For the rest of it our retrievers had brought back a couple of small local teal. I think Billy must have shot those, for Arnold had a sheepish look on his face.

'Time we went back.' Without waiting for comment, Billy set off boldly away from the tank.

Trees that only a short while ago had looked like the grate in a celestial fireplace now took on the attributes of secondary jungle. Our trip down to the tank had seen us making minor diversions to avoid a tangle of brush. Now we were taking major detours. We weren't lost. By no means were we lost, it was merely that the camp lights weren't where they were supposed to be. In fact there weren't any lights at all. Anyway, Billy seemed to be completely confident as he marched on through the darkness.

The sudden appearance of the security fence in front of us was as much a surprise to Billy as it was a shock to me. For me, because there were no lights on in the camp, and for Billy, because it was supposed to be some distance away to our left.

We stopped for a moment to discuss what to do next. It was apparent that the camp was on full alert. It was also obvious that we were armed and suspiciously dressed in anything but a uniform. 'Oh, bollockksss' I thought, 'we are as sure as shit going to get challenged and shot or put in jail.'

On the other hand, we were going to be extremely embarrassed trying to explain the whole thing away. Just what were we doing plodding around in the dark outside the camp, armed to the teeth, during a major alert?
Ah, well, when you're in the shit that deep you put on all your lights and plough on regardless. Which is exactly what we did. Taking the easy downhill option, we fed off to the right along the perimeter track and eventually found the overgrown taxiway. Chattering away to each other like schoolkids on a nature walk, we marched along. Full of confidence. Full of shit. I could hear the rattle of magazines being fitted, and the soft metallic click of safety catches coming off sounded like thunder to me.

Out of pure apprehension my scrotum had shrivelled to walnut size and was working hard towards pea size. We stopped some distance short of the main gate while Billy went forward to explain who we were. Me, the survival instinct went into overdrive; I made sure that there was at least one labourer between me and the nearest Sangar. Twenty minutes later we were sitting comfortably in the Officers Mess, listening in mock awe to the story of how the local Police Station had just recently come under attack. The Duty Constable in Vavuniya had switched off all the lights in the Station and had stood by to be overrun. The Duty Inspector had immediately called on the Army at Vavuniya Camp for support, only to find that they too were under attack.

It transpired that just about sunset the Tigers had opened up with at least three shotguns from somewhere out near the tank. Heavy-gauge pellets had rained down on the corrugated tin roofs of the camp like hailstones. I seemed to remember having a go at a couple of high birds.

Billy, Feroze and me sniggered quietly and uncontrollably to ourselves.

The Brigadier, taking an after, dinner coffee and cigarette, finally spoke. 'Tim, I think I should congratulate you on your evening's shooting. You seem to have had quite a large bag. Perhaps we can share it at supper tomorrow evening.'

'Certainly, Sir. It would be my pleasure,' I replied politely. Having been congratulated and receiving a mild bollocking in one go, I was quite happy to let it rest at that.

The following evening our Brigadier took great pleasure in a most splendid meal of roast duck.

Billy and Feroze promised that they would speak to Brigadier Denzil and try to arrange some time off for me before I left Sri Lanka and take me to their tea plantations around Negalle and Nuwara Eliya and show me some real shooting.

14

Fever, and Feverish Activity

Vavuniya stands halfway between Katunayaka and Jaffna. Unserviceable aircraft were, more often than not, changed out by the simple expedient of taking them to Katunayaka and getting it fixed while-you-wait. A sort of Quik-fit repair station. Unserviceable aircraft from KKS were brought to Vavuniya and exchanged for one of our fit ones.

The same applied to casualty evacuation. We often took casualties direct to the Military Hospital in Colombo and stayed overnight in Katunayaka. There was generally no pressing need to get back to Vavuniya. The good thing about it was that we were able to stock up on our dwindling supply of Whiteface goodies rather more easily than previously in Jaffna.

In early December a casualty from a Talladi convoy needed urgent surgery in Colombo. It was an opportunity to stock up on Christmas goodies. Just as well, really, for I didn't get a day off for well over a month after that. Even Christmas Day was spent thundering around the outstations, taking casualties from Mankulam, Mullaittivu and Puliyankulam to the Civil Hospital in Anuradhapura. There was no unspoken truce or cease-fire. There was no '*HeiligeNacht*' sung wistfully across 'no-man's land'.

Arriving at the instructors' bungalow on one such trip, I was surprised to find Greg back in residence. He looked like something out of Kuching Market. A reject from Belsen; he was a walking shadow, a ghost that breathed. He looked bloody awful.

'Hell's bells, Greg. What's up, what's wrong with you? Have you got the flu or something?' He was gaunt to the point of being emaciated. I was more than a little concerned.

'I've been away on the East Coast,' he mumbled, as if that were reason enough. 'I don't feel that well. I must have caught something while I was there.'

'Greg, have you seen a doctor? Have you spoken to the company about it?'

Greg shrugged his shoulders. He seemed almost lifeless in his movements.

Marching across the room, I picked up the phone. Riffling quickly through the sheets of hand-written numbers, I found the one we needed and called the office in town. No, as ever, Ken wasn't around to be contacted. Nor did they have a car available. When it came to their aviators, Keenie Meenie Services didn't appear to give a shit. If they really were playing mind games, then we were decidedly the social outgroup. They could send out letters exhorting us to look after our health whilst we lived eight yards from Froggy Pond at KKS. They couldn't give a shit whilst we were in town.

'Greg, what's the name of the hospital that we are supposed to use?' I demanded. 'You're going to see a doctor.'

An hour later I was pacing along the enclosed veranda of a private hospital in the residential district on the north edge of Colombo. It hadn't taken long to whistle up one of the local taxis that we used to go out drinking on the rare occasions when we were in town.

The staff nurse who had met us on arrival had been birdlike and efficient. The Matron in charge that day had been a bustling hive of activity and very positive about it all. The moment that she clapped eyes on Greg's skeletal form she had whisked him off into a side ward and called for a doctor.

Me? Well, she had hustled me out of the room onto the veranda and had all but commanded me to keep out of the way before she bustled off. Fearsome lady, I wasn't about to argue.

We chatted through the louvered door and windows whilst I had a cigarette and waited. One and a half cigarettes later the doctor arrived and disappeared into Greg's room. The door was firmly shut in my face.

A short time later the doctor re-emerged followed by the Matron, like a galleon in full sail. 'Mr Streater will stay with us for a while. I think he has Dengue fever. The doctor will confirm that in a short while'. She spoke in capital letters. She commanded, I listened. What else could I do? As a Dog of War I was just a pup, and anyway I'd never heard of Dengue fever.

'I'd appreciate it if you could call a taxi for me. I'll go and get his necessities from his room.' There was nothing more that I could do.

Dengue fever, an acute, short-lived feverish illness. A virus transmitted by mosquitoes. It depletes the red blood cells. He had got it on the East Coast. It was not all that he would get from the East Coast.

An hour and a half later I left him to the tender ministrations of the Matron and her staff nurse. He had his overnight gear, some books, and enough cigarettes to last him for a few days. I left for a night on the beer before going back upcountry. Christmas had come and gone almost unnoticed.

Almost a month had passed without a single day off. Greg was fit again and back at work somewhere. Gone were the days of Flying Instruction and lazy afternoons. As for me, I'd done well to make a good impression on the Army at Vavuniya. It was probably due to that 'good impression' that I was allowed some time off in Katunayaka, several days of it.

Kicking the bungalow door open, I shouldered my way through with my bags. Squince struggled up from an easy chair. Dropping my bags in a heap at my feet, I shook his outstretched hand.

'Hey, me old lad, how ya doin'? Certainly I was glad to see him again. 'How about we go out for a few beers?'

'I've been here for a few days, and I won't be leaving for a while yet.'

He looked really fit and happy enough. No bloody wonder. He was getting his wife out from the UK and was in the process of jacking up a rented bungalow on the outskirts of Negombo for them to live in.

'Christ, Squince, that'll slow you down a bit. It'll be like getting married again.'

What I wanted to say was that I was immediately concerned for their safety, living in Negombo while her husband was out at work. Work? Well, yes. Him, me, Greg, it was work. I shook myself mentally. 'Bollocks,' I thought, 'not my problem.'

Easy to think, perhaps, but I was concerned. There were enough Tamils in the area. Bloody hell, enough waiters and bar staff in the Blue Oceanic who knew what a day's work meant for us.

'We'll just have to have a stag party for you.' Typical stiff upper lip stuff that, very British. Change the subject and it'll go away.

Still, DB and Greg had brought their wives over for a holiday last summer. Ah, what the hell.

'Come on then, we'll stay at the Oceanic,' I suggested. A real lazy bastard, me. It meant I wouldn't have to unpack my overnight bag. Donald said nothing he just upped and ordered a taxi on the phone. He must have been in Katunayaka for some time, for he knew the number without even looking it up in the book.

Really, I don't know why or how I felt so at ease. Maybe it was because we'd been allowed a little time off. It was as if we were going out for the evening back home. Sort of natural that we should be there. The bar staff in the Blue Oceanic were not people to dance in attendance on us, just people we knew going about their daily business, just like us.

As soon as we had booked in and dumped our bags, we took off for the restaurant across the road for a beer and some grub. The place was like a morgue and we needed something a little livelier, like a nightclub, like Browns Bar.

Ten minutes later Squince was waving his Police Pass in front of him like a shield. He talked our way into Browns Bar without paying the entrance fee. 'We're from the uh, Drug Squad,' he muttered. It seemed to work a treat, for an hour or so. Then we were braced by an off-duty Detective. We left at a scamper through the toilet window and headed back to the restaurant.

We should have said Paedophile Squad, maybe we'd have been all right.

Giggling like a couple of schoolboys playing truant, we sat ourselves at a table on the roadside patio and ordered some more beers and a couple of standard blood-drained steaks.

We hadn't been there long when a slack handful of baby pilots, fresh out of the bag trainees from Air Lanka, pitched up. Somehow they knew who or what we were, and started praising our undoubted bravery and valorous deeds. The beers were already gone and we were on to Arak by then. Rocket fuel, brain-melting fluid. I was in no mood for a discussion on the subject of bravery and decided to read their tea leaves for then.

'If you guys think it's so bloody wonderful, why the hell don't you join the Air Force and have a go yourselves?' I muttered from behind a mouthful of steak.

'Captain, we are praising you for working for us,' piped up one of them.

'Young man, I'm on my day off. The hangar doors are firmly

shut. Now, why don't you fuck off and leave me in peace,' I spluttered from behind a mouthful of chips.

Some of the locals at the bar moved threateningly towards us.

'But you are helping us, helping Sri Lanka,' cried another. 'You are good men.'

Pushing my now-empty plate to one side I picked up my glass and downed it in one. This was going to turn nasty, and I didn't want to spill my drink.

'If you chaps think it's so fucking heroic, why don't you join up and take part in it instead of hiding in a civil airline like a bunch of fucking tarts?'

'You are not being very nice,' said another baby pilot. He was bloody right.

'Ahh, fuck off somewhere else son, and grow up. Just leave me in peace.'

The biggest one took a lunge across the table at me. Sheeit, but he was really angry. I think I must have upset him somehow.

What happened next I don't quite know. Squince probably stuck out a foot and tripped him up. The guys at the bar moved in. This, I knew, was going to be untidy.

In seconds there was a rolling heap of bodies on the patio that tumbled into the street. Surprisingly, the guys at the bar were taking our part. Being streetwise fighters, Rugged Jungle Fighters and Roughy Toughy Pilots, me and Squince took advantage of the melee in the shadows and sauntered off to the hotel. We left them there struggling in a heap and hitting each other for all they were worth. Aye, it was a grand feeling to be accepted as one of the locals.

Tuesday, 13 January 1987. Back in Vavuniya a couple of days later, I found that I'd been accepted there as well. I'd brought them a replacement Trooper from Kat. Down at the heli-pad the engineers had greeted me warmly. All the way up through the camp I'd been nodded at and helloed to like an old friend. The guard on the main gate gave half a wave, not sure if he should salute a Whiteface. The postman grinned, a young Subaltern smiled. 'Good afternoon.' Passing the side-gunners' billet, I was surprised with a chorus of 'Hello Captain'. I smiled and waved back.

It was great, like a dose of tonic it picked me up. Like a big wave breaking around me; it swept me along.

Later that evening as I sat cooling down after my daily run, the Brigade Major pulled up a chair and sat with me for a while. He gently quizzed me on my theories for helicopter operations. The very ideas that I'd discussed with the Tracker Captain. Obviously the word had got about that I had some different thoughts on the subject.

Hell's bells, it was only the sensible utilisation of resources. Standard Operating Procedures (SOPs). Nobody could ever put it down to me, and I didn't want him to.

The idea was simple. Each district had a couple of helicopters in support, enough for the daily grind of coconuts and cabbages but not enough for major or sustained operations. My answer was to borrow Gunships and Troopers from the other main outstations for a day or two and launch airborne cordon and search operations without warning on the Tiger strongholds and training camps. Simple, really. Rather than a lumbering three-day wind-up to the cordon and search of a village, we'd catch the buggers with their sarongs about their knees.

One could only hope that the aircraft would be up to it. After three years of constant use, the aircraft were beginning to show the strain. Chip Light warnings were becoming more frequent. Hydraulic system failures kept the engineers working all night. Rotor brake systems that stuck on were a pain in the arse that had to be investigated. Constant high-power operations were creating cracks in the superstructure that had to be fixed.

A huge crack had been found in one of the side-gun mounts on the Trooper that I'd brought back from Katunayaka. There was no replacement for it.

'Captain Smith, we have an operation in Kilinochchi today. You will fly the Trooper without the side-gun mount on the starboard side'.

That was Gagan, the Flight Lieutenant in charge of the Vavuniya detachment at the time. He really expected me to stumble around an operational area without a starboard side-gun. Bad enough to be kept in the dark. Even worse to do so without a side-gun. Roshan stood sheepishly at his shoulder. You could be sure that Gagan wouldn't fly it, and Roshan had obviously expressed his delight at flying any other aircraft. That left it to me.

Had it been Jaffna two months earlier, I would have told them to poke it up their arse in no uncertain terms. Now we were in

Vavuniya, and me an accepted part of the Army's team, Brigadier Denzil's team.

'No. No bloody way. The crew would be at risk, and so would the aircraft.'

'Tim, we need the Trooper for the Operation.' Roshan put in his bit. Knowing Roshan, he didn't want to get stuck with flying it if I refused to. It was time to accept the inevitable and adapt to the situation.

'The side-gunner can use a general-purpose machine gun.' Stunned silence and bog-eyed, querulous looks greeted my statement.

Positive thinking on my feet, hell's teeth, whatever next. Feeling very much alive to the situation, I was doing just that. Anyway, I didn't really want to be totally undefended on one side of the cab. The feeling was great. After seven months of being buggered around I was, at last, taking charge, in a small way, in control of the situation.

'He can use a rifle sling to secure it to his monkey harness in case he drops it'.

The side-gunner standing nearby looked from one to the other of us. He didn't know what to do for the best. Perhaps he sensed who had the upper hand. He looked at me for a moment longer than necessary. 'Go to the Armoury and draw up a GPMG and a rifle sling. Tell them that I sent you, tell them it's for the Operation at Kilinochchi today.' The gunner turned and looked at his Officers. Roshan nodded. The gunner grinned and left at a trot for the Armoury.

A couple of miles north of Kilinochchi stand a huddle of buildings at a crossroads. Intelligence led us to believe that the Tiger might be found hiding there. Intelligence, the sort of information that Billy and Feroze were picking up in the Tamil speaking shops, restaurants and bars around the Northern Province.

Air support for the Operation was brought up by the simple expedient of holding the daily re-supply Trooper from KKS on the heli-pad and bringing up the second Trooper from Vavuniya when the Army at Kilinochchi were ready to start. We were briefed in the air on the way up.

Immediately on arrival we picked up a Stop Group for insertion on the road going east out of the village. As soon as that was done we topped it up with the Search Party.

Tall trees surrounded the heli-pad at Kilinochchi and power lines on the approach made it a real bugger to get into and a real struggle to get out with a full load of armed troops on board. The turbulence created by two helicopters working at the same time made takeoff and landing extremely difficult. As the second to go, we struggled out of there with precious little to spare in terms of speed or power. There was really no time to be wasted if the Stop Group were to be inserted in strength. We elected to stay at low level for the short run-up to Paranthan. Thumping along at 100 feet above the rice paddies, we struggled to keep up with the lead Trooper. Down in the paddies, knee-deep in water, the workers looked up in fear and anger. One of them turned and ran along the mud walls towards a house in a small coconut grove nearby.

'Gunners, stand by.' Roshan looked across the cockpit at me in surprise. The rattle of weapons being brought to the ready came to me over the beat of the blades and the roar of the engines.

'What is it, what have you seen?' Roshan's querulous voice came on the intercom.

'There's activity in the rice paddies, Roshan. People running for no good reason.'

'Number two gunner, what's happening on your side?'

Number two gunner was the man without a gun mount; the gunner with the hand-held machine gun. I felt very vulnerable.

'A man has stopped running and is pointing at us. The others have disappeared.'

We had already gone well past the running field hands and were rapidly closing on the landing site, where Roger, some distance ahead of us, had started his descent and was flaring off speed to land. Too late to do anything about the pointing man. Pointing, pointing at what?

Ahead of us in the lead Trooper, Roger was already putting his skids down and taking his bloody time about it. He was also too far back on the small landing site that he had selected, and he'd left us with very little space to get down on. He would have to move quickly if we were to put in the Stop Group as one unit.

Still Roger fannied about, flying as perfectly as ever, but with very little thought of practical, tactical efficiency. I willed him to get a move on as we drew closer to the landing site – as we came ever closer to having to abort the landing and expose the soldiery in the back to another sweep over the agitated workers in the rice paddy. He must have read my mind. With seconds to spare, Roger lifted out of the way.

The troops he'd had on board were ambling about the landing site like they were on a bloody picnic. Until we went sliding through them, that is, then they jumped for cover.

Our own section of infanteers, properly briefed by our gunners, leapt for the cover of the surrounding bushes as soon as we had slid to a halt. We pulled pitch almost as soon as we had landed.

Swinging away from the site right-handed, away from Paranthan, we chased Roger back to Kilinochchi for the next load of troops. Coming abeam the house in the rice paddies, we took a small rattling of small arms fire from the area but had no time to waste on retaliation.

With our next load on board we backed up to the far end of the hard-packed and dusty landing site. In a storm of dust I pulled all the power we had available and struggled to get airborne.

Going back towards Paranthan we again stayed at low level and called on our number two gunner to stand by for an engagement from the house in the coconut grove as we went by. Somehow having the GPMG in his hands seemed to slow him down, for he had to ask what he should do when a crackle of gunfire came from our right.

'Shoot the bastard. Brace yourself against your monkey harness. Fire from the hip and watch the tracer rounds. Fire. Fire.' I didn't need the intercom as I shouted back at him.

The first tentative burst of fire came from the cabin, then a longer burst as our gunner got the idea. Looking back at the coconut grove, I watched in fascination as the tracer carved a flickering arc across the rice paddies to disappear into the house. 'Not bad,' I thought, 'not bad at all.'

The Search Group had started moving out towards the cross-roads in the middle of the village. From house to house they went, dashing from one garden to the next, taking cover where they could find it, searching each house as they came to it, and moving on until they came up against resistance. They were having problems getting past the village school. They had tried to outflank it but got pinned down. Unable to move any further, they called on us for help. We'd already lifted from the dusty heli-pad with yet another load of follow-up troops. Swinging out of our approach to the landing site, I set us up to bring down some fire on the school.

'Captain, where do I fire, what do I aim at?' Our number two gunner was still uneasy about his ability to use his hand-held machine gun.

'First, fire at the school playground. You will see the dust as the bullets strike the ground.'

'Yes, Captain.'

'When you are sure of your aim, fire into the buildings. That is where the terrorists are hiding.'

'Yes, Captain.'

A burst of fire rattled from the rear of the cabin. He was quickly gaining confidence with his new role. The whole burst, some 20 rounds of it, raised dust slap in the middle of the playground. There were no more questions as he hosed down the school buildings with more accuracy than I'd ever seen before.

That young man deserved a medal for his efforts. It couldn't have been that easy, built like a racing snake and hanging out there on the end of a monkey harness. Looking back on it, I should have had Roshan put him up for some sort of commendation. He certainly gained the respectful awe of the infantry section in the cabin that watched him at work.

Running back to Kilinochchi to stand easy and await further developments, we came across the man from the coconut grove again. This time he was on his pushbike, pedalling like mad for Paranthan. He wanted to join the party.

Without thought of what he was doing, I swung a tight orbit around him. Our number one side-gunner opened up on him without hesitation and blew him off his bike in a flailing, flopping rag-doll heap into the ditch. He really shouldn't have pissed me off earlier in the day. Another dead Tiger.

The Op went on. Search Groups from Kilinochchi, to the south, and those that we had inserted from the east eventually tied the Tiger down in the centre of the village. They had holed up for a last-ditch defence in some derelict factory buildings.

The Army called us in to try and locate them in the rambling maze of corrugated tin sheds. It was a near-impossible task. We ended up hosing down the whole area with machine-gun fire from the side-guns. All to no avail, for at the end they still popped up and harassed the Search Parties with hit-and-run sniper fire. Hard bastards.

Von Clausewitz had got that bit absolutely right. To come to

Mortar Kilinochchi

grips with the Tiger a lot of innocent civilians would have to die; the Sri Lankan Government would lose the moral and political edge. They already had. In a final effort to dislodge them, the Artillery were called in, and we were asked to observe and correct the fall of shot for them. Bugger the village, blow 'em away, literally.

We set ourselves up in a high and lazy figure-of-eight orbit to the north of Paranthan and called for ranging fire. This was going to be easy. This I could do.

'Hello Golf Two One, this is Charlie Hotel Five Three Seven. Fire mission Battery, over.'

Years had been spent practising this with the Air Corps. The map reference and the direction of fire were passed. Everything was ready to go. It really should have been a piece of cake. I'd watched the gun crews at work in Kilinochchi earlier in the day.

'Three guns in adjustment. At my command adjust fire, over.' I wanted three guns to be used, because seeing the fall of shot in the warren of tin sheds and shacks wasn't going to be easy.

'Fire, over.'

'Fire. Shot One Eight, out.'

Now that was a surprise. Shot One Eight. Time of flight 18

seconds. The gunners expected the shot to be in the air for 18 seconds.

'So where in hell is the gun position?' the thought scalded through my brain like a Vindaloo through a drunkard's arse. Holding our position, we looked intently into the target area. The rounds arrived smack on time, but some distance south of the target. No problem there.

'Add Four Hundred. Adjust fire, over.'

Too easy, the next lot would rip the village apart. Tiger, Tiger burning bright, yess, burn. The next salvo arrived smack on time again, but a further 400 metres to the south. Then I knew for sure then what had been bothering me since the initial call of 'Shot One Eight' had raised the hairs on the back of my neck.

The gun position was at Elephant Pass. The guns were firing from behind us. All those shells had merrily whistled their way through the same piece of airspace that we were sat in. Oh, shit. Why hadn't I bothered to double-check the co-ordinates of the gun position? Why didn't my ever so clever SL co-pilot tell me where it was?

'Drop Eight Hundred, fire for effect, out.'

Ah well, the next lot would arrive very shortly. Three rounds from each of the guns would fill the air over Paranthan with more aerial scrap metal than I cared to be a part of, and I really wouldn't want to be in those tin shed factory buildings when nine rounds of 105mm HE arrived. The Army could sort out the rest of it while we got to hell out of that busy patch of sky.

The clearing of Paranthan went on. God knows what they found when the Infantry finally cleared the crossroads.

Later that afternoon we were tasked to pick up the Stop Group to the west of the village. Namal had arrived at lunchtime to relieve the other crew, who were needed elsewhere. Good old Namal, proud and haughty as ever.

'I will lead the pick-up. You can follow us, we know where to go.' Namal strutted off to his Trooper with his co-pilot trotting along behind him. Something had definitely got up his arse.

Ten minutes later both machines were struggling skywards. At 4000 feet we levelled off and thumped our way towards the pick-up area, Namal leading some half a mile in front.

'We are going down.' Namal's voice on the radio broke the silence. It was great to let someone else take the lead, great to sit back and let someone else do the thinking and make the decisions.

'The pick-up point is on the south-west edge of the plantation in front of us.' Watching from behind, I was mildly surprised to see the Trooper drop into a high-speed spiral descent, just as I had shown him at Karainagar so many months before.

'This should be interesting,' I thought, and had to admire him as he went. A nice tight spiral and a good recovery at the bottom. At least he had learned something from our time together at KKS.

Dropping through the same piece of airspace, we levelled off some 400 yards behind and were preparing to land in tight formation for the pick-up when three tight little mushroom clouds of grey smoke appeared in the air across our front. Hmm, airburst grenades. Shit, it was time to be elsewhere, the Tigers had set this up very nicely.

'Overshooting, Namal, we're overshooting. Rolling left behind you.'

The adrenaline surge was tremendous. Fear clutched my gut like a dose of Froggy Pond skitters. Pulling away from the ground into a rapid full power climb, I turned to orbit the area, trying to identify the firing point. The bastards couldn't do this to me. A wave of cold rage swept over me, filled me with a deep impersonal hatred.

The Tactical Radio erupted in a flurry of babbling speech. Those useless buggers on the ground had called us into a killing zone and then wanted us to go back and fetch them out.

'Get on the Tac-radio and find out where those bloody Tigers are firing from.' No time for pleasantries, just orders. Bugger the Sri Lankans, they'd be the death of me if I didn't take charge.

Follow me he had said, follow me. Now the haughty little bastard was waiting around for me to take charge.

The guys on the ground were next to useless. They were unable to describe where the hostile fire was coming from. They couldn't decide on what was east or west, and in all probability were head-down and arse-up in a ditch somewhere inside the plantation. Certainly they had no intention of engaging the bastards responsible for their own plight, and had no thought of helping us to support them.

How could you help people like that? They were about as much use as a broken leg at an arse-kicking party. The radio erupted into another jabber of noise as the poor bloody infantry in the plantation realised that their pick-up was about to be postponed. From

1500 feet we rattled every possible firing point in the area with a dose of medicinal side-gun fire in an attempt to give Namal some cover for a pick-up. No way. No sooner did he get within a quarter mile of the pick-up point he came under heavy fire. Whoever was down there had enough 40mm airburst grenades and machine guns to make our lives a misery. In the end Namal decided that he had taken enough. 'We go back to Kilinochchi' he called on the radio, and we buggered off.

The Stop Group marched out unhindered the following day. For all the cock-ups, the operation was in many ways successful. It had proved that helicopter support could be drummed up quickly, that Stop Groups could be inserted swiftly and accurately before the Tigers could withdraw or respond, that artillery fire could be directed accurately onto hard points; once we knew where the gun position was of course.

It also meant that the hours that I'd spent talking to the Tracker Captain had meant something; someone was listening at last.

15

The Hunt Goes On

The Trackers had been dropped into the jungle on the edge of the Madu Elephant Sanctuary. They were out looking for Tigers. After several days of radio silence they checked in on HF (High Frequency Radio), requesting extraction. They'd made a successful contact the previous night. Their cover was blown, and it was time to get out.

There was no doubt that I was pleased to have been asked to fly the sortie. I'd been busy elsewhere for the insertion and had missed it, Roshan was down to fly with me, and as ever, he elected to fly in the co-pilot's seat, nothing new in that.

Leaving Vavuniya, we climbed to the normal cruise height and set off just as though we were going out to Talladi. Keep the bad guys guessing was the game. About ten kilometres short of the pick-up point we let down to low level and turned away from the standard track to follow a stream that led into the pick up point (PUP). Once settled along the river line, I let down even further. With the skids in the tree tops, we wound our way along the river until a tank, just beyond the PUP, came into sight. A Tracker stepped briefly out of the bushes, lifted his arms to indicate the LS, and stepped back into the bushes. It was enough.

Flaring into a quickstop, I flung the Trooper into the small clearing that the Trackers were using for an LS. It was tight, not only that they were under fire. I spot-turned the chopper until the tail was pointing at the tank and taxied into the bushes, where we were almost out of sight of the Tigers. The rattle of gunfire from immediately behind us increased as the Trackers laid down covering fire for us.

This wasn't an extraction, it was a Cas-evac. Why the bloody hell didn't anybody back at base think to tell us that much? Did they think I wouldn't go? They didn't want to go themselves, that was it, and they had applied the same thinking process to me that they applied to themselves. It's always the same. The bastards that don't trust themselves can't be trusted and, of course, don't trust anybody else.

The Trackers were worth working for. They were out there now, laying down covering fire for me while I did what they expected of me. That's the way it works. That's how I knew that the next thing would be a hot extraction for the rest of them. That's when I decided that I would be back to pick up the rest of them, no one else, me. Mind you, I didn't expect Roshan or Namal to volunteer for a hot extraction.

'Roshan, get on to the Tracker Lieutenant out there.' We would be doing more than our bit when we left the site. 'Wave him over here.'

Roshan looked at me strangely. He was probably having his doubts about flying with me, some doubts about my intentions. He did as he was asked.

'Ask him where the Tigers are firing from. Tell him we'll engage them on take-off. Tell him we'll do the same when we come back.'

Part of the team does all in their power for the rest of the team. That's the way it should work anyway.

Ken Who and his band of bastards back in Colombo should be seeing this. The bunch of dipshits in Jaffna should be seeing this. In that respect it was so much different than in KKS. In Jaffna there was no team. In Keenie Meenie Services there was no team.

'They are firing from the earth wall at the far end of the tank. They are using the tank wall as cover.'

'Well done, Roshan. Now brief the gunners. They will have little time to shoot at the Tigers, but I want them to do their best.'

Roshan's figure of eight nose roll was the best answer I would or could get.

The casualties were already being loaded and Roshan was chattering away in Sinhalese to the gunners. This would be a good departure.

Lifting into a hover, I pulled up until we were clear of the bushes surrounding us and then swung right, pointing the nose back down our approach path. The number two gunner opened as soon as he could see the far end of the tank, as soon as he could see the tank wall. We departed in a chatter of machine-gun music, leaving a trail of gunsmoke in our downwash.

An hour or so later we were back. Confident with the approach line, we poled into the LS somewhat quicker than before, but this time I held the Trooper a little higher as I swung round into the cover of the bushes. High enough to give the number one gunner a view of the tank wall before we sank out of sight to land. It was gratifying to hear him open up as soon as he could see the target.

'Blow the bastards away' I thought.

The Trackers were ready for us. No sooner had the skids touched down than they were boarding. Run in, turn, kneel, and rattle off a burst as the rest of the group recovered to do the same. Run in, turn kneel, rattle off a burst as their mates boarded. Me hollering at the number one gunner to cover them as the last few scrambled aboard, hollering at the number two gunner to 'Stand by, we're taking off. Fire when you see the target.' The sweating faces of the Trackers grinning at me as they clambered aboard with a quick thumbs up that said 'Nice one'.

Strangely enough, when the last wave came on board the firing stopped. A brief silence; an unexpected cessation. The sweating, grinning faces caught in freeze frame. Almost as if everything was going in slow motion. That adrenalin-pumping slow motion that comes just before the crash. Had I looked, I could have counted the blades as they went round.

The Trooper was swinging around, seeming to drift around in silence, it took forever, and then the number two gunner was firing, the spell was broken. The stream fled beneath us as we accelerated away. The gunner stopped firing as we levelled on the treetops and were lost from sight to the ground behind us.

The Trackers had been blooded. They had proved that such operations were viable. Ken Who and his boys had produced something worth having. What a crying bloody shame that he hadn't seen them at work with the aviators for whom he had so little time.

I saw it, in slow motion. In my mind's eye I still see the sweating, grinning faces and smile a quiet inward smile.

Somewhere in the depths of a Royal Mail Returned Letter Branch is a mass of my notes, made at the time on scraps of paper and sent home for safety, lost now forever. The notes are not necessary the remaining few months in Sri Lanka are etched on my memory.

Whether there were other Tracker groups at other bases I did not know. I preferred to think that ours was the only one. Whatever the truth might have been, I was proud to have been a small but integral part of the Trackers' success.

After that, Air-Ground Ops took a higher profile all over. Operations were mounted from other bases, and we were moved on a day-to-day basis to other Districts to provide helicopter support.

Although many hours were flown on Ops in Batticaloa and China Bay, they didn't seem to go off with the unqualified success that we'd had in Vavuniya. On one such 'one-day op' at Batticaloa I flew well over six hours, making insertions with Search Teams and shifting Stop Groups around, all high-pressure flying, coming under fire on a regular basis without even thinking about it. Day-to-day stuff, you know, normal.

With the SL habit of telling us a lot less than we needed to know, I never knew if an Op was a winner or just another Sri Lankan cock-up. Not that it mattered, the angry Whiteface from KKS of just a few months earlier would now turn on any target and brass it up unmercifully without further thought. I wasn't just part of the team, I was the team; not the 'I' of me, all of me submerged in the team. Something that Ken Bloody Who and his mind games rhetoric could never have achieved.

Only months before I had decried DB for being a gung-ho, lead-slinging asshole. Now, although the safety of the crew and the machine were always in the front of my mind, I was more than ready to take on any target that cared to pop its head over the parapet.

So, there we were then, yet another Op in China Bay. Was it just another Army fuck-up or was it not? Whatever, it dragged its weary self on into the night.

Landing on the heli-pads at China Bay just before dark, Roshan and me I walked up the hill to meet Greg and find out what was going on.

The camp was really picturesque. Eucalyptus and flame trees were scattered through the camp, their gnarled and twisted trunks and branches looking almost Chinese. Single-storey accommodation, bungalows with wooden verandas, clung to the steep hillside. Footpaths swung back and forth between them up the hill.

In a bungalow somewhere near the top I met Greg. He seemed distracted, but being Greg, he greeted me with his usual charming grin and contagious bonhomie.

'Smudger, me old lad. How y' doing?'

'Fine, Greg, fine. What's going on here then?'

'Ah, it's a fuck-up, Tim. They've been at it all day, now there's a patrol stuck up on the high ground north of here., They want us to fetch them out. They don't seem to realise that it's dark.' Greg had obviously had enough of the situation and was ready to chuck his hand in on the deal.

The Sri Lankan pilots weren't giving any lead in the affair and had left it to us to sort out. They seemed to think that we would dig them out of the shit as we had always done in the past. The only difference now was not only were we in the dark on the tactical front, it was also nighttime. We were totally in the dark.

An earlier attempt to extract the patrol had been beaten off by heavy ground fire from the Tigers. Now it was my turn.

There was virtually no briefing for the sortie. Just that we were going to pick up a patrol. How the hell we were supposed to do it over strange ground, I couldn't fathom. The Sri Lankan pilots had, as ever, buggered off to a briefing on their own and came back to the bungalow some time later.

Roshan was my man that night. His briefing was brief. 'We have to pick up a patrol that is stuck in the jungle,' he said, when I next met him an hour or so later. Stuck. Stuck with wounded, stuck lost, stuck under fire. Stuck what? Fucking brilliant briefing.

Down on the heli-pad a short time later, I cranked up Five Three Seven, still not knowing where we were going or what we were really doing when we got there. The sortie turned out to be a complete and utter farce.

Out over the high ground some time later, we located the patrol by the tracer rounds that lit the sky from their position. Orbiting to try and identify a landing site and pick them up, we came under some fairly heavy fire. Green tracer rounds arched into the sky from all around the patrol. Green fingers of light that reached out to try and stroke us from existence.

We retaliated, orbiting left and right. Red tracer going down, green tracer coming back up at us. It was utterly fucking stupid. We couldn't even see a landing site. It was black down there, black as the inside of a witch's hat. There wasn't a star in the sky, no moon; just a vast blanket of cloud.

Brief glimpses of the ground showed us a dusty grey ribbon of road going east to west. Equally brief glimpses of the map showed a bloody great big power line crossing it nearby. Smoking hole stuff, that. Tigers all over the place and a patrol that wouldn't or couldn't tell where they wanted us to land.

Every time we set up to land on the road, the patrol would chip in that we were in the wrong place. Every time we went somewhere else, we came under fire from the Tigers, red and green crisscrossing the sky as we hacked around trying to do something for the poor bloody infantry patrol stuck there on the high ground north of China Bay.

'Bollocks, Roshan. Bollocks to it. There is nothing we can do here.'

'You are right. We should go back.'

So we left them to it and went back to the camp with the flame trees and the winding paths going up the hill.

Somehow Roshan organised some sleeping space for the crew. We went our separate ways. With nothing better to do, I got my head down and slept for a couple of hours.

We left the next day, returning to Vavuniya. What happened to the patrol I don't know. What I do know is that Greg went out for them again.

What I found out later was that a charming gentleman, a friend of mine more used to the order of the classroom, more in tune with the training environment of Katunayaka, went out for them again in the dark. Immediately afterwards he suffered some sort of stroke and was later Medevaced back to the UK, having lost the use of his left side.

I had gone out and tried it. Me, by now something of a complete bloody headbanger, more used to coming under fire than most of them, I had tried and given it up for a bad job. Fear had crawled up my back and knotted my guts. Apprehension had tightened my scrotum to a peanut. It happened with every contact and I'd got used to it. What Greg must have felt I cannot imagine, but it pushed his system over the top.

But then the Sri Lankan Air Force had always found it hard to tell the Army that it was their own bucket of shit and to empty it as best they could.

Back in Vavuniya the situation was changing day by day. The Mad Major from Mankulam, my old Armoured Squadron friend, was promoted and posted to Talladi.

He moved in with his normal gusto and verve. In no time at all he had a trooper appointed as pig man and another as fish man. There was an unending supply of pork and smoked fish for the table. Anything above and beyond their own Mess needs was used to barter for fresh fruit and vegetables from the traders that went through the Vehicle Check Point (VCP) on the causeway just outside the camp.

The country around Talladi was more suited to armoured cars anyway, being flat and open. The Tigers would find their lives just a little trickier with Karunatilika around.

The airstrips at Mankulam and Mullaitivu were finished, and the new 18-seater Chinese STOL planes started lifting the load off the convoys. The question of how they were going to land 748s at Mankulam was answered.

Namal spotted a green van acting suspiciously on his way out to Talaimannar. He investigated it on the way back in the standard Namal manner. He went in low and close and not too fast. The Tigers responded by unleashing an RPG7 in his direction.

The missile struck a soldier sitting on the outside seat in the cabin and shattered his elbow. From there it struck the upright cabin post and severely bent it. Continuing on its way, it ricocheted inches in front of the number two gunner's face. Passing through the rear cabin wall, it destroyed the number two engine intake and lodged itself in the firewall between the engines. All that without an explosion.

The hero of the hour then flew back to Vavuniya on the remaining engine and landed safely. Well, that's what he was trained to do.

The engineers took off the cowlings to investigate the damage to the engine and found the missile lodged there in the firewall. They subsequently broke all previous records for the standing quarter mile.

Lucky, lucky boy. The safety pin was still in the damn thing. So lucky. What a shame that Greg wasn't so bloody lucky. For me, they could have taken the safety pin out and blown the bloodthirsty little 'ommming' Buddhist bastard away.

Operations took on greater importance. I found myself deeply involved, with no time to think of consequences, of the morality of things as I had in Jaffna. In Vavuniya I was so deeply involved, so much a part of the team.

Somehow Brigadier Denzil had managed to organise six

RPG7 Hole

RPG7 Damage (1)

Troopers for a cordon and search on a coastal village. They thundered in from their different bases just before sun-up. During the briefing the Troopers were refuelled and made ready by the engineers. Before dawn had crept over the horizon we got airborne and headed out into the sunrise. Daylight was just waking the village as we thundered out of the jungle at tree-top height and swung over the beach before turning in towards the village to land. A small lagoon stretched southwards behind the village, cutting it off from the jungle and any instant escape. It was a bad spot for a Tiger to spend the night.

Flashing across the beach, we streamed our six Troopers full of infantry into the village. They weren't Trackers, just ordinary soldiers. Sliding to a stop just yards behind the first Trooper, I bellowed like a bull to get them out and on the ground. The last man out had to jump. There was no way I was going to fuck around, pleading with them to get out. There were two more runs to do, and we needed to get back before they found themselves faced with more Tigers than they could handle.

Roger in the lead Trooper was flying as 'nicely' as ever and getting in the bloody way. We were already airborne by time he got back into the hover. We almost overtook him on the way out.

Timing was of the essence. Stoke 'em up with squaddies and then put in the Stop Groups. The Trackers were already out, forming a screen in the jungle. Anybody that escaped the village would have to cross the lagoon and make several miles in the jungle before they came up against them.

A short time later we slid to a stop in the same skid marks that we had left on the first landing and dumped another truckload of squaddies into the village. The side gunners had got the idea and chivvied them out onto the ground before they had a chance to say 'but'. The poor buggers didn't even know that there were 60 or so of their mates already out there, covering the second wave.

The Stop Groups were next, and so it went on. Moving them around like pawns on a chessboard, picking up a redundant group here and dropping them somewhere else, where they were needed.

Fairly late in the afternoon, we started going out to pick up the captured Tigers, rushing about in an attempt to get the job done before darkness tipped the scales the other way until darkness gave them the chance to slip away.

Hurtling into makeshift LS's on the edges of towns and villages

Tigers in the Back

to pick them up; using the main rotor blades to chop our way through bushes and small trees to make our own Landing Sites in places. Bound and blindfolded under armed guard, we brought them back to Vavuniya.

The engineers were goggle-eyed to see how close the tail rotor came to the ground in the mad-assed flaring quick stops that were used to get on the deck as quickly as possible. The tail rotor blades were covered in green stain from grass and weeds. The tail rotor's protective bar, the hockey stick, was covered in mud.

Royce was his usual petulant self and wanted to complain to the engineers that I had damaged the tail rotor. The smiles and laughs and rolling nose figures of eight from the engineers told him gently to bugger off.

The whole bloody operation had been brilliant. It was an opportunity to shine, and shine we did, like a bloody beacon.

'Bugger you Ken Who, bugger the Tigers, bugger them all.'

During that hectic period I gave no thought as to whether or not I was doing the right thing, nary a thought as to the morality of it all. My reluctance of only three months before had disappeared, dissipated like a fart in the breeze, like piss in the ocean.

After two straight months of operational flying, it was time for a break. I'd been given a few days off. Billy had already arranged to

Nuwara Eliya

have me met at the Taj Samudra and driven up to the Pittakande Tea Plantation at Mawatagama.

There was a minor cock-up in meeting Billy at the Taj. For a while I fretted, believing that the whole trip would never come off. Eventually it was his wife, Jennifer, who turned up after a day of shopping in town. Loading my gear in the back of a bloody great big 4WD truck, we set off up into the Central Highlands.

It was a wonderful experience. A tremendous tour through some of the most stunning scenery I've ever seen. At Nurawa Eliya we stopped briefly and bought something to nibble on. Who would ever have thought that chillied cadju (cashew) nuts could taste so good?

As night fell we left the main road and took a rutted and potholed track through steep-sided valleys up onto the estate. Clinging to the hillside, the track was like a switchback. One moment the headlights were lost in the undergrowth, the next they picked out the low clouds that hung in the trees on the valley sides. Mountain streams crossed over the road in places, in others under rickety bridges that I doubted would last much longer.

Eventually we drove up out of the gorge-like valley and onto the

The central highlands near Nuwara Eliya

hilltop. Out on the end of the hill was Billy's bungalow. Built there many years before by the British to make the most of the cool air moving up and down the valley, it commanded an absolutely staggering view. Inside it was all parquet floors, with ceiling fans chugging softly in the gloom.

Arnold had already arrived with Valerie, his wife. Dinner would be served quite soon due to our late arrival. I washed and cleaned my teeth, changing quickly into a fresh shirt and slacks.

Maybe that's why the whisky and water didn't taste as it should have. Either that, or maybe the water up there had a taste of its own. It didn't matter, for it was bloody wonderful to sit down to dinner with the four of them, knowing that tomorrow wouldn't bring another day of coconuts and Cas-evacs.

At five o'clock the next morning Billy's HouseBoy brought me tea. Before the sun had cracked the dark of night, we were loaded up and ready to go. I'd been presented with a magnificent side-by-side for the day. A Churchill, one of a boxed, handcrafted pair, made many years before.

'Here are some cartridges for you, Tim.' Billy handed over half a dozen cartridges, one of which was decidedly a home-loaded solid shot; through a Churchill! 'The solid shot you put in the second barrel for emergencies,' he explained with a smile.

'What's it for, elephants?' I asked, stuffing the cartridges into my pocket.

'You will see, maybe,' he replied with one of his broad smiles.

Some time later we met up with the rest of the party and set off on our first drive. Although I'd had the opportunity to go for wild boar in Germany, I had never been able to fit it around my duties. It would be a whole new experience.

The feeling of friendship, of easy-going camaraderie, was really quite something else. The beaters were all Tamils. Plantation workers, young and old, led by a stately old chap that had known Billy since he was a boy. The dogs were a pack of mongrels that, had I seen them on the street, I would normally have given a wide berth.

The first stand was in open ground above a grove of eucalyptus trees. Fortunately we drew a blank, for I could only stand there in wonderment at the scenery, at the sunshine striking off the piebald bark of the eucalyptus, the leaves fluttering dark and bright in the early morning breeze, against a backdrop of vertiginous hillside. I could only stand there and wonder what sort of life one could expect there without the troubles of Jaffna and the East Coast.

The first stand

We moved on foot to a second stand, slightly off the shoulder of the hill. Standing in the cool dappled shadows of a winding track, where I had been placed as the most advantageous spot for the drive, I was almost lost in reverie when the sound of crashing came from the undergrowth down the hill to my front.

Not knowing what to expect, I slid the safety off and watched my front. A couple of young wild boar suddenly broke out of the undergrowth. Seeing me on the track, they both broke to my right and were gone so quickly that I could only stand open-mouthed in amazement at their speed and agility.

'Bollocks, you really buggered that one,' I muttered to myself quite disgusted that I'd not even got the gun into my shoulder.

Another thrashing in the scrub brought the gun into my shoulder, pointing to where the first two had broken out. Faster than I'd thought possible, yet another young boar had appeared and turned away. Swinging fast, I'd almost caught up with the little bugger when it turned again and cleared the bank onto the track in a prodigious leap, and was gone as quickly as the first two.

The game cart

About to lower my 12 bore in a fit of self-disgust, a flicker of movement caught my left eye. Instinctively I aimed, tracked, and fired as the little bugger leapt the bank and cleared the track. 'Bugger, bugger, bugger,' I hissed at myself feeling sure that I'd caught it square. However, it had still charged on up the bank and out of sight, seemingly regardless.

Walking out into the open a few minutes later, I was astounded to find that I had indeed caught it square on. The beaters had found it on the edge of the trees, stone dead. There was a great slapping of backs and shaking of hands. There was also a great deal of piss-taking about the size of it – about as big as a full-grown labrador. I didn't think it that small and was really pleased with myself. The beaters were chuffed anyway, for it would supplement their diet for a day or so. What I couldn't fathom was the need for a solid shot up the second barrel 'for emergencies'.

'Ah, what the hell,' I thought, 'maybe it's for Tigers.'

The final drive that day was on the edge of a tea plantation where a big old boar had been bothering the tea-pluckers for some time. The tea bushes grow together at the top and cover the ground

My Final Tally

completely, leaving cool and shaded tunnels beneath. The tea-pluckers wade through this sea of green without being able to see what's going on about their ankles. A bad-tempered, territorial old boar doesn't come high on their list of recommended toe-nibbling friends.

At the top of the hill was an area of scrub where it was thought he would be lying up. The remainder of the guns were lined out facing the scrub, whilst I was sent off down the hill behind a chain link fence 'just in case he went that way'. Actually, I'd had my shot for the day and would give over the best spot for the others.

Stood kicking my heels, waiting for the drive to start, I decided to open a gate and go through to the other side of the fence for a better shot should it be necessary. Several minutes later I heard a veritable fusillade of shots, certainly a couple of 12-bore and one high velocity.

'That'll be Arnold or Billy,' I thought, as I gazed idly up the hillside towards where they were. They both carried re-chambered .303 Lee Enfields.

Suddenly the bushes in front of me started waving about furiously. The line of jiggling branches moved quite quickly towards a gap where a footpath passed through the scrub. Although still a hundred yards away, I was on guard. Just as well really, for a boar the size of a donkey came charging along the path and disappeared back into the bushes considerably closer to me.

'Bugger me,' I mused, 'that sod will come up against the chain link fence and me very soon.' I legged it, lickety spit, for the gate, putting the chain link fence between me and it. I didn't see it again and was quite pleased, for I felt that one solid shot 'for emergencies' would hardly stop such an enormous and decidedly pissed-off pig.

Talking about it a few minutes later, I discovered that the monster had broken from the scrub at the top of the hill and found itself confronted by Sam, Billy, and Arnold. Definitely unhappy about being disturbed, it had charged Arnold, who managed, by a magnificent feat of acrobatics, to leap in the air and shoot it at the same time. Unfortunately he didn't leap high enough. Well, the bloody thing stood at least three-foot high at the shoulder. Struck on the left shin, Arnold was knocked arse over head onto the ground and was unable to partake in any further action. Sam gave

Billy and his ghillie

it one barrel before it disappeared back into the brush in my direction.

Maybe I was right to put the fence between me and it. Having been hit twice, it was still going like a train when I saw it. I can't admit having ever seen anything that displayed so much raw power, and was secretly glad that I hadn't see it any closer than I did. I certainly knew what 'for emergencies' meant.

We tracked that old boar down the hillside for some while, but were unable to find more than the occasional splash of fresh blood to show that it had been that way. In the end we gave up and left it there somewhere, licking its wounds, hoping that the tea-pluckers wouldn't be unfortunate enough to come across it in the next few days.

Supper that evening was a jovial affair, full of male ego, whisky and succulent wild boar. During the whole time I had hardly thought of how I came to be there. The friendship of Billy and Arnold was such that I truly felt a part of it all.

All too soon it was time to put my head down; the trip back to reality would start at five the next morning. The trip down the hill was spent in virtual silence as I took in all that I'd missed on the way up just two days before in the dark.

That night was spent in the Taj. Out of boredom I sank a few whiskies and wondered why the hell I ever bothered to come down off the hill. My chuff chart said 32 days to go. None of them would be as good as the last two had been. Still, I had some photographs to remind me of them in the future.

16

Lucky Thirteen?

Walking up through the camp at Vavuniya again it was obvious that I'd become part of the scenery. The nods and waves I got were still very friendly, but not the joyous greeting I'd received on my last return.

There had been talk of the Indian Army moving onto the Jaffna Peninsula as a peacekeeping force. There had also been mutterings among the Whitefaces of an improvement in the accuracy of the Tamils' shooting. We had often wondered when the Tamils would bring in their own Whitefaces, their own 'military advisors'. My feelings were that they already had.

Chris E was now the KKS man. I hoped that he'd come out in one piece.

Morose and moody, I spent my time counting down on the days to do on my chuff chart. Evening runs went by with the grim determination to fill in some time, just to finish another day. Maybe my attitude showed. Certainly my role had changed. More and more often I seemed to be involved in Cas-evac and air tests.

Possibly somebody somewhere felt that I'd done enough with the Trackers and the development on the aerial ops side of things; perhaps it was time for someone else to take the lead. Whatever the case, I was happy to trundle up and down the line and take casualties to the hospitals in Anuradhapura and Colombo. At least that's what I thought. Having dealt out so much death and destruction over the last eleven months, to see the results in close-up so often brought a tremendous sadness over me. So many bodybags. So many young lives, on both sides.

How many sucking chest wounds? How often had I looked back into the cabin to see thighbones sticking out of young flesh? How often had I looked back into eyes wide open in death? Up and down the line to the hospitals in Colombo and Anuradhapura, and back again with more the next day, and the next.

Out to China Bay to watch green tracer rounds flicker through the night sky once more and swap them, in the crack, rattle and slap of machine-gun fencing, red tracer for green. The following day we would take the wounded to a well-practiced emergency ward in Anuradhapura.

Even as I write this I can feel the tightening in my chest and taste the bitter thickness in my throat. I'd been into Anuradhapura with wounded three times that day and taken more into Colombo. I wanted out. Twenty-eight days to do.

My trip up to the tea plantations had been a mistake; too much contrast, so many shades of grey. People, families at home, enjoying a normal home life. It made me realise that when Roger or Roshan, or any of the local pilots, disappeared for a few days, they went home; home to their wives and families. Three weeks on and one week off. They had a reason for fighting this crummy action. They were fighting for their country and their people. Me, well I was fighting the sodding taxman, for a bloody hole in my roof, where the rain came in. Tell that to some kid's mother as he is finally laid to rest. Tell her he died for a hole in some Englishman's roof; he died because of the British Government's vague idea of political influence in the region.

The last few days passed in a dreamlike state. Up and down the line of Route 9, changing out the poor bloody infantry on R&R. Trying to keep things tight, but not quite managing it. Trying to maintain the façade of being the switched-on cookie that I was supposed to be.

Going in and out of the LS at Kokavil had always been a tricky affair. The site was really too small. The supporting stays for the transmitter mast got in the way. Because they were 'way out on a limb' we always carried the maximum possible load.

How we didn't fly into those stays during that last fortnight I don't know. We fluttered in and out of there like a pre-Christmas turkey. In fact we probably would have done better with a couple of pounds of chestnut stuffing up my arse. Had the Tigers been prowling under the take-off path, they'd have taken us out for sure. Basically we were too heavy, there was always too much fuel on board for the load we had to carry.

Again, out at Talladi I allowed myself to be diverted, literally and mentally. I stayed too long trying to help the Armoured Squadron out of a hole during a local VCP Op. I'd taken part in similar Ops in NI. We'd called them Operation Canister then, after the shotgun-like 20-pounder canister round used by the Armoured Corps.

The armoured cars were out on a mobile road block operation around Pallamadu and Kaliyadi along the coast to the north. They'd taken some casualties and, rather than wait for them to be brought in, we went out to fetch them.

We stayed well beyond our return time. When we finally left for Vavuniya we were well into our fuel reserve. The last 15 miles were spent in a long shallow dive to get back to base with more than fumes in the tank. Cursing myself for a bloody fool, we thundered on at tree-top height directly over the spot where Namal had picked up an RPG7 in his number two engine. Like a pheasant at a driven shoot. Fortunately for us, the 'guns' were engaged elsewhere.

So March staggered into April. I continued to run in the evenings and was physically quite fit. Skin, bone, cartilage and muscle. Mentally I was totally shot out, blown away, in bits. Flakey. Arak was easy enough to get hold of in the Officers Mess. Before coming away from Colombo the last time round I'd bought two cartons of wine. They were both gone. Not an alky; just a bit flakey. I was ready for out.

When Roger knocked on my door at three-thirty in the morning on 1 April, he politely asked if I wouldn't mind going up to KKS. I thought that he was joking, April Fools Day and all that.

'Piss off Roger, I'm going home in eight days.'

I didn't even bother to lift my head off the pillow. Roger left without arguing. Who went in my place? I don't know.

The very next day, 2 April, Namal and Chris E were flying top-cover for the morning re-supply plane's arrival at KKS. They came under heavy fire from a 12.7mm heavy machine gun and sustained some serious damage. The early Avro 748 was also hit hard. They lost one passenger, and another was severely wounded. April Fool? No doubt now as to whether or not the Tigers had help. Things don't improve overnight unless you bring in professionals.

Well, Namal never was any good on top-cover, but more to the point the Tigers had hit them both. I was seriously convinced that the LTTE had at last found some outside help. Whiteface, eh! Military advisors, maybe. They are decried as mercenaries in polite circles and treated like shit by established governments.

The great problem was that there were so few people in authority that would listen to a Whiteface theory. In Vavuniya we had been extremely fortunate to have Brigadier Denzil and the Trackers.

In Jaffna there was, and probably still is, a prime case to use surveillance helicopters. A couple of Jet Rangers would have done the trick. Sat at 3000 or 4000 feet over the city, they could have kept an eye on the whole of the north-west end of the Peninsula with a pair of stabilised binoculars and kept a watchful eye on the Tigers as they prowled the undergrowth. With the right radio link to Headquarters, all movement around Jaffna and KKS could have been monitored and acted on where necessary.

But no, the Whitefaces were spread out as thinly as possible to supplement the complete dickheads they called operational pilots. The Namals and the Royces, the Rogers and Roshans, the operational pilots who should have been in padded cells, short trousers, basic training establishments or a school classroom, in any order.

On 6 April I flew my last operational sorties in Sri Lanka. I wasn't sad to give a one-fingered salute to each outstation as I went by.

Mullaitivu, where a soldier had died to capture oil paintings. Just to the north, the hospital at Puthukkudiyiruppu and my first Dust-off with Roshan. Further north along the coast to Chundikulam, where a fast-boat had burned like a funeral pyre. Odduchudan, Mankulam and the Mad Major. Talladi and Iluppaikkadavai. Coming home with vapours in the fuel tank. Uyilankulam and the Madu Road. Cold, hot and covert insertions. Dust-off, night or day and hot extractions. Not sad to see them go, not one bit. Sad though, almost angry, that in many cases it had all been one self-imposed and self-generated fuck-up after another.

That evening I didn't run. As ever, I didn't know what was happening the next day. What I did know was that soon I would be on my way home. Most of my gear was packed, only the operational stuff remained ready for use.

When Brigadier Denzil wished me 'good luck in the future' at supper, I knew I was leaving the next day. Karunatilaka, the Mad Major, was in Vavuniya for some meeting or other and wished me the best. 'Tim, here is my address in Colombo. Come and stay for an evening, have supper with us.' As ever, his eyes had twinkled as he spoke. 'Call my wife at home, and she will send our driver to fetch you.'

His handshake was as firm and his voice as friendly as it had always been. I knew that I would not take him up on the offer. He would have talked me into a second tour over a good bottle of port.

'I'll give you a call when I've finished at the office.' I lied, through my teeth I'd lied.

My desire to get out of that place was only exceeded by my lack of understanding. Lack of understanding that my thoughts, my memories, would remain with me wherever I went.

Four days to go. My chuff chart had a big zero around Saturday 11 April 1987.

Climbing aboard the 748, I felt a surge of relief. There was no one to see me off. Nobody to wave goodbye. There were no thoughts of 'at last' or 'thank heaven', just an indescribable feeling of relief.

At Ratamalana I was surprised to be met by a driver from 4 Squadron. 'Unusually well organised,' I thought, but then was not surprised to find out that he'd been there to deliver someone else and had recognised me as he was walking out.

It came as no surprise that the company didn't know I was arriving.

The bungalow was a complete and utter pigsty. There had been no one in residence to keep it even half-tidy. Greg had been in a UK hospital the past month. Squince had moved into a rented bungalow in Negombo with his wife weeks before.

My dreams of sitting on the veranda with a tall cool glass had never come to fruition. I had no desire to stay there a minute longer than I had to.

The following day I handed in my gear at the Quartermaster's Stores.

'Vests, PT, Red, One.'

'Yeah, here they are.' God, but it took me back to my days in the mob.

'Shoes, PT, Pairs, One.'

'Yep, never used 'em.'

'Complete with laces. There are supposed to be two laces, there is only one.' The storeman was adamant.

'Jesus fuckin' Christ, it's only a fuckin' lace.'

'Complete with laces,' chanted the storeman again. Ducking

below the counter, I took a lace out of my desert boots. Standing again, I folded it neatly and laid it on the counter.

'It does not match the other one. It is not a pair.'

Ducking again, I removed the other lace from my desert boots and laid it on the counter alongside its mate. 'Complete with laces, one fuckin' pair,' I growled, and gave him a look that would normally have frightened small children. He smiled and put them with the plimsolls.

In the pursuit of peace I'd left well over a 150 bodies littered around northern Sri Lanka, and the fucking storeman wanted a matching pair of laces.

Slap, slap, slapping my way through the camp with no laces in my shoes, I headed for the Armoury.

'T56, One. Cleaning Kit, One. Magazines, Four. One hundred and twenty rounds.'

'One, two, three, four, five,'

Ten minutes later I was all but complete.

'Vests, Protective, One.'

'What?'

'Flak jacket, Captain, your flak jacket.'

'Oh, yeah. Sorry, me old lad, I handed it in at the Squadron Stores last November.'

'No problem, Captain.'

That bit was too easy, I'd finished, done it, no problem even. Well, time enough to get downtown to the company Office in Kollupitiya and collect my ticket for the big silver bird to UK. There was also the matter of last month's expenses to collect and, before I broke my neck slapping around, a pair of laces for my desert boots.

Resplendent with my new matching laces purchased in the shack by the railway crossing and my air ticket in my wallet, the rest of that day was devoted to spending my expenses shopping for souvenirs in the Fort. I was being a bloody tourist.

By eight o'clock that evening I had fed and watered and was propping up the bar in the Taj when the public address system broke my half-pissed reverie.

'Would Captain Smeeth please come to reception. Captain Smeeth to reception, please.'

Ambling through to reception a couple of minutes later I was surprised to see Kapila waiting for me.

'Hullo Kapila, what the hell are you doing here?'

'Tim. Hi, I've just come from Headquarters around the corner. There is a problem with your Flak Jacket.'

Kapila was one of the few that had ever had the courage or grace to use my first name.

'Kapila, I handed it in to the Squadron Stores at Katunayaka when I went on leave last November. You know I haven't worn a flak jacket since last summer. You've seen me.'

'It cannot be found. They say you will not be permitted to leave the country until it is found.' Kapila's tone was sympathetic, but there was no doubting the seriousness of his message. They would not allow me to leave.

I had three days to sort it out. 'Bugger. Bollocks and double bollocks,' I thought.

'Ah, Kapila. I have only my overnight bag here. Tomorrow I am going to stay at the Blue Oceanic. All my gear is at the bungalow, packed ready to go home. You can look in that if you want, I don't really need a flak jacket for a souvenir.'

'I know, Tim. I will do what I can.'

'Yeah, come to my room. You can look in my bag here.'

Ten minutes later Kapila returned to Headquarters. Having looked at my tiny overnight bag, he left without bothering to look inside it. He at least trusted me. Totally depressed, I returned to the bar and finished the job of getting pissed. It could have been six months back, mood swings, up and down like a bloody yo-yo. Foul-tempered and blackhearted, I propped myself against the bar like an unexploded bomb.

In my room two hours later I was about to hit the sack when a knock at the door had me wondering what the hell was going on. It was Roger this time, in uniform.

'Hi, Roger. Come in. What can I do for you?'

'Headquarters has decided that you can go. You may leave the country.'

The relief was wonderful. I had thought that he'd come to arrest me, or some such.

'Great, Roger. Thanks very much. I shall see you at the Squadron tomorrow, maybe.'

'No, I'm at Headquarters for a few days. See you.' He turned and left.

No explanations, nothing. I reckon that they must have sent

someone to the bungalow and searched through my bags as soon as Kapila had got back to the office two hours before. Ah, what the hell. I was cleared; I was free to go.

The following day saw me moving in to the Blue Oceanic. It was cheaper and closer to the airport. I'd gathered my bags from the bungalow on the way. I was ready for the off. Just one more night to waste away. What the hell could I do to fill the time?

A coach had just dumped a load of tourists in the hotel foyer. 'Yes,' I thought, 'maybe pick up a piece of white beaver tonight.'

The rest of the day was spent wandering around Negombo. A beer here and another one there, just killing time. Supper in the restaurant across the road and a gentle wander back to the Oceanic to see what was going on.

The sound of music met me in the street. 'Yes, yesss, beaver hunting time,' I grinned to myself. The restaurant was packed. German tourists filled every table. '*Wunderschon. Vielen dank*, Kuoni Tours.'

As casually as possible when your balls are aching fit to burst, I wandered towards the darkened dance hall. The floor was mobbed, women all over the place, gently jigging away to the local version of James Last. Light summery dresses, clinging in seductive shadows to waists and thighs, cleavages, bosoms and bums. All moving alluringly in the dim dance floor light. Moving in closer, I scanned the crowd for a target. The hunter moving in for the kill.

The music stopped, the lights went up and my eyes fell out. Every one of them was at least fifty, every one of them a grey-haired German Frau.

'Bollocks, it's grab-a-granny night.'

Thoroughly disgusted with the situation, I buggered off back to the bar and spent the remainder of the night throwing VSOA down my throat and hoping on hope that the lovely Erika of a year ago would appear at my side and take me away from it all. I went to bed alone and totally drunk.

Breakfast was taken late and did nothing for the rocking hangover that pounded in my skull like a pod-gun. Grabbing up my gear, I booked out and headed for the Airport Garden Hotel. One step closer to departure, and maybe I'd find something there to ease my loins. For some unknown reason I felt as randy as a butcher's dog. Maybe I shouldn't have been so choosy at the Blue Oceanic.

Lunch was late, liquid and spread into supper. My final fling in Sri Lanka had been flung, all to no avail. No backslapping farewells, no uproarious last night on the town.

That last weekend was a load of shite. From 'Complete with laces, pairs one', through to 'They won't allow you to leave the country', and onwards and upwards to 'grab-a-granny night'. The whole weekend was nothing worth remembering, but strangely enough I remember it well.

At nine-thirty I called for a taxi and dragged my alcohol-soaked and unhappy self to the airport. This time I was more than ready for the dry bar in the departure lounge. My camera bag held a mini travelling bar, complete with plastic beakers to drink from. Sadly there were no bimbos to watch this time. Nothing to distract me whilst I waited for the one a.m. departure.

Nothing but a head full of memories that crowd in on me whenever my back is turned, whenever I've had a few jars and my guard is down. No, I wouldn't be back, I wouldn't ever need to go back, for I carry it with me wherever I go.

Epilogue

On my return it was planned to take three months out. Then suddenly, within a few weeks of getting back a friend needed a helping hand. It was a godsend really. By the end of May I was flying the gas pipelines in the North of England and Scotland. The pay wasn't spectacular, but the job was excellent therapy. Thumping along at 300 feet and 80 miles an hour, there was nothing to think of but the kilometres of gas pipe line rolling out behind and the next fuel stop ahead.

Away in Scotland I didn't have to suffer the atmosphere at home, the almost tangible air of antagonism between my wife and my son. During the evenings in bed and breakfast, I had no time to reflect on the past. I was too busy studying the weather and planning how we would tackle the next day's quota of pipeline.

The shorter week in the North of England meant I was at home from Wednesday night to the following Monday morning, when the whole process started all over again. Those days were spent walking the hillsides at Robert and Anna's, or out shooting pigeons. Unfortunately the evenings gave me the time to reflect on the past, time for morbid introspection. I looked forward to Monday morning, when I could escape from it all again.

Fortune was on my side with my choice of Aviation Medical Examiner, Dr Pat Honeyman. On my return to the UK I was due for my annual Aviation Medical Examination. I walked out of the surgery not knowing how lucky I was to have that Medical Certificate in my hand. The Medical Certificate is an integral part of a Flying Licence, without it the Licence is not valid. It was only on my next visit to his surgery, a year later, that I realised just how flaky I had been on the previous occasion, how emotionally unstable I had been.

Many years have gone by since then; much has changed.

1995, late April, it's an early summer. The road stretches before me, gently curving. The sound of the stainless steel exhaust on the

1000cc V-twin engine beneath me is a joy to the ears. It's good to be alive.

The car before me needs to be overtaken. The fool behind the wheel is weaving the car all over the road. I pull out to overtake; a quick look behind and then back to the front. The fool is across the white line with the brakes hard on. The tarmac comes up to hit me and the lights go out.

It's 1996, summertime. The sun is behind me as I approach the beach at 500 feet. The broken clouds scatter a patchwork of shadows over the fields inland. They look like rice paddies. The trees look like coconut palms. 500 feet, we're too high! I look left and right for firing points and dump the collective lever for a fast descent and start to weave left and right. I shake myself and level off.

Swinging left-hand down, I line myself up on the airstrip at Dimlington and start my final approach for the helipad of the North Sea Gas Terminal. This has happened too many times lately. Fortunately today I'm single crew and empty; there are no passengers in the back.

This has been going on for several months now, ever since I slammed my head on the tarmac. The frequency is increasing. I wonder how long it will be before I start taking hard evasive manoeuvres with a load of oilies in the back.

It's time to get out.

1998. Late summer, and it's gorgeous. The little shed that I built for the pigs last year needs a bit of cleaning out. The smell of hot grass is beautiful. The peace and quiet is almost tangible.

A dull thumping noise breaks the silence growing louder, getting rapidly closer. I know the noise. It's a helicopter, a Bell 412, a Trooper with side guns. It's low and thunders directly overhead. When it's gone I uncurl from a foetal ball in the dirt and lie waiting for the trembling to stop.

2000. Midsummer. The sound of rotor blades breaks the silence. I run out to see what it is. It's one of those nice new-fangled things; fuck-all good as a Gunship though. Now that's got to be better. Thirteen years, eh!

The mood swings are still there, but gentler now, and the bouts of morbid introspection. After thirteen years I still see the lady in the blue sari, I still see a boat burning on the beach, men struggling with death in the water.

The sound of bullets slapping past the window is muted now, but in my mind's eye I still see the fountains of water leaping beneath us as we came away from Point Pedro. Old men, like scarecrows, still hang grotesquely tangled in the branches of a tree.

It is all still there, locked in my mind. It is still rock and roll, but to a longer, slower beat.

Lucky thirteen?

Tired, so tired. Slowly, deeply soul-stirringly sad.

Kant, Nietzsche, Clausewitz (On War), Dixon, (The Psychology of Military Incompetence). They were all so right, all so tragically right. (The last one with an answer to it all was nailed to a piece of wood.) That's what humans do best. So many Tigers tried to save their small piece of Humanity. I nailed them to the ground.

So sad, soul-stirringly sad.

Tim